Introduction
to Excel 2/e

David C. Kuncicky

Florida State University

Prentice Hall
Upper Saddle River, NJ 07458

Library of Congress Cataloging-in-Publication Data
Kuncicky, David C.
    Introduction to Excel 2/e / David C. Kuncicky.
      p.   cm. — (ESource—the Prentice Hall engineering source)
    Includes index.
    ISBN 0–13–016881–5
    1. Microsoft Excel for Windows. 2. Business--Computer programs. 3. Electronic spreadsheets. I. Title. II. Series.

    HF5548.4.M523 K86 2000
    005.369--dc21

                      00-035701

Vice-president of editorial development, ECS: **MARCIA HORTON**
Acquisitions editor: **ERIC SVENDSEN**
Associate editor: **JOE RUSSO**
Vice-president of production and manufacturing: **DAVID W. RICCARDI**
Executive managing editor: **VINCE O' BRIEN**
Managing editor: **DAVID A. GEORGE**
Production editor: **AUDRI ANNA BAZLEN**
Cover director: **JAYNE CONTE**
Manufacturing buyer: **PAT BROWN**
Editorial assistant: **KRISTEN BLANCO**
Market manager: **DANNY HOYT**

© 2001 by Prentice-Hall, Inc.
Upper Saddle River, New Jersey 07458

The author and publisher of this book have used their best efforts in
preparing this book. These efforts include the development, research,
and testing of the theories to determine their effectiveness.
Printed in the United States of America.

10 9 8 7 6 5 4 3 2 1

ISBN 0-13-016881-5

Prentice-Hall International (UK) Limited, *London*
Prentice-Hall of Australia Pty. Limited, *Sydney*
Prentice-Hall Canada, Inc., Toronto
Prentice-Hall Hispanoamericana, S.A., *Mexico*
Prentice-Hall of India Private Limited, *New Delhi*
Prentice-Hall of Japan, Inc., *Tokyo*
Pearson Education (Singapore) Pte. Ltd., *Singapore*
Editoria Prentice-Hall do Brasil, Ltda., *Rio de Janeiro*

About ESource

ESource—The Prentice Hall Engineering Source
—www.prenhall.com/esource

ESource—The Prentice Hall Engineering Source gives professors the power to harness the full potential of their text and their first-year engineering course. More than just a collection of books, ESource is a unique publishing system revolving around the ESource website—www.prenhall.com/esource. ESource enables you to put your stamp on your book just as you do your course. It lets you:

Control   You choose exactly what chapter or sections are in your book and in what order they appear. Of course, you can choose the entire book if you'd like and stay with the authors' original order.

Optimize   Get the most from your book and your course. ESource lets you produce the optimal text for your students needs.

Customize   You can add your own material anywhere in your text's presentation, and your final product will arrive at your bookstore as a professionally formatted text.

ESource ACCESS

Starting in the fall of 2000, professors who choose to bundle two or more texts from the ESource series for their class, or use an ESource custom book will be providing their students with complete access to the library of ESource content. All bundles and custom books will come with a student password that gives web ESource ACCESS to all information on the site. This passcode is free and is valid for one year after initial log-on. We've designed ESource ACCESS to provides students a flexible, searchable, on-line resource.

ESource Content

All the content in ESource was written by educators specifically for freshman/first-year students. Authors tried to strike a balanced level of presentation, an approach that was neither formulaic nor trivial, and one that did not focus too heavily on advanced topics that most introductory students do not encounter until later classes. Because many professors do not have extensive time to cover these topics in the classroom, authors prepared each text with the idea that many students would use it for self-instruction and independent study. Students should be able to use this content to learn the software tool or subject on their own.

While authors had the freedom to write texts in a style appropriate to their particular subject, all followed certain guidelines created to promote a consistency that makes students comfortable. Namely, every chapter opens with a clear set of **Objectives**, includes **Practice Boxes** throughout the chapter, and ends with a number of **Problems**, and a list of **Key Terms**. **Applications Boxes** are spread throughout the book with the intent of giving students a real-world perspective of engineering. **Success Boxes** provide the student with advice about college study skills, and help students avoid the common pitfalls of first-year students. In addition, this series contains an entire book titled *Engineering Success* by Peter Schiavone of the University of Alberta intended to expose students quickly to what it takes to be an engineering student.

Creating Your Book

Using ESource is simple. You preview the content either on-line or through examination copies of the books you can request on-line, from your PH sales rep, or by calling 1-800-526-0485. Create an on-line outline of the content you want, in the order you want, using ESource's simple interface. Either type or cut and paste your own material and insert it into the text flow. You can preview the overall organization of the text you've created at anytime (please note, since this preview is immediate, it comes unformatted.), then press another button and receive an order number for your own custom book. If you are not ready to order, do nothing—ESource will save your work. You can come back at any time and change, re-arrange, or add more material to your creation. You are in control. Once you're finished and you have an ISBN, give it to your bookstore and your book will arrive on their shelves six weeks after they order. Your custom desk copies with their instructor supplements will arrive at your address at the same time.

To learn more about this new system for creating the perfect textbook, go to www.prenhall.com/esource. You can either go through the on-line walkthrough of how to create a book, or experiment yourself.

Supplements

Adopters of ESource receive an instructor's CD that contains professor and student code from the books in the series, as well as other instruction aides provided by authors. The website also holds approximately **350 Powerpoint transparencies** created by Jack Leifer of Univ. of Kentucky—Paducah available to download. Professors can either follow these transparencies as pre-prepared lectures or use them as the basis for their own custom presentations.

Titles in the ESource Series

Introduction to UNIX
0-13-095135-8
David I. Schwartz

Introduction to AutoCAD 2000
0-13-016732-0
Mark Dix and Paul Riley

Introduction to Maple
0-13-095133-1
David I. Schwartz

Introduction to Word
0-13-254764-3
David C. Kuncicky

Introduction to Excel, 2/e
0-13-016881-5
David C. Kuncicky

Introduction to Mathcad
0-13-937493-0
Ronald W. Larsen

Introduction to AutoCAD, R. 14
0-13-011001-9
Mark Dix and Paul Riley

Introduction to the Internet, 3/e
0-13-031355-6
Scott D. James

Design Concepts for Engineers
0-13-081369-9
Mark N. Horenstein

Engineering Design—A Day in the Life of Four Engineers
0-13-085089-6
Mark N. Horenstein

Engineering Ethics
0-13-784224-4
Charles B. Fleddermann

Engineering Success
0-13-080859-8
Peter Schiavone

Mathematics Review
0-13-011501-0
Peter Schiavone

Introduction to C
0-13-011854-0
Delores Etter

Introduction to C++
0-13-011855-9
Delores Etter

Introduction to MATLAB
0-13-013149-0
Delores Etter with David C. Kuncicky

Titles in the ESource Series

Introduction to FORTRAN 90
0-13-013146-6
Larry Nyhoff and Sanford Lesetma

Introduction to Java
0-13-919416-9
Stephen J. Chapman

Introduction to Engineering Analysis
0-13-016733-9
Kirk D. Hagen

Introduction to PowerPoint
0-13-040214-1
Jack Leifer

Graphics Concepts
0-13-030687-8
Richard M. Lueptow

Graphics Concepts with Pro/ENGINEER
0-13-014154-2
Richard M. Lueptow, Jim Steger, and Michael T. Snyder

Graphics Concepts with SolidWorks
0-13-014155-0
Richard M. Lueptow and Michael Minbiole

Introduction to Visual Basic 6.0
0-13-026813-5
David I. Schneider

Introduction to Mathcad 2000
0-13-020007-7
Ronald W. Larsen

About the Authors

N o project could ever come to pass without a group of authors who have the vision and the courage to turn a stack of blank paper into a book. The authors in this series worked diligently to produce their books, provide the building blocks of the series.

Delores M. Etter is a Professor of Electrical and Computer Engineering at the University of Colorado. Dr. Etter was a faculty member at the University of New Mexico and also a Visiting Professor at Stanford University. Dr. Etter was responsible for the Freshman Engineering Program at the University of  New Mexico and is active in the Integrated Teaching Laboratory at the University of Colorado. She was elected a Fellow of the Institute of Electrical and Electronics Engineers for her contributions to education and for her technical leadership in digital signal processing. In addition to writing best-selling textbooks for engineering computing, Dr. Etter has also published research in the area of adaptive signal processing.

Sanford Leestma is a Professor of Mathematics and Computer Science at Calvin College, and received his Ph.D. from New Mexico State University. He has been the long-time co-author of successful textbooks on Fortran, Pascal, and data structures in Pascal. His current research interest are in the areas of algorithms and numerical computation.

Larry Nyhoff is a Professor of Mathematics and Computer Science at Calvin College. After doing bachelor's work at Calvin, and Master's work at Michigan, he received a Ph.D. from Michigan State and also did graduate work in computer science at Western Michigan. Dr.  Nyhoff has taught at Calvin for the past 34 years—mathematics at first and computer science for the past several years. He has co-authored several computer science textbooks since 1981 including titles on Fortran and C++, as well as a brand new title on Data Structures in C++.

Acknowledgments: We express our sincere appreciation to all who helped in the preparation of this module, especially our acquisitions editor Alan Apt, managing editor Laura Steele, developmental editor Sandra Chavez, and production editor Judy Winthrop. We also thank Larry Genalo for several examples and exercises and Erin Fulp for the Internet address application in Chapter 10. We appreciate the insightful review provided by Bart Childs. We thank our families—Shar, Jeff, Dawn, Rebecca, Megan, Sara, Greg, Julie, Joshua, Derek, Tom, Joan; Marge, Michelle, Sandy, Lory, Michael—for being patient and understanding. We thank God for allowing us to write this text.

Mark Dix began working with AutoCAD in 1985 as a programmer for CAD Support Associates, Inc. He helped design a system for creating estimates and bills of material directly from AutoCAD drawing databases for use in the automated conveyor industry. This system became  the basis for systems still widely in use today. In 1986 he began collaborating with Paul Riley to create AutoCAD training materials, combining Riley's background in industrial design and training with Dix's background in writing, curriculum development, and programming. Dix and Riley have created tutorial and teaching methods for every AutoCAD release since Version 2.5. Mr. Dix has a Master of Education from the University of Massachusetts. He is currently the Director of Dearborn Academy High School in Arlington, Massachusetts.

Paul Riley is an author, instructor, and designer specializing in graphics and design for multimedia. He is a founding partner of CAD Support Associates, a contract service and professional training organization for computer-aided design. His 15 years of business experi-  ence and 20 years of teaching experience are supported by degrees in education and computer science. Paul has taught AutoCAD at the University of Massachusetts at Lowell and is presently teaching AutoCAD at Mt. Ida College in Newton, Massachusetts. He has developed a program, Computer-aided Design for Professionals that is highly regarded by corporate clients and has been an ongoing success since 1982.

Scott D. James is a staff lecturer at Kettering University (formerly GMI Engineering & Management Institute) in Flint, Michigan. He is currently pursuing a Ph.D. in Systems Engineering with an emphasis on software engineering and computer-integrated manufacturing. Scott decided on writing textbooks after he found a void in the books that were available. "I really wanted a book that showed how to do things in good detail but in a clear and concise way. Many of the books on the market are full of fluff and force you to dig out the really important facts." Scott decided on teaching as a profession after several years in the computer industry. "I thought that it was really important to know what it was like outside of academia. I wanted to provide students with classes that were up to date and provide the information that is really used and needed."
Acknowledgments: Scott would like to acknowledge his family for the time to work on the text and his students and peers at Kettering who offered helpful critiques of the materials that eventually became the book.

Charles B. Fleddermann is a professor in the Department of Electrical and Computer Engineering at the University of New Mexico in Albuquerque, New Mexico. All of his degrees are in electrical engineering: his Bachelor's degree from the University of Notre Dame, and the Master's and Ph.D. from the University of Illinois at Urbana-Champaign. Prof. Fleddermann developed an engineering ethics course for his department in response to the ABET requirement to incorporate ethics topics into the undergraduate engineering curriculum. *Engineering Ethics* was written as a vehicle for presenting ethical theory, analysis, and problem solving to engineering undergraduates in a concise and readily accessible way.
Acknowledgments: I would like to thank Profs. Charles Harris and Michael Rabins of Texas A & M University whose NSF sponsored workshops on engineering ethics got me started thinking in this field. Special thanks to my wife Liz, who proofread the manuscript for this book, provided many useful suggestions, and who helped me learn how to teach "soft" topics to engineers.

David I. Schwartz is an Assistant Professor in the Computer Science Department at Cornell University and earned his B.S., M.S., and Ph.D. degrees in Civil Engineering from State University of New York at Buffalo. Throughout his graduate studies, Schwartz combined principles of computer science to applications of civil engineering. He became interested in helping students learn how to apply software tools for solving a variety of engineering problems. He teaches his students to learn incrementally and practice frequently to gain the maturity to tackle other subjects. In his spare time, Schwartz plays drums in a variety of bands.
Acknowledgments: I dedicate my books to my family, friends, and students who all helped in so many ways. Many thanks go to the schools of Civil Engineering and Engineering & Applied Science at State University of New York at Buffalo where I originally developed and tested my UNIX and Maple books. I greatly appreciate the opportunity to explore my goals and all the help from everyone at the Computer Science Department at Cornell. Eric Svendsen and everyone at Prentice Hall also deserve my gratitude for helping to make these books a reality. Many thanks, also, to those who submitted interviews and images.

Ron Larsen is an Associate Professor of Chemical Engineering at Montana State University, and received his Ph.D. from the Pennsylvania State University. He was initially attracted to engineering by the challenges the profession offers, but also appreciates that engineering is a serving profession. Some of the greatest challenges he has faced while teaching have involved non-traditional teaching methods, including evening courses for practicing engineers and teaching through an interpreter at the Mongolian National University. These experiences have provided tremendous opportunities to learn new ways to communicate technical material. He tries to incorporate the skills he has learned in non-traditional arenas to improve his lectures, written materials, and learning programs. Dr. Larsen views modern software as one of the new tools that will radically alter the way engineers work, and his book *Introduction to Mathcad* was written to help young engineers prepare to meet the challenges of an ever-changing workplace.
Acknowledgments: To my students at Montana State University who have endured the rough drafts and typos, and who still allow me to experiment with their classes—my sincere thanks.

Peter Schiavone is a professor and student advisor in the Department of Mechanical Engineering at the University of Alberta, Canada. He received his Ph.D. from the University of Strathclyde, U.K. in 1988. He has authored several books in the area of student academic success as well as numerous papers in international scientific research journals. Dr. Schiavone has worked in private industry in several different areas of engineering including aerospace and systems engineering. He founded the first Mathematics Resource Center at the University of Alberta, a unit designed specifically to teach new students the necessary *survival skills* in mathematics and the physical sciences required for success in first-year engineering. This led to the Students' Union Gold Key Award for outstanding contributions to the university. Dr. Schiavone lectures regularly to freshman engineering students and to new engineering professors on engineering success, in particular about maximizing students' academic performance. He wrote the book *Engineering Success* in order to share the *secrets of success in engineering study*: the most effective, tried and tested methods used by the most successful engineering students.

Acknowledgements: Thanks to Eric Svendsen for his encouragement and support; to Richard Felder for being such an inspiration; to my wife Linda for sharing my dreams and believing in me; and to Francesca and Antonio for putting up with Dad when working on the text.

Mark N. Horenstein is a Professor in the Department of Electrical and Computer Engineering at Boston University. He has degrees in Electrical Engineering from M.I.T. and U.C. Berkeley and has been involved in teaching engineering design for the greater part of his academic career. He
devised and developed the senior design project class taken by all electrical and computer engineering students at Boston University. In this class, the students work for a virtual engineering company developing products and systems for real-world engineering and social-service clients. Many of the design projects developed in his class have been aimed at assistive technologies for individuals with disabilities.

Acknowledgments: I would like to thank Prof. James Bethune, the architect of the Peak Performance event at Boston University, for his permission to highlight the competition in my text. Several of the ideas relating to brainstorming and teamwork were derived from a workshop on engineering design offered by Prof. Charles Lovas of Southern Methodist University. The principles of estimation were derived in part from a freshman engineering problem posed by Prof. Thomas Kincaid of Boston University.

Kirk D. Hagen is a professor at Weber State University in Ogden, Utah. He has taught introductory-level engineering courses and upper-division thermal science courses at WSU since 1993. He received his B.S. degree in physics from Weber State College and his M.S. degree
in mechanical engineering from Utah State University, after which he worked as a thermal designer/analyst in the aerospace and electronics industries. After several years of engineering practice, he resumed his formal education, earning his Ph.D. in mechanical engineering at the University of Utah. Hagen is the author of an undergraduate heat transfer text. Having drawn upon his industrial and teaching experience, he strongly believes that engineering students must develop effective analytical problem solving abilities. His book, *Introduction to Engineering Analysis*, was written to help beginning engineering students learn a systematic approach to engineering analysis.

Richard M. Lueptow is the Charles Deering McCormick Professor of Teaching Excellence and Associate Professor of Mechanical Engineering at Northwestern University. He is a native of Wisconsin and received his doctorate from the Massachusetts Institute of Technology in 1986. He teaches design, fluid mechanics, and
spectral analysis techniques. "In my design class I saw a need for a self-paced tutorial for my students to learn CAD software quickly and easily. I worked with several students a few years ago to develop just this type of tutorial, which has since evolved into a book. My goal is to introduce students to engineering graphics and CAD, while showing them how much fun it can be." Rich has an active research program on rotating filtration, Taylor Couette flow, granular flow, fire suppression, and acoustics. He has five patents and over 40 refereed journal and proceedings papers along with many other articles, abstracts, and presentations.

Acknowledgments: Thanks to my talented and hard-working co-authors as well as the many colleagues and students who took the tutorial for a "test drive." Special thanks to Mike Minbiole for his major contributions to Graphics Concepts with SolidWorks. Thanks also to Northwestern University for the time to work on a book. Most of all, thanks to my loving wife, Maiya, and my children, Hannah and Kyle, for supporting me in this endeavor. (Photo courtesy of Evanston Photographic Studios, Inc.)

Jack Leifer is an Assistant Professor in the Department of Mechanical Engineering at the University of Kentucky Extended Campus Program in Paducah, and was previously with the Department of Mathematical Sciences and Engineering at the University of South Carolina—
Aiken. He received his Ph.D. in Mechanical Engineering from the University of Texas at Austin in December 1995.

His current research interests include the modeling of sensors for manufacturing, and the use of Artificial Neural Networks to predict corrosion.

Acknowledgements: I'd like to thank my colleagues at USC—Aiken, especially Professors Mike May and Laurene Fausett, for their encouragement and feedback; Eric Svendsen and Joe Russo of Prentice Hall, for their useful suggestions and flexibility with deadlines; and my parents, Felice and Morton Leifer, for being there and providing support (as always) as I completed this book.

David C. Kuncicky is a native Floridian. He earned his Baccalaureate in psychology, Master's in computer science, and Ph.D. in computer science from Florida State University. He has served as a faculty member in the Department of Electrical Engineering at the FAMU–FSU College of Engineering and the Department of Computer Science at Florida State University. He has taught computer science and computer engineering courses for over 15 years. He has published research in the areas of intelligent hybrid systems and neural networks. He is currently the Director of Engineering at Bioreason, Inc. in Sante Fe, New Mexico.

Acknowledgments: Thanks to Steffie and Helen for putting up with my late nights and long weekends at the computer. Thanks also to the helpful and insightful technical reviews by Jerry Ralya, Kathy Kitto, Avi Singhal, Thomas Hill, Ron Eaglin, Larry Richards, and Susan Freeman. I appreciate the patience of Eric Svendsen and Joe Russo of Prentice Hall for gently guiding me through this project. Finally, thanks to Susan Bassett for having faith in my abilities, and for providing continued tutelage and support.

Jim Steger is currently Chief Technical Officer and cofounder of an Internet applications company. He graduated with a Bachelor of Science degree in Mechanical Engineering from Northwestern University. His prior work included mechanical engineering assignments at Motorola and Acco Brands. At Motorola, Jim worked on part design for two-way radios and was one of the lead mechanical engineers on a cellular phone product line. At Acco Brands, Jim was the sole engineer on numerous office product designs. His Worx stapler has won design awards in the United States and in Europe. Jim has been a Pro/Engineer user for over six years.

Acknowledgments: Many thanks to my co-authors, especially Rich Lueptow for his leadership on this project. I would also like to thank my family for their continuous support.

David I. Schneider holds an A.B. degree from Oberlin College and a Ph.D. degree in Mathematics from MIT. He has taught for 34 years, primarily at the University of Maryland. Dr. Schneider has authored 28 books, with one-half of them computer programming books. He has developed three customized software packages that are supplied as supplements to over 55 mathematics textbooks. His involvement with computers dates back to 1962, when he programmed a special purpose computer at MIT's Lincoln Laboratory to correct errors in a communications system.

Michael T. Snyder is President of Internet startup Appointments123.com. He is a native of Chicago, and he received his Bachelor of Science degree in Mechanical Engineering from the University of Notre Dame. Mike also graduated with honors from Northwestern University's Kellogg Graduate School of Management in 1999 with his Masters of Management degree. Before Appointments123.com, Mike was a mechanical engineer in new product development for Motorola Cellular and Acco Office Products. He has received four patents for his mechanical design work. "Pro/Engineer was an invaluable design tool for me, and I am glad to help students learn the basics of Pro/Engineer."

Acknowledgments: Thanks to Rich Lueptow and Jim Steger for inviting me to be a part of this great project. Of course, thanks to my wife Gretchen for her support in my various projects.

Stephen J. Chapman received a BS in Electrical Engineering from Louisiana State University (1975), an MSE in Electrical Engineering from the University of Central Florida (1979), and pursued further graduate studies at Rice University. Mr. Chapman is currently Manager of Technical Systems for Brithish Aerospace Australia, in Melbourne, Australia. In this position, he provides technical direction and design authority for the work of younger engineers within the company. He is also continuing to teach at local universities on a part-time basis.

Mr. Chapman is a Senior Member of the Institute of Electrical and Electronics Engineers (and several of its component societies). He is also a member of the Association for Computing Machinery and the Institution of Engineers (Australia).

Reviewers

ESource benefited from a wealth of reviewers who on the series from its initial idea stage to its completion. Reviewers read manuscripts and contributed insightful comments that helped the authors write great books. We would like to thank everyone who helped us with this project.

Concept Document

Naeem Abdurrahman *University of Texas, Austin*
Grant Baker *University of Alaska, Anchorage*
Betty Barr *University of Houston*
William Beckwith *Clemson University*
Ramzi Bualuan *University of Notre Dame*
Dale Calkins *University of Washington*
Arthur Clausing *University of Illinois at Urbana–Champaign*
John Glover *University of Houston*
A.S. Hodel *Auburn University*
Denise Jackson *University of Tennessee, Knoxville*
Kathleen Kitto *Western Washington University*
Terry Kohutek *Texas A&M University*
Larry Richards *University of Virginia*
Avi Singhal *Arizona State University*
Joseph Wujek *University of California, Berkeley*
Mandochehr Zoghi *University of Dayton*

Books

Stephen Allan *Utah State University*
Naeem Abdurrahman *University of Texas, Austin*
Anil Bajaj *Purdue University*
Grant Baker *University of Alaska—Anchorage*
Betty Burr *University of Houston*
William Beckwith *Clemson University*
Haym Benaroya *Rutgers University*
Tom Bledsaw *ITT Technical Institute*
Tom Bryson *University of Missouri, Rolla*
Ramzi Bualuan *University of Notre Dame*
Dan Budny *Purdue University*
Dale Calkins *University of Washington*
Arthur Clausing *University of Illinois*
James Devine *University of South Florida*

Patrick Fitzhorn *Colorado State University*
Dale Elifrits *University of Missouri, Rolla*
Frank Gerlitz *Washtenaw College*
John Glover *University of Houston*
John Graham *University of North Carolina—Charlotte*
Malcom Heimer *Florida International University*
A.S. Hodel *Auburn University*
Vern Johnson *University of Arizona*
Kathleen Kitto *Western Washington University*
Robert Montgomery *Purdue University*
Mark Nagurka *Marquette University*
Romarathnam Narasimhan *University of Miami*
Larry Richards *University of Virginia*
Marc H. Richman *Brown University*
Avi Singhal *Arizona State University*
Tim Sykes *Houston Community College*
Thomas Hill *SUNY at Buffalo*
Michael S. Wells *Tennessee Tech University*
Joseph Wujek *University of California, Berkeley*
Edward Young *University of South Carolina*
Mandochehr Zoghi *University of Dayton*
John Biddle *California State Polytechnic University*
Fred Boadu *Duke University*
Harish Cherukuri *University of North Carolina—Charlotte*
Barry Crittendon *Virginia Polytechnic and State University*
Ron Eaglin *University of Central Florida*
Susan Freeman *Northeastern University*
Frank Gerlitz *Washtenaw Community College*
Otto Gygax *Oregon State University*
Donald Herling *Oregon State University*
James N. Jensen *SUNY at Buffalo*
Autar Kaw *University of South Florida*
Kenneth Klika *University of Akron*
Terry L. Kohutek *Texas A&M University*
Melvin J. Maron *University of Louisville*
Soronadi Nnaji *Florida A&M University*
Michael Peshkin *Northwestern University*
Randy Shih *Oregon Institute of Technology*
Neil R. Thompson *University of Waterloo*
Garry Young *Oklahoma State University*

Contents

9   EXCEL AND THE WORLD WIDE WEB   161

APPENDIX A: COMMONLY USED FUNCTIONS 173

INDEX 175

1

Engineering and Electronic Worksheets

1.1 INTRODUCTION TO WORKSHEETS

A *spreadsheet* is a rectangular grid composed of addressable units called *cells*. A cell may contain numerical data, textual data, macros, or formulas. Spreadsheet application programs were originally intended to be used for financial calculations. The original electronic spreadsheets resembled the paper spreadsheets of an accountant. One characteristic of electronic spreadsheets that gives them power over their paper counterparts is the ability to automatically recalculate all dependent values whenever a parameter is changed. Over time, more and more functionality has been added to spreadsheet application programs. These include graphing functions, database functions, and the ability to access the World Wide Web. A large number of analytical tools are now available within spreadsheet applications. These include scientific and engineering tools, statistical tools, data mapping tools, and financial analysis tools.

As an engineering student, you may find that an advanced spreadsheet program such as Microsoft Excel® will suffice for many of your computational and presentation needs. For example, Excel® may be used to manage small databases. If you wish to manage large or sophisticated databases, however, a specialized database application such as Microsoft Access® or Oracle® is preferable. You can use the Analysis Toolpack in Excel to perform mathematical analysis. If the analysis is large or sophisticated, however, you may want to use a specialized mathematical package such as MathCAD® or MATLAB®. The same concept is true for graphing (Harvard Graphics®) or statistical analysis (SPSS®).

Microsoft Excel® uses the term *worksheet* to denote a spreadsheet. A worksheet can contain more items than a

OBJECTIVES

After reading this chapter, you should be able to

- Understand the worksheet as an interface for engineering computation
- Understand the steps of the engineering method
- Understand engineering design and computers
- Understand how to use this book

traditional spreadsheet including charts, links to Web pages, Visual Basic modules, and macros. We will treat the two terms synonymously in this text. A collection of worksheets that is stored in a single file is called a *workbook*.

1.2 ENGINEERING METHODS

Engineers are problem solvers. The ability to solve technical problems successfully is both an art and a science. The successful solution of engineering problems requires a broad background in a variety of technical areas such as mathematics, physics, and computational science. Successful problem resolution of engineering problems also requires a set of nontechnical skills. Common sense and good judgment are examples of important nontechnical abilities. Engineering solutions often involve balancing several competing factors.

An example of such a trade-off is cost versus reliability. For example, it costs money to remove impurities from an Integrated Circuit (IC) during manufacture. Impurities are directly related to the reliability of the chip. As the manufacturing and testing processes are improved to produce a more and more reliable chip, the costs continue to increase (probably at a higher than linear rate). A design decision could be made that balances these two competing factors. We could express it in this way: A chip is reliable if there is a 90% probability that the chip will not fail in five years.

Another essential skill for engineers is the ability to collect and analyze data. We must be able to organize and communicate our results both verbally and in written form. The analysis and presentation of data using Microsoft Excel® is the core topic of this book. In order to understand the role and importance of data analysis in the engineering profession let us first look at a variation of a problem-solving process called the *engineering method*. The engineering method consists of a series of steps that help an engineer break the solution of a problem into smaller, logical phases. This method has been described many times in slightly different terms. One version of the method's steps is

- *Problem definition*
- *Information gathering*
- *Selection of the appropriate theory or methodology*
- *Collection of simplifying assumptions*
- *Solution and refinement*
- *Testing and verification*

Each of these steps will be described in the following sections. Within each of the six steps, an engineer typically analyses or presents some form of data.

1.2.1 Problem Definition

The precise definition of a problem can be one of the most difficult phases of solving a problem. Often a client (or instructor) will present a problem with ambiguous specifications. At times, the client does not completely understand the problem. It is worth the effort to obtain missing requirements and reduce ambiguities as early as possible in the design process. A clear and precise written statement of a problem at this stage will save much wasted expenditure of energy later.

1.2.2   Information Gathering

To specificy a problem properly, the engineer must gather relevant information. At a minimum, this involves a thorough review of the relevant technical areas. This includes a review of previous solutions to similar problems. The engineer may also perform experiments to test underlying assumptions that are needed before a problem solution can be devised. The experiments may involve laboratory testing or use computer modeling.

For example, you might be asked to improve the drilling technology used at a particular offshore drilling site. The first thing to do would be to review reports of previous solutions used at this site and other sites. Perhaps you would obtain and analyze core samples from different depths at the drilling site. You might also take seismic readings and perform computer modeling using these data.

The engineer must be able to effectively communicate the results of testing and data collection. This often involves the use of tables and charts, as described in Chapter 5.

1.2.3   Selection of the Appropriate Theory
or Methodology

A variety of scientific principles may be used to formulate a problem solution. The engineer's educational background and training contribute strongly to the ability to succeed in this step. However, after a theory or set of principles is chosen, it must be presented to others. Scientific principles are often expressed using mathematics. Chapter 4 describes how to create and use formulas within a spreadsheet.

1.2.4   Collection of Simplifying Assumptions

A theory is an abstraction of how the world works. To solve real-world problems, we need to simplify the solution by making assumptions about some of the theory's components. As an example, suppose you were given the job of designing a kiln. Part of the design process involves calculating the heat loss from the kiln. If you make the assumption that the convective loss is negligible, then the calculation has to account only for heat loss due to conduction and radiation. Excel provides a number of tools for viewing and analyzing data from different perspectives. These include trend analysis, goal seeking, pivot tables, and maps. They are discussed in Chapter 6.

1.2.5   Solution and Refinement

Engineering problems are frequently solved iteratively. A common scenario is for an engineer to test and refine potential solutions to a problem using Excel. After the engineer is satisfied that the solution works for small data sets, then the solution may be translated to a programming language such as C or FORTRAN. The resulting program can then be executed on a powerful workstation or a supercomputer using large data sets. This use of a worksheet is called building a *prototype*. A spreadsheet package such as Excel is useful for building prototypes because solutions can be developed quickly and modified easily.

1.2.6   Testing and Verification

Final testing and verification of a problem solution are critical before the solution is implemented. Many times, misplaced decimal points or incorrect unit conversion produce unreasonable answers. Solutions can also be tested by choosing the endpoints of parameter ranges. In this way, the limits of the solution are tested. In many cases, it is impossible to test all the possible input sets. For example, consider a control unit with eight input controls, each of which has ten calibration settings. There are 100 million possible input combinations for the control unit. It would be unreasonable to test every combination, so we choose a representative sample and present our results statistically. In Chapter 6, we discuss the statistical functions available in the Analysis Toolpack®.

1.3 ISSUES IN ENGINEERING AND DATA ANALYSIS

1.3.1 Group Problem Solving

Engineers rarely work alone into today's environment. Teams of engineers work together in every stage of the design and problem-solving process. The ability to work well in a group is an important skill to be learned. One group task is the solution of engineering problems in a collaborative manner. When working in a group, it is necessary to incorporate each group member's input without inadvertently destroying the work of another member. It is also necessary to maintain historical versions of the groups work. In Chapter 8, we will discuss some of the tools that Excel provides to assist with collaboration. These include means for tracking changes, sharing a workbook, and protecting a workbook.

1.3.2 Document Transfer

During the group design process, data may be manipulated by a variety of application programs. Issues of data transfer and functional compatibility are more important than in the past. Prior to the 1990s, the design process generally occurred within a single organization that was located at a single geographical site. All engineers who worked on a project tended to use the same software and hardware. Today, members of design teams are likely to work from different geographical locations and may use different application programs and different computer architectures. The elements of a design project may pass hands many times during the design process. The ability to move data among software applications, operating systems, and hardware is important. The methods for importing and exporting data between Excel and other application programs are discussed in Chapter 8. The use of the Internet has become a major method of communicating ideas, transferring documents, and publishing information. The use of the Internet and Excel is discussed in Chapter 9.

1.3.3 Standardized Units

Since engineers from different sites and organizations tend to communicate and work more than ever as a team, it is important that the technical language that they speak be the same. This technical language consists of mathematical notation and a system of units. The International System of Units (SI) is designed to be the basis for a worldwide standard for measurement. As an engineering student, you should become familiar with the SI system and with the methods for converting units among SI and other systems.

1.4 HOW TO USE THIS BOOK

This book is intended get the engineering student up and running with Excel 97 as quickly as possible. Examples are geared toward engineering and mathematical problems. Read the book while sitting in front of a computer. Learn to use Excel by re-creating each example in the text. Perform the instructions in the boxes labeled **Practice!**. Many of the worksheets used to develop the examples in this book are available for download via anonymous File Transfer Protocol from

    `ftp.eng.fsu.edu/pub/kuncick/excel/`

or point your Web browser to

    `ftp://ftp.eng.fsu.edu/pub/kuncick/excel/`

Chapter 9 discusses how to import worksheets from an FTP site directly into a local worksheet.

This book is not intended to be a complete reference manual for Excel. It is much too short for that purpose. Many books on the market are more appropriate for use as a complete reference manual. However, if you are sitting at the computer, one of the best reference manuals is at your fingertips. The on-line Excel help tools provide an excellent resource if properly used. Chapter 2 covers the use of on-line help.

1.4.1 Typographic Conventions Used in This Book

Throughout the text, the following conventions will be used.

Selection with the Mouse. The book frequently asks you to move the mouse cursor over a particular item and then click and release the left mouse button. This action is repeated so many times in the text that it will be abbreviated as

> Choose **Item**.

If the mouse button is not to be released or if the right mouse button is to be used, this will be stated explicitly.

Bold Items. A button, icon, or menu item you select with the mouse will be typed in bold face. A key you should press is also typed in bold face. For example, if you are asked to choose the menu item at the top of the screen that is labeled *File*, it will be written as

> Choose **File** from the Menu bar.

Multiple Selections. The book frequently refers to selections that require more than one step. For example, to see a print preview perform the following steps:

1. Choose **File** from the Menu bar (at the top of the screen).
2. Choose **Print Preview** from the drop-down menu that appears after performing step 1.

Multiple selections such as this will be abbreviated by separating choices with a comma. For example, the two steps listed above will be denoted as

> Choose **File**, **Print Preview** from the Menu bar.

Multiple Keystrokes. If you are asked to press multiple keys, the book separates the keys with a plus sign. For example, to undo a typing change you can simultaneously press the **Ctrl** key and the **Z** key. This will be described as

> To undo typing press **Ctrl** + **Z**; to redo typing press **Ctrl** + **Y**.

Literal Expressions. Underlines indicate a word or phrase that is a literal transcription. For example, the Title bar at the top of the screen should contain the text Microsoft Excel.

Key Terms. The first time a key term is used it is italicized.

KEY TERMS

cells

collection of simplifying
 assumptions

engineering method

information gathering

problem definition

prototype

selection of theory
 or methodology

solution and refinement

spreadsheet

testing and verification

workbook

worksheet

Problems

1. Visit the U.S. National Institute of Science and Technology (NIST) Physics Labo-
    ratory's Web site about the International System of Units (SI) at http://phys-
    ics.nist.gov/Divisions/Div840/SI.html

    Click on the menu item labeled *In-depth Information on the SI, the Modern Met-
    ric System* and locate the table for SI Base Units. Use Table 1 – 1 to fill in the
    missing entries.

TABLE 1-1   SI Base Units

QUANTITY	NAME	SYMBOL
length		m
	kilogram	kg
time	second	
electric current	ampere	
temperature		K
	mole	mol
luminous intensity		cd

2. The electronic spreadsheet has played an important role in the history of com-
    puting. The following links discuss the history of electronic spreadsheets. Access
    the following Web sites with your Web browser and then answer the following
    questions.

    Power, Daniel. *A Brief History of Spreadsheets*, at URL

    `http://dss.cba.uni.edu/dss/sshistory.html,`

    visited November 24, 1999.

    Browne, Christopher. *Historical Background on Spreadsheets*, at URL

    `http://www.ntlug.org/~cbbrowne/spreadsheets.html,`

    visited November 24, 1999.

    Mattessich, Richard. *Early History of the Spreadsheet*, at URL

    `http://www.j-walk.com/ss/history/spreadsh.htm,`

    visited November 24, 1999.

    a. What is the name of the first marketed electronic spreadsheet that was
        partly responsible for the early success of the Apple computer?

    b. What spreadsheet application remains the most widely sold software
        application in the world (as of 1998)?

2

Microsoft Excel Basics

2.1 UNDERSTANDING THE EXCEL 97 SCREEN

This chapter introduces you to Microsoft Excel. The chapter was written for a student who is not familiar with Microsoft Excel and it is designed to get you up and running as soon as possible. The preferred way to use this chapter is for you to sit at a computer and execute each of the examples as you read the chapter.

To start the Microsoft Excel program, place the cursor over the Excel icon and click the left mouse button. The icon will resemble ▨ or ▨. The icon may be on your desktop or may be accessed from the Task bar if you are using Windows 95 or NT. A screen that resembles Figure 2.1 should appear. If the Tip of the Day box appears, close it for now by choosing **Close**. We will return to the Tip of the Day in Section 2.2.6. Try to become familiar with each of the components on this screen since we will use these names throughout the book. Working generally from top to bottom, each of the components will be discussed in turn.

2.1.1 Title Bar

The *Title bar* displays the Excel icon and the name of the worksheet currently being edited. Since we did not specifically open a worksheet, Excel supplies a default name (in out example, *Book1*). You should see several buttons on the right-hand side of the Title bar. These are used to manipulate the window and will be discussed in Section 2.3. Figure 2.2 shows the Title bar from the example screen in Figure 2.1.

OBJECTIVES

After reading this chapter, you should be able to

- Understand the basic Excel screen layout
- Use the toolbars
- Access on-line help using various methods
- Create a new worksheet
- Open an existing worksheet
- Navigate through and edit a worksheet
- Print a worksheet

7

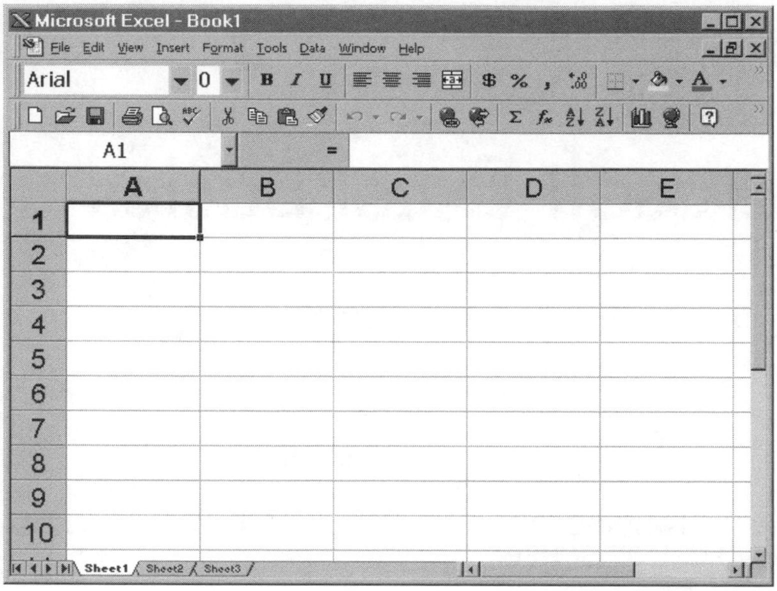

Figure 2.1.   The Excel screen

Figure 2.2.   The title bar

2.1.2   Menu Bar

The *Menu bar* contains a list of menus (see Figure 2.3). If you place the cursor over an item on the Menu bar and click the left mouse button, a drop-down menu will appear. When you place the cursor over an item, the item should change color. While holding the cursor over an item, click the left mouse button to execute the item. Try the following steps:

1.   Place the cursor over the **Window** menu item on the Menu bar.
2.   Place the mouse over the item labeled **Arrange**. Click the left mouse button.

This book will use the following convention as a shortcut to denote the steps listed above:

From the Menu bar choose **Window** and then **Arrange**.

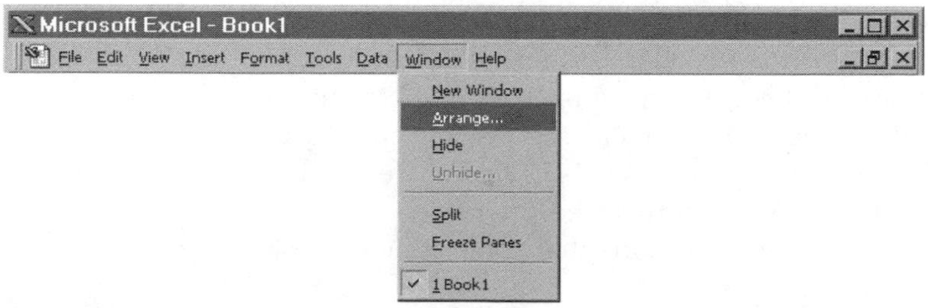

Figure 2.3.   The Menu bar

2.1.3   Toolbars

The next several rows of icons contain various *toolbars*. A toolbar is a group of buttons that are related to a particular topic, for example, drawing. The use of buttons on toolbars is an alternate method of executing commands. Most (but not all) of the commands that can be executed from a toolbar can also be executed from the Menu bar. There are more than a dozen toolbars for various functions.

We will discuss one toolbar now — the Standard toolbar. Some of the other toolbars will be discussed later in the book. Figure 2.4 shows the toolbars from the example screen in Figure 2.1. The toolbars on your screen may not match these exactly. This is because the location and presence of toolbars may be customized. If all of the toolbars were displayed at once on the screen, there would not be much room left for anything else!

Figure 2.4.   Example toolbars

The toolbar in Figure 2.5 is called the Standard toolbar. It contains some of the most frequently used commands. If this toolbar does not appear on your screen, choose **View**, **Toolbars** from the Menu bar and check the box labeled Standard. This will place the Standard toolbar on your screen.

Figure 2.5.   The Standard toolbar

Move the mouse over the toolbar button that looks like this  but don't click the mouse button. The word Print Preview should appear. Clicking the left mouse button on the icon has the same effect as choosing **File**, **Print Preview** from the Menu bar.

The choice and location of toolbars may be customized. To add or remove toolbars from the screen choose **View**, **Toolbars** from the Menu bar. A list of toolbars that resembles Figure 2.6 should appear on your screen. Check any toolbars that you would like to display on the screen.

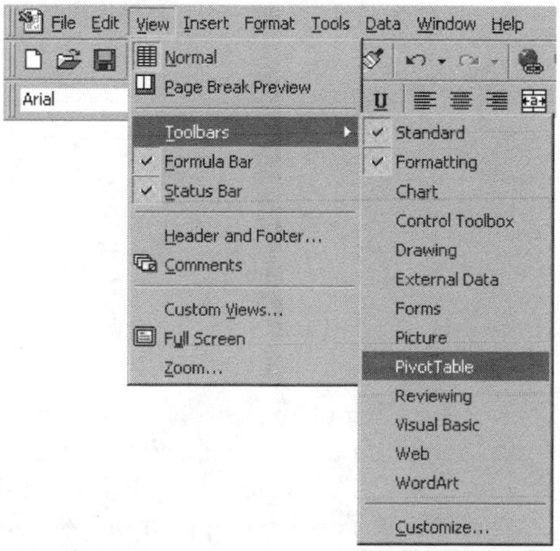

Figure 2.6.   Adding or deleting toolbars

PRACTICE!

Move the mouse slowly over each button on the Standard toolbar without pressing the mouse button. For example, move the mouse cursor over the 📋 icon. The word Paste should appear. Try to locate the equivalent command on the Menu bar. Do this for each of the buttons on the Standard toolbar. Are there any buttons that don't have an equivalent Menu bar item? What about the ⊞ icon?

Once a toolbar appears on the screen, it may be moved by dragging the toolbar with the mouse. This is accomplished by moving the cursor to the left side of the toolbar (there are two vertical lines on the left side of each toolbar) and dragging the toolbar to a new location. Toolbars may be placed along the left-hand side of the screen or in a separate box anywhere on the screen. Figure 2.7 shows the Standard toolbar placed along the left side of the screen, the Formatting toolbar placed at the top of the screen, and the PivotTable toolbar placed near the center of the screen.

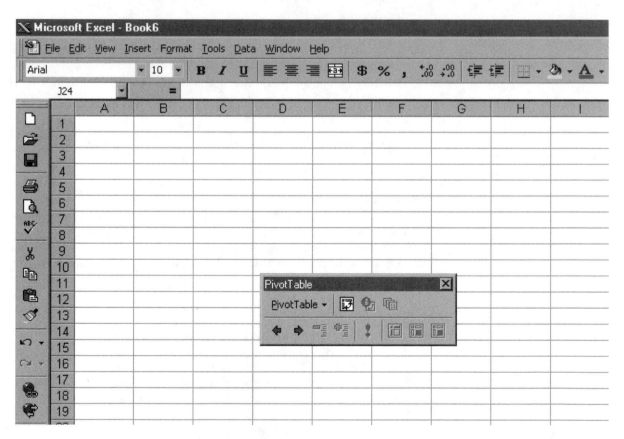

Figure 2.7.   Example of customized toolbars

2.1.4   Formula Bar

The Formula bar displays the formula or constant value for the selected cell. Figure 2.8 shows an example of a Formula bar, which appears immediately below the Formatting toolbar. The selected cell is B5 and the formula for cell B5 is =SUM(B3,B4). If the Formula bar does not appear on your screen, choose **View** from the Menu bar and check the box labeled formula Bar. The maximum length for a formula is 1,024 characters.

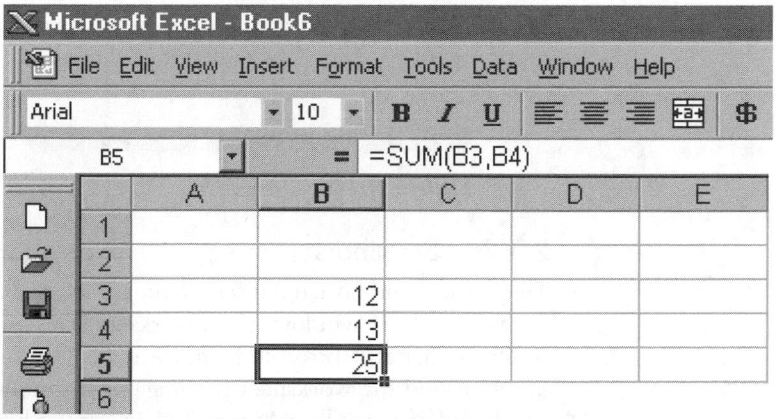

Figure 2.8.   The Formula bar

2.1.5   Workbook Window

The Workbook window is the area on the screen where data are entered. The maximum size for a worksheet is 65,536 rows by 256 columns. The columns are labeled A, B, C, ..., AA, AB, ... IV and the rows are labeled 1, 2, 3, ..., 65,536. An entire column can be selected by clicking the left mouse button on the column label. An entire row can be selected by clicking on the row label. The entire worksheet can be selected by clicking on the blank box in the top-left corner of the workbook window. Figure 2.9 depicts a workbook window with column C selected.

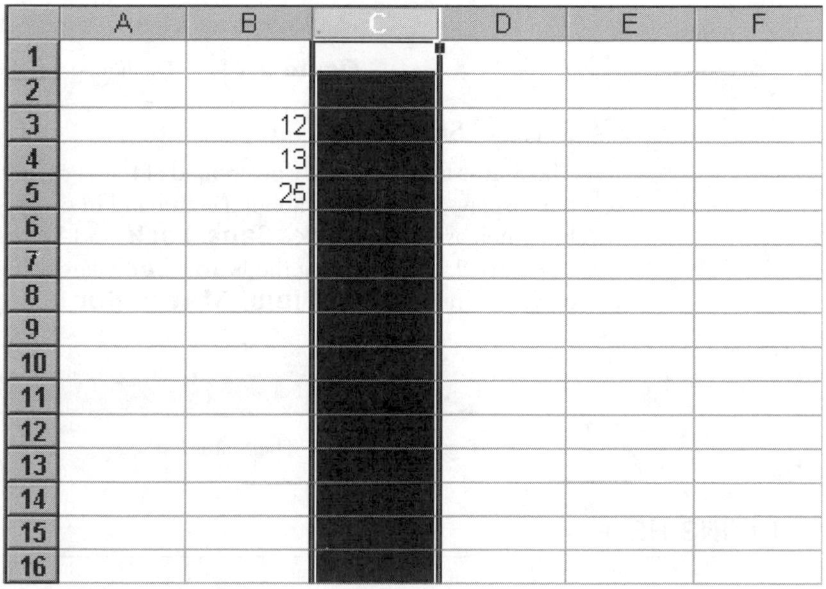

Figure 2.9.   The Workbook window

2.1.6   Sheet Tabs

The Sheet Tab bar is positioned bottom of the screen. The Sheet Tab bar lists the work-sheets in the workbook (see Figure 2.10). You can move quickly from sheet to sheet by selecting a sheet tab. If there are more sheets that are visible on the sheet tab bar, then you can use the arrows to the left of the sheet tabs to move from sheet to sheet. By default, Excel creates three worksheets when you create a new workbook. There is a maximum of 255 sheets in a default workbook.

Figure 2.10.   Sheet tabs

2.1.7   Scrollbars

The vertical and horizontal *scrollbars* are located along the right-hand side and bottom of the Workbook window. Many worksheets are much larger than the visible window. A scrollbar makes it possible to move quickly to any position on a worksheet. You can move around the worksheet by dragging a scrollbar, or you can click on the arrows at either end of a scrollbar. Figure 2.11 shows the horizontal and vertical scrollbars.

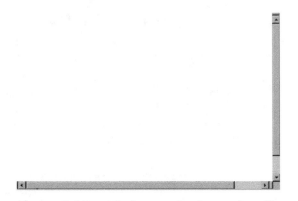

Figure 2.11.   The horizontal and vertical scrollbars

2.1.8   Status Bar

The Status bar is normally positioned at the very bottom of the Excel screen. The Status bar displays information about a command in progress and displays the status of certain keys such as **Num Lock**, **Caps Lock**, and **Scrol Lock**. The Status bar is depicted in Figure 2.12 as showing the **Num Lock** key turned on. If the status bar is not visible on your screen, choose **View**, **Status Bar** from the Menu bar.

Figure 2.12.   The Status bar

2.2   GETTING HELP

Excel contains a large on-line help system. To access the help menu, choose **Help** from the Menu bar. There is a variety of ways to obtain help. These include

- Choosing a section from the table of contents
- Searching an index
- Searching for keywords in the help text
- Using the Office Assistant

- Using the What's This feature
- Learning from the Tip of the Day
- Accessing help from the World Wide Web
- Accessing special help for Lotus 1-2-3 users

Each of these methods will be discussed in the following sections.

2.2.1   Choosing from the Table of Contents

This method is useful if you have time to read about a general topic. Reading through the topics could serve as a tutorial. This is not the method to use if you have a specific question and you want an immediate answer. To access the Table of Contents, choose **Help**, **Contents and Index** from the Menu bar and select the **Contents** tab. A good first selection for you to read is titled **Getting Help**.

2.2.2   Searching the Help Index

To access the Help Index, choose **Help**, **Contents and Index** from the Menu bar and select the **Index** tab. A dialog box that resembles Figure 2.13 should appear.

Type in a key word or words and choose a topic from the displayed list. For example, type shortcut keys and select **Microsoft Excel** from the list. Now choose the **Display** button. A Help dialog box that resembles Figure 2.14 will appear. Choose any ⏩ button to see information about a selected topic. If you would like to print a help topic, then choose **Options**, **Print Topic** from the Help dialog box.

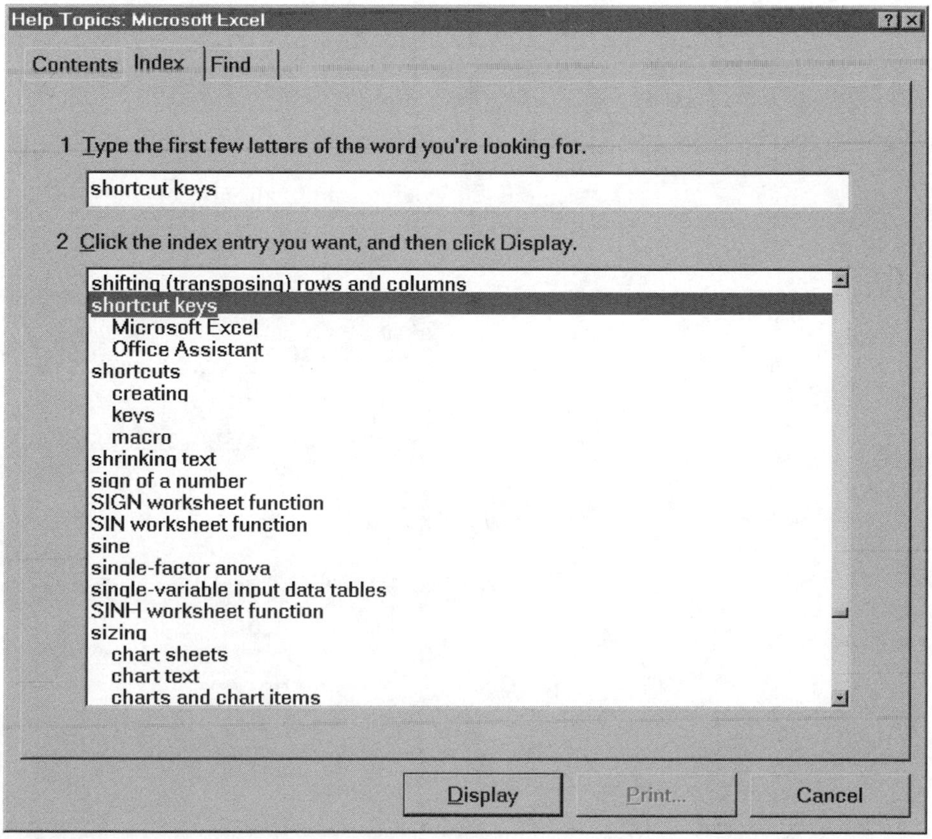

Figure 2.13.   The Help Topics dialog box

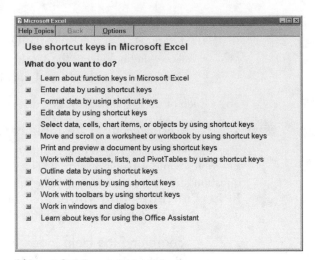

Figure 2.14.   A Help dialog box

2.2.3   Searching for Keywords in the Help Text

This option provides a more exhaustive search capability by building a database of all words in the help text. Before the search can proceed, the database must be built. Fortunately, you only have to build the list once. To access the keyword search feature, choose **Help**, **Contents and Index** from the Menu bar and select the **Find** tab. A dialog box will appear. Perform the steps listed in the dialog box:

1.   Type in a keyword.

2.   Select a matching word to narrow the search.

3.   Select a topic from the list.

Figure 2.15 demonstrates the use of the keyword search feature to locate help about hyperlinks.

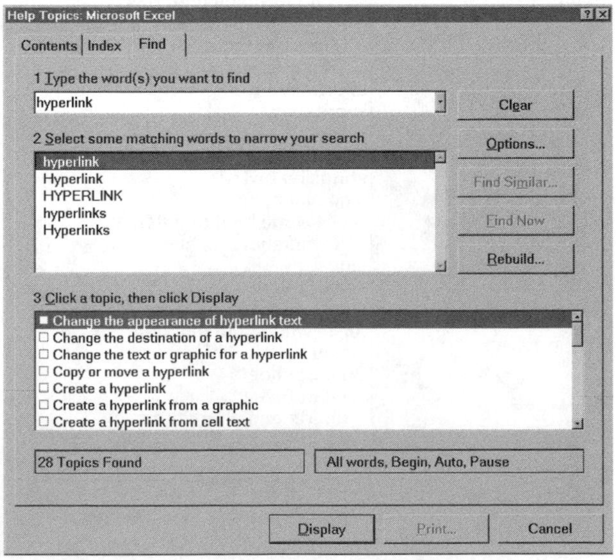

Figure 2.15.   Example of keyword search

2.2.4 Using the Office Assistant

The Office Assistant is a new feature of the Office 97 products. This feature is intended to guide you through many tasks interactively. The Office Assistant has several personalities, including an animated paper clip and an animated Albert Einstein. To change the personality of the Office Assistant, choose the [?] button on the Standard toolbar. When the Office Assistant dialog box appears, choose **Options**, then **Gallery**. The [Next >] and [<Back] buttons can be used to view the various Office Assistant personalities. The Office Assistant has a search feature similar to the keyword and index searches mentioned above. As you gain proficiency with Excel, you may reach a point where you no longer want to use the Office Assistant. To make the Office Assistant go away, choose the [● Close] button on the Office Assistant picture.

2.2.5 Using the What's This Feature

If you would like to learn about a button or other graphic item on the screen, the **What's This** feature may be helpful. Choose **Help**, **What's This** from the Menu bar. Your cursor should change to the following shape [?]. Now move the mouse to the icon or graphic item that you want to learn about and click the left mouse button. A help box will appear and your cursor will return to its original shape.

2.2.6 Learning from the Tip of the Day

If you would like Excel to provide you with a helpful tip each time you start up the Word program, open the Office Assistant by choosing the [?] icon from the Standard toolbar. Then choose **Options** and select the **Options** tab. Click the item labeled **Show the Tip of the Day at Startup**.

2.2.7 Accessing Help from the World Wide Web

A wealth of information about Microsoft Excel is available on the World Wide Web. To access an Excel-related Web site, choose **Help**, **Microsoft on the Web** and choose one of the items on the drop-down menu. For example, select **Free Stuff** and you will be connected to a Microsoft site where you can download a new Office Assistant personality.

If these links do not work, you may not be connected to the Internet. To access the World Wide Web, you must have access to the Internet through your school or a private *Internet Service Provider* (ISP).

2.2.8 Accessing Special Help for Lotus 1-2-3 Users

If you are a Lotus 1-2-3 user, you can access a help section that explains the differences between Lotus 1-2-3 and Excel commands. Choose **Help**, **Lotus 1-2-3 Help** from the Menu bar.

2.3 MANIPULATING WINDOWS

It is a good idea to spend some time getting used to manipulating windows before we actually begin to create a workbook. Excel allows you to keep more than one workbook open at a time. This is helpful when you are copying text or objects from one worksheet to another. There are three important buttons on the Title bar of every workbook and the same three buttons appear on the main Excel Title bar. These buttons are used to control the window and are listed in Table 2-1. The functions of each control button are explained below.

TABLE 2-1 The Window Control Buttons

BUTTON	NAME
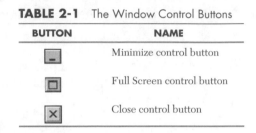	Minimize control button
	Full Screen control button
	Close control button

2.3.1 Minimize Control Button

The Minimize *control button* reduces the window to an icon in the main Excel window. The name of the workbook is displayed on the icon. Figure 2.16 depicts three workbooks. Book 6 is open and Books 7 and 8 are minimized. To restore a minimized document, double-click the worksheet's icon. When minimized, the document is not closed and it remains in computer memory. This is useful if you plan to use the document again shortly since the document will not have to be retrieved from disk.

Figure 2.16. Example of minimized workbooks

2.3.2 Full Screen Control Button

The *Full Screen control button* allows you to maximize the amount of real estate that your document or application occupies on the screen. Choose the ▢ icon on the Title bar to expand the document or application to full screen size. Choose the ▣ icon to reduce a full screen document or application to a smaller window size.

2.3.3 Close Control Button

The *Close control button* will close your workbook or application. If there are unsaved changes, an alert box will appear that reminds you to save your work. The alert box is depicted in Figure 2.17. If you choose **No**, the document or application will be closed without saving. If you choose **Cancel**, the workbook or application will not be closed and you will be returned to your workbook or application.

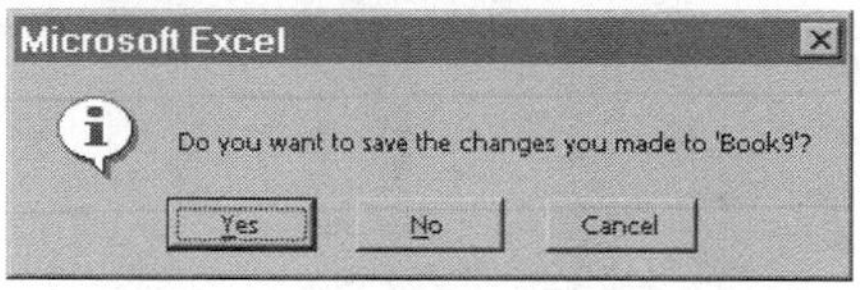

Figure 2.17. Alert box for saving changes

2.4 CREATING AND SAVING WORKSHEETS AND WORKBOOKS

2.4.1 Introduction to Templates

A *template* is a workbook that has some of its cells filled in. If you use similar formatting for many documents, you will benefit from creating and using a template. You may build your own template or customize preformatted templates and, in time, create a library of your own template styles.

2.4.2 Creating and Opening Documents

To create a new document, choose **File**, **New** from the Menu bar. The New dialog box should appear as depicted in Figure 2.18. The tabs on this dialog box refer to several groups of templates. Choose one of the tabs and click on a template. For example, choose the **Spreadsheet Solutions** tab and select **Invoice**. Once you have selected a template, click **OK** to create the new document. As you can see, much of the tedious formatting used to create an invoice has already been done for you.

If you want to create a new blank workbook, a quick method is to click on the ☐ button on the Standard toolbar. You will not be asked to choose from the template list.

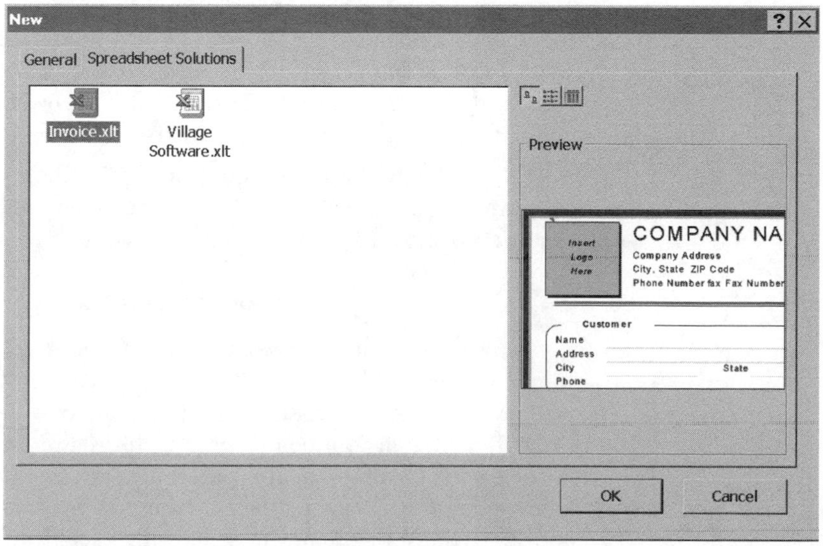

Figure 2.18. The New dialog box

To open an existing document choose **File**, **Open** from the Menu bar or choose the  button on the Standard toolbar. The Open dialog box should appear as depicted in Figure 2.19. From this dialog box, you can type in a path and file name, or you can browse the file system to locate a file. If the file system is very large, you may want to use the search function to locate files of a given name or files that contain a certain string of text.

Open			? X
Look in:	⬜ COP 5770		
📄FFT.xls			Open
📄Logplot Example.xls			Cancel
📄Matrix Addition.xls			Advanced...
📄Quadratic Example.xls			
📄XY Scatter Example.xls			

Find files that match these search criteria:

File name: [   ] Text or property: [   ] Find Now

Files of type: Microsoft Excel Files (*.xl*; *) Last modified: any time New Search

5 file(s) found.

Figure 2.19. The Open dialog box

2.4.3 Naming Documents

It is important to develop a methodical and consistent method for naming documents. Over time, the number of documents you maintain will grow larger and it will become harder to locate or keep track them. Documents that are related should be grouped together in a separate folder. Do not use the default workbook names, Book1, Book2, Book3, and so on or chaos will soon ensue. If documents are not given meaningful names, the documents may inadvertently be overwritten. Documents that have very general names, for example, **Spreadsheet**, will be difficult to locate later.

By default, Excel documents are given the extension xls. Unless you are specifically creating a template (.xlt), ASCII text document (.txt), or other special type of document, you should use the default extension.

2.4.4 Opening Workbooks with Macros

A *macro* is a recording of a group of tasks that are stored in a Visual Basic module. A set of frequently repeated commands can be stored and then executed with a single mouse click whenever needed. Macros are very powerful tools. However, macros can contain viruses that infect files on your computer. For this reason, you should enable macros only if you are certain of the origin of the document. For example, if you followed the above example and opened the invoice template, a warning box that resembles Figure 2.20 should have appeared. Since this template came with Excel, you can assume that it is safe and click **Enable Macros**. If you are unsure of the source of a macro, you should check the document using virus protection software before opening the document. Virus protection software is not provided with Microsoft Excel and must be purchased separately.

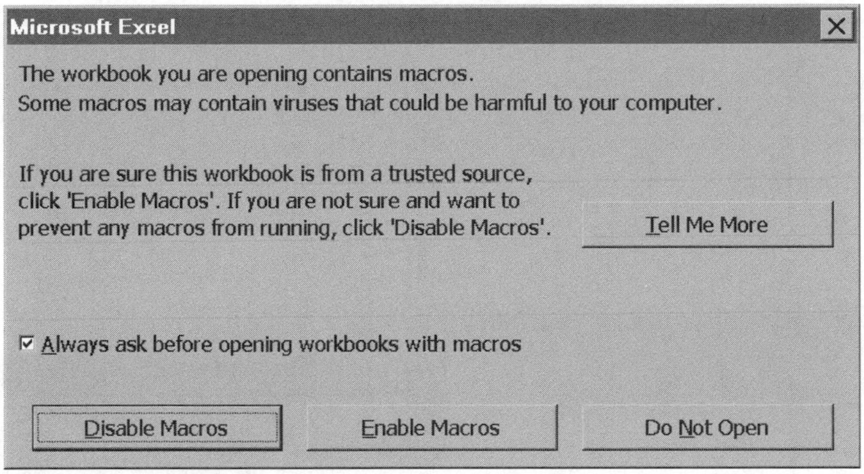

Figure 2.20.   The Macro Warning dialog box

2.4.5   Saving Documents

To save a document for the first time, choose **File**, then **Save As** from the Menu bar. The Save As dialog box should appear as depicted in Figure 2.21. Choose a folder in which to save the document by selecting the ▼ button on the right side of the box labeled **Save In**. Then type in (or select) a name for your document.

As mentioned in Section 2.4.3 on naming documents, it is wise to carefully choose a meaningful name for your document. Once a document has been given a name, it may be reopened and edited. To save an open document that already has a name, choose **File**, **Save** from the Menu bar, or choose the ⊟ button from the Standard toolbar. If you are unsure of the name of the current working document, you can view it in the Title bar.

Saving documents frequently is an important task. It is also important to make backup copies of your important documents on floppy disks or some other physical device. There are many tales of woe from students (and professors) who have lost hours of work after a power failure.

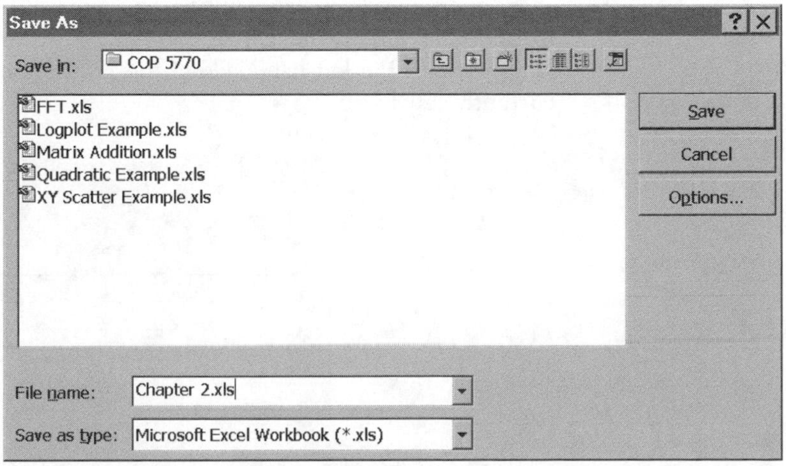

Figure 2.21.   The Save As dialog box

Fortunately, Excel has several *AutoSave* features that make the frequent saving of documents an easy task. The task of making frequent backup copies to a different medium, for example, floppy disk or tape, is something you must perform yourself, however.

To set the AutoSave features, choose **Tools**, **AutoSave**. (If the AutoSave option does not appear on the Tools menu you can add it to the menu by choosing **Tools**, **Add-Ins**, then checking the **AutoSave** box and clicking **OK**.) The AutoSave dialog box should appear as depicted in Figure 2.22. From the AutoSave dialog box you can choose

- How often to AutoSave (Ten minutes is a good starting choice.)
- Save all open workbooks or only the active workbook (The latter is a good starting choice.)
- Prompt before saving (The prompt can quickly get annoying so you may want to uncheck this item.)

Figure 2.22.   The AutoSave dialog box

2.5   EDITING A WORKSHEET

In addition to AutoSave, many other options may be set. To view the current settings choose **Tools**, **Options** from the Menu bar and browse through the various tabs. We recommend that you leave the default settings for now if you are a new Excel user.

2.5.1   Moving around a Worksheet

There are several methods of moving from place to place in an Excel worksheet. If the worksheet is relatively small, any of these methods will work equally well. As a worksheet grows in size, movement becomes more difficult and you can save a lot of time by learning the various movement methods. The current cell number is displayed in the Name box on the left-hand side of the Formula bar. Figure 2.23 shows that H5 is the currently active cell.

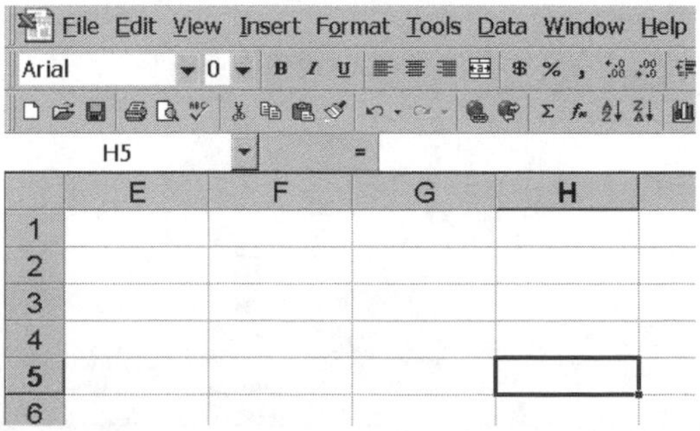

Figure 2.23.   The Name box

The general methods for moving around a document are:

- Movement using the keyboard
- Movement using the mouse
- Movement using the Go To dialog box

Movement Using the Keyboard

The keyboard may be used to select a worksheet from a workbook. The keyboard may also be used to navigate around a single worksheet quickly and effectively. There are many key combinations for moving and through a worksheet and among worksheets. Table 2-2 lists the most frequently used combinations.

TABLE 2-2   Movement within a Worksheet Using the Keyboard

KEY COMBINATION	ACTION
Ctrl + Page Down	Select next worksheet
Ctrl + Page Up	Select previous worksheet
⇐	Move one cell (column) to the left
⇒	Move one cell (column) to the right
⇑	Move up one cell (row)
⇓	Move down one cell (row)
Page Down	Move down one window
Page Up	Move up one window
Ctrl + ⇒	Move to right column of worksheet
Ctrl + ⇓	Move to bottom row of worksheet

Movement Using the Mouse

The mouse may be used to select a worksheet and to move within a worksheet. To select a worksheet, choose a tab from the Sheet Tab bar as depicted in Figure 2.10.

One method of moving around a worksheet with the mouse is to click on a cell. This is most useful if the new insertion point is located on the same screen. If the desired location is on a different page, then the scrollbars and scrolling arrows maybe used to move quickly to a distant location. Figure 2.24 shows the vertical scrollbar and arrows.

Figure 2.24. The vertical scrollbar

Movement Using the Go To Dialog Box

Open the Go To dialog box by choosing **Edit**, **Go To** from the Menu bar, or press the **F5** key. The Go To dialog box will appear as depicted in Figure 2.25. A history of previous references is kept in the Go To window so recently visited cells can be located quickly.

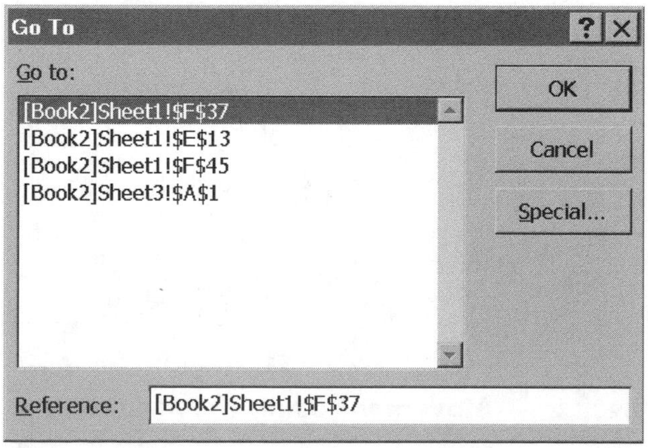

Figure 2.25. The Go To dialog box

Click the **Special** button on the Go To dialog box and the Go To Special dialog box should appear as depicted in Figure 2.26. You can select items from this dialog box to locate and browse a particular type of item. For example, Figure 2.26 shows that only cells containing formulas are to be located.

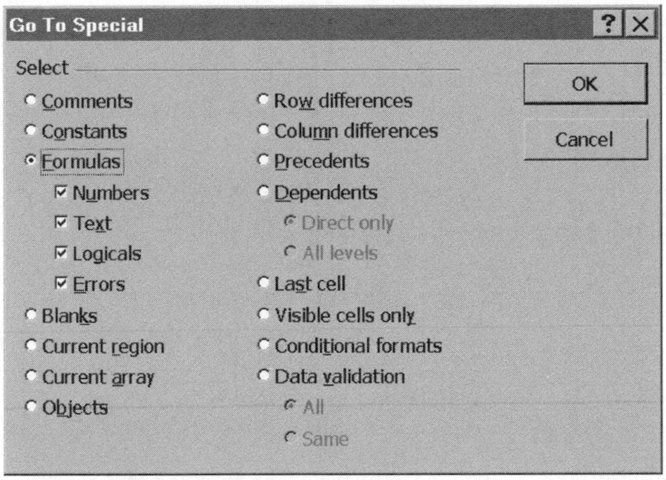

Figure 2.26. The Go To Special dialog box

2.5.2   Selecting a Region

Much of the time spent in spreadsheet preparation involves moving, copying, and deleting regions of cells or other objects. In this section, we will be selecting regions of cells, but the same principles apply to regions that contain charts, formulas, and other objects. Before an action can be applied to a region, the region must be selected. The selection process can be performed by using either the mouse or the keyboard.

To select a region of text with the mouse, move the mouse to the beginning of the region, click, and drag to the end of the region. As you drag the mouse, the selected region will be highlighted.

To select a region of text that is larger than one screen, drag the mouse to the bottom of the screen. If you hold the mouse at the bottom of the screen without releasing the mouse button, the selected region will continue to grow and the screen will scroll downward. This takes a little practice.

An alternative method for selecting large regions of a document is

1.   Click the mouse on one corner of the region that you wish to select.
2.   Hold down the **Shift** key and scroll to the ending location using one of the arrow keys, the **Page Up** key, or the **Page Down** key.

To select the entire worksheet, choose the **Select All** button at the top-left corner of the worksheet. The Select All button is depicted in Figure 2.27. This is useful if you are applying a change to every cell in a worksheet.

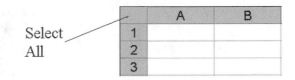

Figure 2.27.   The Select All button

If you make a mistake and incorrectly select a region, click the mouse cursor anywhere on the document window before you apply an action (such as delete). If the highlighting disappears, you have deselected the region.

PRACTICE!

Try the following exercise to practice selecting regions.

1. Place the cursor over cell B3 and type the number 5.
2. Press the down arrow key.
3. Type the number 6.
4. Press the down arrow key.
5. Type the number 7.
6. With the mouse, place the cursor over cell B5, hold down the left mouse button, and drag the mouse until cells B5, B4, and B3 are all highlighted.
7. Now choose the AutoSum button ∑ on the Standard toolbar.

A new cell will be added that contains the sum of cells B3, B4, and B5. The results should resemble Figure 2.28.

	A	B
1		
2		
3		5
4		6
5		7
6		18

Figure 2.28.   The AutoSum feature

2.5.3   Cutting, Moving, Copying, and Pasting

Once a region has been selected, several actions may be taken such as delete, move, copy, and paste. As usual, there are a variety of ways to accomplish these actions. One method uses the right mouse button, which has been unused up to now.

Cutting a Region

Cutting a region places it on the clipboard. To cut a region by using the mouse, first select the region using one of the methods described above. Then choose **Edit**, **Cut** from the Menu bar. The cut region will be highlighted by a rotating dashed line. An alternate method is to click the right mouse button and choose **Cut** from the Quick Edit menu that appears. The Quick Edit menu is depicted in Figure 2.29.

✂ Cu̲t
▤ C̲opy
▤ P̲aste
Paste S̲pecial...
I̲nsert...
D̲elete...
Clear Co̲ntents
▭ Insert Co̲mment
▭ F̲ormat Cells...
Pic̲k From List...

Figure 2.29.   The Quick Edit menu

Moving a Region

A region may be moved by first cutting the region and then pasting it to a new location. Try this by selecting a region, clicking the right mouse button, and choosing **Cut** from the Quick Edit menu. Now place the insertion point in a new location, and either

- Create a region of the same size and shape as the cut region, or
- Select a single cell.

Click the right mouse button, and choose **Paste** from the Quick Edit menu. The original region of cells should now appear in the new location. If you do not create the new region with the same size and shape, an error box will appear to prompt you.

An advantage of the cut and paste method of moving a region is that the region may be moved across documents and even across applications. You can cut a region from an Excel worksheet and paste the region into a Word document.

An alternate method for moving a region is to select the region and click and hold down the left mouse button anywhere on the edge of the region. Now drag the region to the new location. When the selected region point is in the correct location, release the mouse button.

Copying a Region

Copying a region is similar to moving a region except that the original copy of the region remains intact. To copy a region, first select the region to be copied. Choose **Edit**, and then **Copy** from the Menu bar. Place the insertion point in the new location and choose **Edit**, **Paste** from the Menu bar to make a copy. The last action can be performed as many times as needed if multiple copies are to be made.

An alternate method is to click the right mouse button and use the Quick Edit menu to perform the same actions. The copy and paste method can be used to copy regions to another document or another application.

2.5.4   Inserting and Deleting Cells

New cells may be added to a worksheet and cells may be deleted. To delete a region of cells, first select the region and choose **Edit**, **Delete** from the Menu bar. An alternate method is to click the right mouse button and select **Delete** from the Quick Edit menu. In either case, the Delete dialog box should appear as depicted in Figure 2.30.

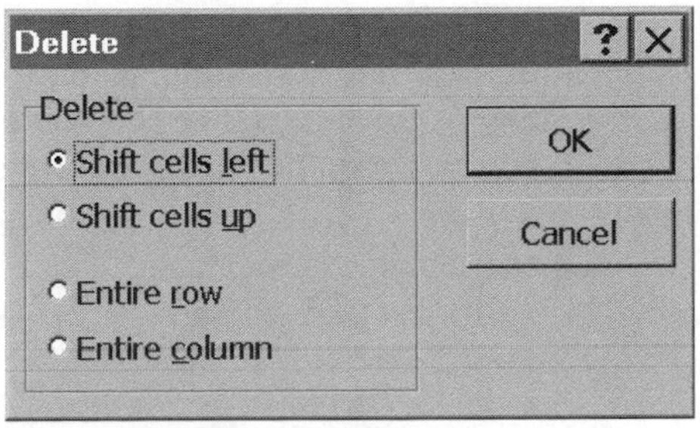

Figure 2.30.   The Delete dialog box

Choose the direction to shift the remaining cells in the worksheet. If you want to clear the contents of a region of cells without shifting, then click the right mouse button and choose **Clear** Contents from the Quick Edit menu.

You can insert new cells, rows, columns, or an entire worksheet by selecting **Insert** from the Menu bar as depicted in Figure 2.31.

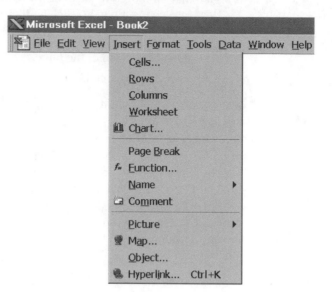

Figure 2.31.   Inserting cells, rows, columns, and worksheets

2.5.5   Shortcut Keys

There is another method of executing Excel commands. This method uses combinations of keys on the keyboard and bypasses the mouse altogether. For example, to execute the copy and paste functions using shortcut keys, first select a cell by placing the mouse cursor over the cell. Simultaneously hold down the **Ctrl** key and the key for the letter **C**. Throughout the book, the plus sign will denote keys that are to be pressed simultaneously; for example, the previous sentence will be worded, Press the **Ctrl + C** keys.

Using this shortcut to copy has the same effect as choosing the 🔳 button from the Standard toolbar (or choosing **Edit**, Copy from the Menu bar). To paste the contents of the cell to a new location, first select a new cell in which to copy by moving the mouse cursor. Now press **Ctrl + V**. Using this shortcut to copy has the same effect as choosing the 🔳 button from the Standard toolbar (or choosing **Edit**, **Paste** from the Menu bar).

Now you know three ways of executing the cut and paste functions. Why does Excel have so many ways of performing the same function? The reason is that users with different levels of experience have different needs. The novice user may have trouble finding commands. Using the Menu bar is a good method for the novice since the command names are listed and the commands are usually in the same place. As the novice gains experience, the toolbars become more useful since a toolbar button is faster to execute than a Menu bar selection. As a user becomes very proficient with Excel and learns to type at a rapid rate, the shortcut keys become the quickest way to execute a command. Movement of the fingers from keyboard to the mouse is avoided. The downside of using keyboard shortcuts is that they have to be memorized.

This book will teach you only a few keyboard shortcuts. As you become more proficient in Excel, you might consider learning and memorizing the keyboard shortcuts for several of your most frequently used commands. One method of learning shortcuts is to look at the right-hand side of the Menu bar items. For example, choose **Edit** from the Menu bar and note that the shortcut for **Cut** listed on the menu is **Ctrl + X**.

2.5.6 Undoing Mistakes

Word allows actions to be undone or reversed. To undo the last action, choose **Edit**, **Undo** from the Menu bar or type **Ctrl + Z**. To see the list of recent actions choose the down arrow button ⏷ next to the undo button ↶ ▾ on the Standard toolbar. From this list, you may select one or more actions to be undone. Note that if you select an action on the list, all of the actions above it will also be undone! If you accidentally undo an action then you may redo it by selecting the redo button ↷ ▾ on the Standard toolbar.

2.5.7 Spell Checking

Excel can check the spelling of cells containing text. To check the spelling in a region, first select the region and choose **Tools**, and **Spelling**. Alternate methods are to press the **F7** key or choose ✓ from the Standard toolbar. If Excel finds a spelling mistake then the Spelling dialog box will appear as depicted in Figure 2.32.

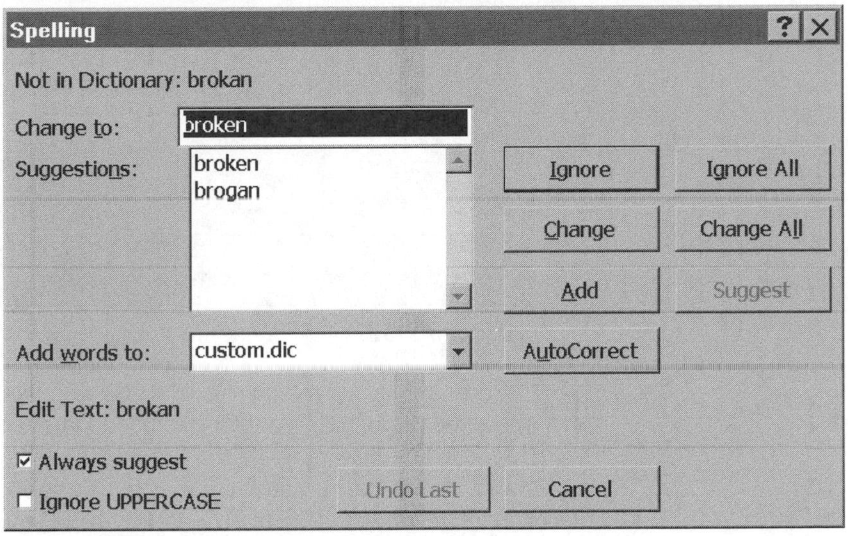

Figure 2.32. The Spelling dialog box

The region containing the mistake is displayed in the top text box. Suggestions for changes are presented in the bottom text box. At any point in the process, you can choose whether to accept or ignore the suggestions. If you choose a suggested correction, you may click the **Change All** button to change all occurrences of the misspelled word in the selected region.

You may add new words to the main dictionary by choosing the **Add** button. This will probably be necessary as you proceed through your coursework since many engineering terms are not in the custom dictionary.

2.5.8 The AutoCorrect Feature

The Excel *AutoCorrect* feature recognizes spelling errors and corrects them automatically. AutoCorrect performs actions such as automatically capitalizing the first letter of a sentence and correcting a word whose first two letters are capitalized. You can test to see if the AutoCorrect feature is turned on for your installation of Excel. Try typing the letters yuo and press the spacebar. Was the word automatically retyped as you? If so, then you have AutoCorrect turned on. To see the AutoCorrect options and dictionary, choose **Tools**, then **AutoCorrect**. The AutoCorrect dialog box will appear as depicted in Figure 2.33.

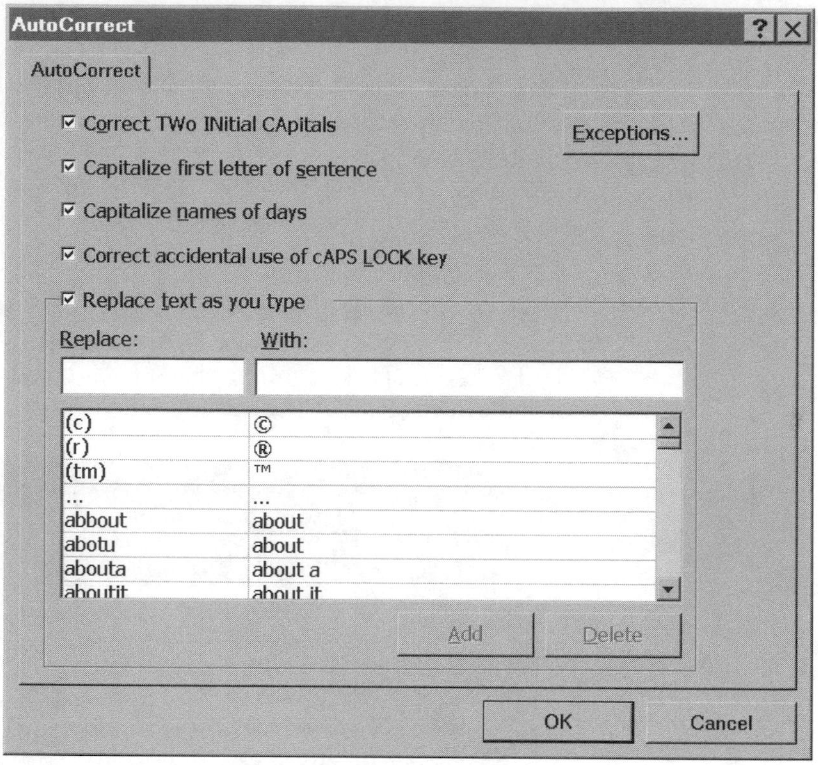

Figure 2.33. The AutoCorrect dialog box

From this dialog box you can select (or deselect) various AutoCorrect options. You can also scroll through the AutoCorrect dictionary, add entries to the dictionary, and add exceptions to the dictionary. This last feature is necessary for exceptions to the selected options. For example, if you have selected the option that automatically converts the second capital letter to lowercase, you may have an occasional exception. One example is the abbreviation for the chemical compound hydrochloric acid, HCl. Another is the abbreviation of megahertz to MHz.

Be careful when adding new entries into the AutoCorrect dictionary. You may inadvertently add an entry for a misspelling that is a legitimate word.

2.6   PREVIEWING AND PRINTING A WORKSHEET

Before attempting to print a document, make sure that your printer is correctly configured. See your operating system documentation for assistance.

2.6.1   Previewing a Worksheet

It is advisable to preview a document before printing it. Many formatting problems can be resolved during the preview process. First, select a region to print and choose **File**, **Print Area**, and **Set Print Area** from the Menu bar. The selected region will now be surrounded by a dashed line.

To preview the document as it will be printed select **File**, **Print Preview** from the Menu bar or choose the ⌕ button from the Standard toolbar. The selected region will be displayed in the same format in which it will be printed. In addition, the Print Preview toolbar is placed on the screen. The Print Preview menu bar is displayed in Figure 2.34. The available options on the Print Preview menu bar are listed in Table 2-3.

| Next | Previous | Zoom | Print... | Setup... | Margins | Page Break Preview | Close | Help |

Figure 2.34.   The Print Preview menu bar

TABLE 2-3 Print Preview Toolbar Options

BUTTON	ACTION
Next	Display next page of the worksheet
Previous	Display previous page of the worksheet
Zoom	Toggle between magnified and normal view
Print	Print the worksheet
Setup	Set the page orientation, margins, page order, etc.
Margins	Graphically set the margins and page stops
Page Break	Graphically set the page breaks
Close	Close this window and return to the worksheet
Help	Special help for the Print Preview menu bar

2.6.2   Printing a Worksheet

To print a document choose **File** and then **Print** from the Menu bar The Print dialog box will appear as depicted in Figure 2.35. To send a job directly without going through the print dialog box, select the 🖶 button on the Standard toolbar. The Print dialog box contains several choices. These include commands for collating, selecting the number of copies to print, and selecting a range of pages. A user may save a great deal of paper by using the Print Preview feature to select and print only those pages that have been modified.

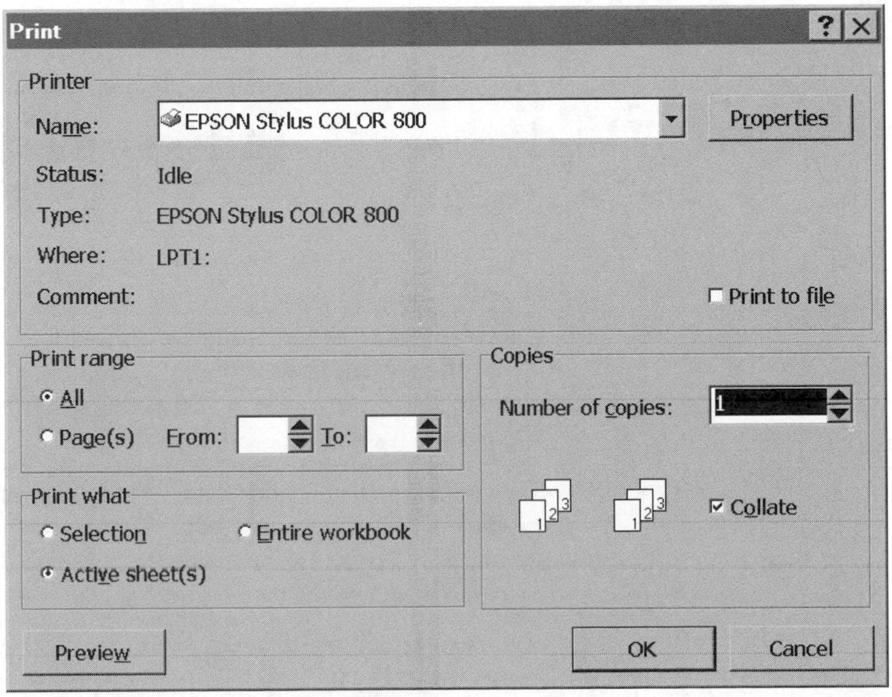

Print	?	×

Printer

Name: EPSON Stylus COLOR 800   ▼   Properties

Status: Idle

Type: EPSON Stylus COLOR 800

Where: LPT1:

Comment: □ Print to file

Print range

⊙ All

○ Page(s) From: [ ] To: [ ]

Print what

○ Selection   ○ Entire workbook

⊙ Active sheet(s)

Copies

Number of copies: [1]

☑ Collate

Preview   OK   Cancel

Figure 2.35.   The Print dialog box

Chapter Summary

In this chapter, you are introduced to Microsoft Excel. The basic Excel components including the Title bar, Menu bar, scrollbars, and various toolbars are presented. Several methods for accessing on-line help are demonstrated. You are guided through the creation of a new worksheet and the basic commands for editing and printing a worksheet.

KEY TERMS

AutoSave	Internet service provider	Status bar
Close control button	macro	template
Formula bar	Menu bar	Title bar
Full Screen control button	Minimize control button	

Problems

1. Practice cutting and pasting regions of cells. Can you cut and paste a region of Excel cells into a Word document? What about an MS-DOS window?

2. As you type, make notes of your most common misspellings. After you have collected a list, add the misspelled words to the AutoCorrect dictionary.

3. Excel is a large and complex application. To see the variety of commands and tools that are available, browse through the various toolbars. Choose **View**, **Toolbars**, **Customize** from the Menu bar. The Customize Toolbar dialog box will appear. Check each of the 22 toolboxes listed in the dialog box. As the toolbars appear on your screen, slowly drag your mouse across the toolbar icons and view the drop-down titles that appear. Figure 2.36 shows the Trace Dependents icon on the Auditing toolbar.

Figure 2.36.   The Auditing toolbar

4. Familiarize yourself with the large volume of on-line help. Choose **Help** and then **Contents and Index** from the Menu bar. The Help Topics dialog box will appear. Select, in turn, the **Contents**, **Index**, and **Find** tabs and scroll through the list that appears in each case.

5. Use the on-line help features of Excel to determine how Excel deals with the Y2K problem. (*Hint*: Y2K means *year 2000*.) Assume you are entering dates of birth in an Excel spreadsheet. If you enter 5/23/19, does Excel record the year to be 1919 or 2019? What about a date entered as 11/14/49?

6. Excel's trigonometric function PI returns an approximation of the mathematical constant π. Use the help feature to determine the number of digits of accuracy that is returned by this function.

3

Entering and Formatting Data

3.1   ENTERING DATA

Cells can be filled with numerical values, text, times, dates, logical values, and formulas. In addition, a cell may contain an error value if Excel cannot evaluate its contents. The basic types of cell values are covered in this section.

3.1.1   Numerical Data

Numerical values containing any of the following symbols can be entered into a cell:

```
0 1 2 3 4 5 6 7 8 9
+ - ( ) , /
$ % .
E e
```

Though numerical values are stored internally with up to 15 digits of precision (including the decimal point), they can be displayed in a variety of formats. To see a list of cell formats, first type a number into a cell and click the right mouse button. The Quick Edit menu will appear as depicted in Figure 3.1.

Select **Format Cells** from the Quick Edit menu. The Format Cells dialog box will appear. Choose the **Number** tab as depicted in Figure 3.2. From this dialog box, the numerical value you entered may be formatted as currency, a date, a fraction, or in scientific notation. When you change the format, the internal representation is not changed; only the method for displaying the value is modified. If the *general format* is selected, Excel will attempt to choose a format based on the contents of the cell. For example, if you type $3.4 into a cell, Excel will automatically convert to *currency format*, and the value will be right-justified and displayed as $3.40.

OBJECTIVES

After reading this chapter, you should be able to

- Enter various types of data into a worksheet
- Enter series of data quickly
- Format rows, columns, and cells
- Apply conditional formatting to a range of cells
- Sort one or more columns of cells

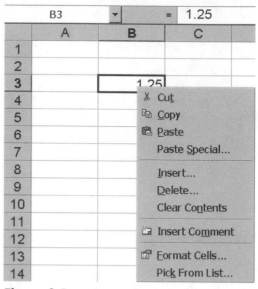

Figure 3.1.   The Quick Edit menu

| B3 | ▼ | = | 1.25 |

	A	B	C
1			
2			
3		1.25	
4			
5			
6			
7			
8			
9			
10			
11			
12			
13			
14			

Quick Edit menu items:
- ✂ Cut
- 🗐 Copy
- 📋 Paste
- Paste Special...
- Insert...
- Delete...
- Clear Contents
- 🗐 Insert Comment
- 🗐 Format Cells...
- Pick From List...

Format Cells

Tabs: Number | Alignment | Font | Border | Patterns | Protection

Category:
- General
- Number
- Currency
- Accounting
- Date
- Time
- Percentage
- Fraction
- Scientific
- Text
- Special
- Custom

Sample
1.25

General format cells have no specific number format.

OK   Cancel

Figure 3.2.   The Format Cells dialog box

3.1.2 Text Data

To treat the contents of a cell as text, first select the cell and apply the text format. Numerical values that are entered into a text cell cannot be used for calculation. You can perform many of the same functions to the contents of a text cell that are used for a Word document. These include changing font size, font type, and performing spell checking.

Once a cell has been stored internally as a number, it is slightly more difficult to convert it to an internal text representation. To do so, first select the cell, change the format to text, press **F2**, and **Enter**.

3.1.3 Date and Time Data

Excel stores dates and times internally as numbers. This allows you to perform arithmetic on dates and times. For example, you can subtract one date from another. If a dash (-) or slash (/) is inserted between two digits, Excel assumes the number is a date. If a colon (:) is used to separate two digits, Excel assumes the number represents time. Excel also recognizes the key characters AM, PM, A, and P to represent A.M. and P.M.

PRACTICE

Try entering data using several formats. First, select cells A1 and A2. Apply the number format to these cells with three decimal places of precision. Then type in the values 1.25 and 2.45, respectively. The results should be right-aligned and represented as 1.250 and 2.450, respectively.

Now select cell A3, choose the AutoSum button **Σ** from the Standard toolbar, and press **Enter**. The value 3.7 should appear in cell A3. Note that only one decimal place is shown. Since you did not specify a format, Excel assumed a general format and displayed only the significant digits.

Let's see how the text formatting differs from numerical formats. Select cells C1 and C2. Apply the text format to these cells and type in the values 1.25 and 2.450, respectively. The results should be left-aligned and the decimal places should appear exactly as you typed them.

Now select cell C4, choose the AutoSum button **Σ** from the Standard toolbar, and press **Enter**. The following formula should appear in cell C4:

```
=SUM()
```

Type C1:C2 inside the parentheses so that the formula looks like

```
=SUM(C1:C2)
```

Press **Enter**. Cell C4 should now contain a zero! This is because Excel cannot sum the text cells, so it returns a zero result. Your worksheet should resemble Figure 3.3.

	A	B	C
1	1.250		1.25
2	2.450		2.450
3	3.7		
4			0

Figure 3.3. Text and numerical formats

3.1.4 Fill Handles

Data entry can be tedious. The use of fill handles allows one to quickly copy a cell into a row or column of cells. Fill handles can also be used to create a series of numbers in a row or column. The *fill handle* appears as a small black square in the bottom-right corner of a selected region. A fill handle is depicted in Figure 3.4. When the mouse is placed over the fill handle, its shape will change to a black cross. Click and hold the right mouse button while dragging the mouse to the right over four or five cells. When the mouse is released, the value in the original cell will be copied into the new cells.

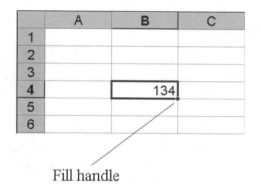

Fill handle

Figure 3.4. Example of a fill handle

The fill handle can also be used to create a series of numbers, dates, or times. The series can be linear or exponential. To see the fill series options, place the mouse over a fill handle, click the right mouse button, and drag the mouse. When the mouse is released, the Fill Series drop-down menu will appear as depicted in Figure 3.5.

Copy Cells
Fill Series
Fill Formats
Fill Values

Fill Days
Fill Weekdays
Fill Months
Fill Years

Linear Trend
Growth Trend
Series...

Figure 3.5. The Fill Series drop-down menu

PRACTICE!

Practice using the fill handle by trying the following steps. First, try copying the contents of a cell. Type the value 1.5 into cell A1. Grab the fill handle with the right mouse button and drag it over cells B1:G1. When you release the mouse button, the value 1.5 should appear in cells A1:G1.

Now try creating a linear series. Type the values 1.5 and 2.5 into cells A3 and B3, respectively. Select the region A3:B3 and grab the fill handle with the right mouse button. Drag the fill handle over the cells C3:G3. Select **Linear Trend** from the drop-down menu.

Finally, create a growth series. Type the values 1.5 and 2.5 into cells A5 and B5, respectively. Select the region A5:B5 and grab the fill handle with the right mouse button. Drag the fill handle over the cells C5:G5. Select **Growth Trend** from the drop-down menu.

The results of your three exercises should resemble Figure 3.6.

	A	B	C	D	E	F	G
1	1.5	1.5	1.5	1.5	1.5	1.5	1.5
2							
3	1.5	2.5	3.5	4.5	5.5	6.5	7.5
4							
5	1.5	2.5	4.166667	6.944444	11.57407	19.29012	32.15021

Figure 3.6. Examples using the fill handle

3.2 FORMATTING WORKSHEETS

3.2.1 Formatting Cells

In the Section 3.1.1, you were shown how to format numerical data. Several other cosmetic formatting options are available for selected cells. These include choice of fonts, colors, borders, shading, and alignment.

To access the cell formatting options, first select a region of cells, choose **Format**, and then **Cells** from the Menu bar. An alternate method is to click the right mouse button and choose **Format Cells** from the Quick Edit menu. The Format Cells dialog box will appear as depicted in Figure 3.7. From this dialog box you may choose one of six tabs to format the font characteristics, alignment within the cell, borders, colors, fill patterns, and password protection of a worksheet.

3.2.2 Formatting Columns and Rows

The primary use of the row and column formatting option is to determine the row height and the column width. You can specify the height and width exactly or you can ask Excel to *AutoFit* the columns and rows for you. The AutoFit function adjusts the selected columns to the minimum width required to fit the data. If the data are changed, the AutoFit may have to be reapplied.

A second use of the row and column formatting option is to hide or uncover a row or column. This may be useful for simplifying the view of a complex worksheet. To view the column (or row) formatting options, first select a region, choose **Format**, and then

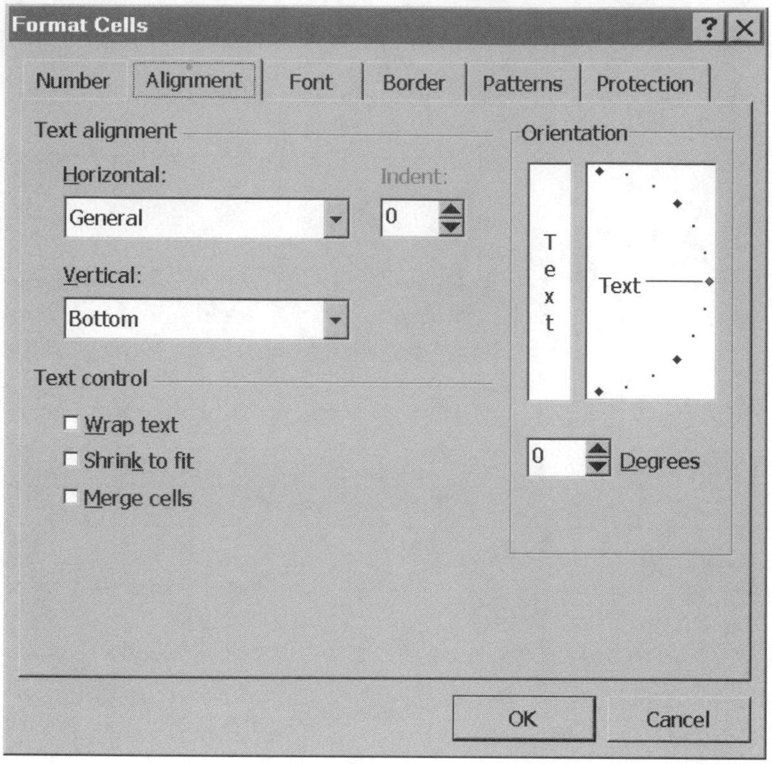

Figure 3.7.   The Format Cells dialog box

Column (or **Row**) from the Menu bar. A drop-down menu will appear as depicted in Figure 3.8.

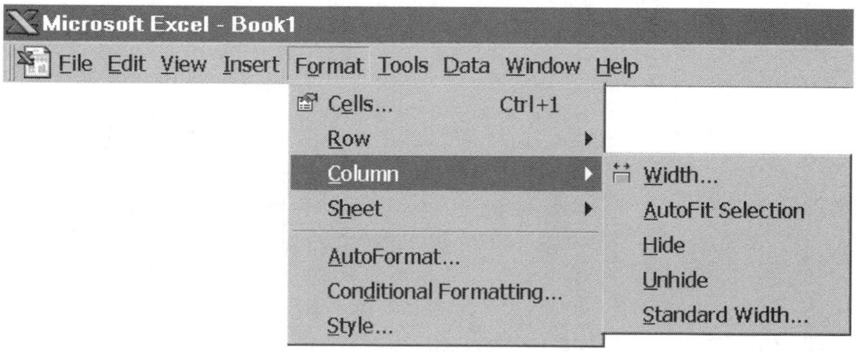

Figure 3.8.   The Column Format drop-down menu

3.2.3   Table AutoFormats

Excel provides a few preformatted table types for convenience. To access the AutoFormat function, first select a region, and choose **Format**, **AutoFormat** from the Menu bar. The AutoFormat dialog box will appear as depicted in Figure 3.9. Browse through the table formats in the list and view the samples in the Sample box.

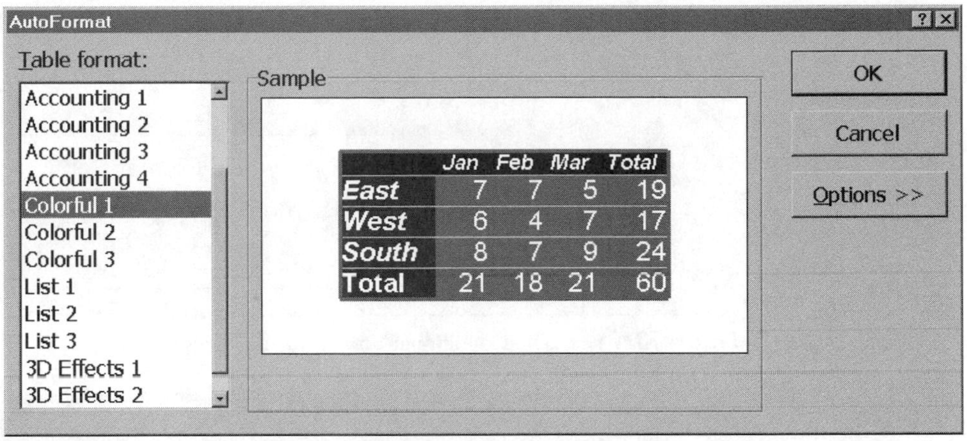

Figure 3.9. The AutoFormat dialog box

3.2.4 Conditional Formatting

Formatting options may be applied conditionally. That is, you may choose logical criteria that are used to format cells. For example, consider the list of temperature data in Figure 3.10. If we want to be alerted when a station's temperature is less than 20 degrees or greater than 51.1 degrees, we can use conditional formatting to highlight cells that meet those criteria.

	A	B
1	Station	Temp (C)
2	A02	23.5
3	A34	23.4
4	B45	53.2
5	A07	72.6
6	C12	12.5
7	B05	34.6

Figure 3.10. Temperature data from several monitoring stations

To initiate conditional formatting, select the region (B2:B7) and choose **Format**, **Conditional Formatting** from the Menu bar. The Conditional Formatting dialog box will appear as depicted in Figure 3.11. Use the pull-down menus to set the criteria *Cell Value is less than 20.0*. Choose the Format button and select a distinctive format for the selected cells, then choose **Add**. The Conditional Formatting dialog box will now expand to include a second condition. Set the second condition to *Cell Value is greater than 51.1*.

The results should resemble Figure 3.12. Now choose OK. The cells with temperatures meeting the criteria should be highlighted.

3.2.5 Sorting

The columns of a selected region may be sorted based on the values in the column. Columns can be sorted in ascending or descending order based on numerical, date or alpha values. The default order type is alphabetical.

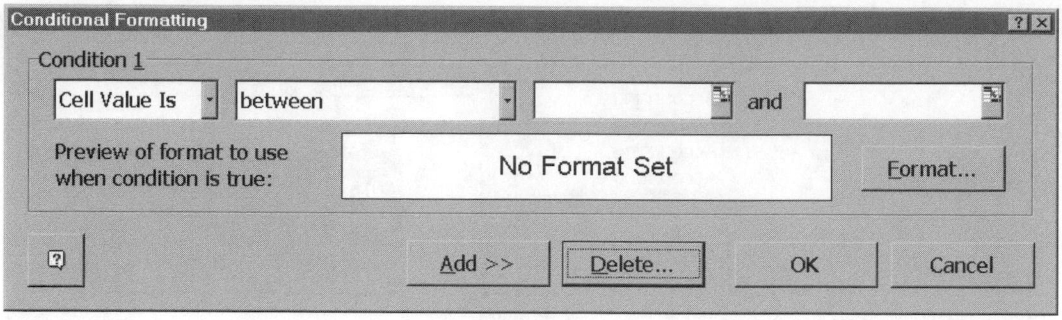

Figure 3.11. The Conditional Formatting dialog box

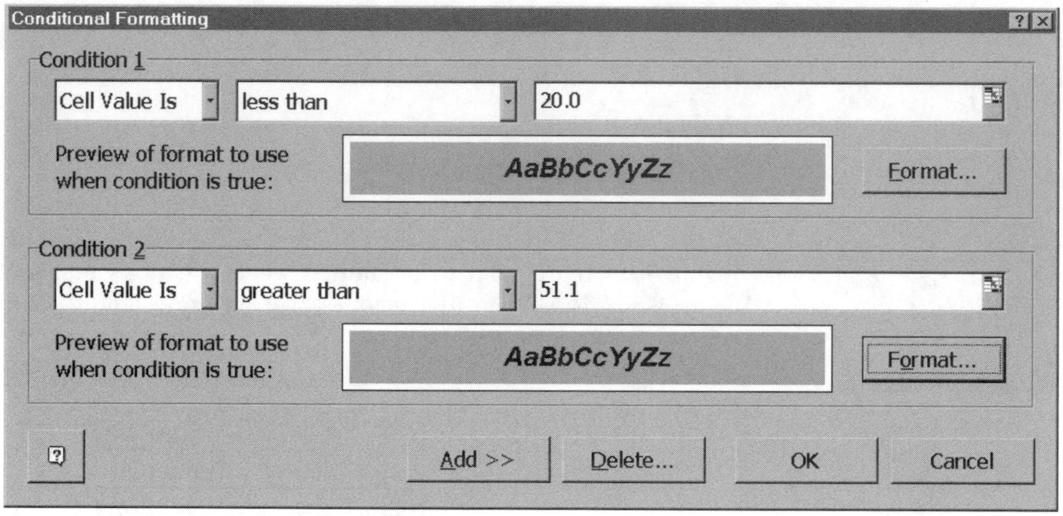

Figure 3.12. Example of conditional cell formats

To sort the temperature data in Figure 3.10 alphabetically on the station code, first select the region (A2:B7). Choose the Sort button 2↓ from the Standard toolbar. The data should be sorted as depicted in Figure 3.13. Note that the cells that were conditionally formatted in Section 3.2.4 are highlighted.

Important: You must select all columns that you want to remain related. For example, if you select column A, but not column B, then column A will be sorted but the cells in column B, will not moved — the temperatures will be no longer be associated with the correct stations.

Sorts that are more complex can be performed by choosing **Data** and then **Sort** from the Menu bar. For example, a sort may be based on more than one column and sorts may be performed on rows instead of columns.

	A	B
1	Station	Temp (C)
2	A02	23.5
3	A07	72.6
4	A34	23.4
5	B05	34.6
6	B45	53.2
7	C12	12.5

Figure 3.13. Temperature data sorted by station

3.2.6 Formatting Entire Worksheets

Several formatting options apply to an entire worksheet. A worksheet can be hidden, renamed, or a different background can be selected. These functions can be accessed by choosing **Format**, **Sheet** from the Menu bar. A workbook can easily grow into a collection of dozens of worksheets. It is helpful to give worksheets meaningful names instead of using the default Sheet 1, Sheet 2, and so on.

APPLICATION

Engineering Economics

Engineering economics involves the study of interest, cash flow patterns, techniques for maximizing net value, depreciation, and inflation. This is an important area of study for all engineers since engineers frequently serve as managers or executive officers of corporations.

The following example demonstrates how John can make a choice between investing $10,000 in a sav-

ings account that he knows will give him 6% growth or in the stock market in a fund that has historically shown 11% growth. John knows that there is no guarantee that the stock fund will continue to return a rate of 11%, but Excel allows him to forecast at 10-year intervals the growth differential between 6% and 11%, and he can use this information to decide if it would be worth it to take a chance that it will

Accumulated Capital		
Age	6% Growth	11% Growth
18	$10,000	$10,000
28	$17,908	$28,394
38	$32,071	$80,623
48	$57,435	$228,923
58	$102,857	$650,009
68	$184,202	$1,845,648

John's analysis shows that, if the stock market does return 11%, at retirement age, he will end up with 10 times as much money than if he puts the $10,000 into a savings account at 6%.

HOW'D HE DO THAT?

If John invested $10,000 in an account that paid 6% interest (6% APR—*Annual Percentage Rate*), one year later he would receive an interest payment of

$$0.06 \times \$10,000 = \$600$$

When the interest is added to the account, the value of the account after one year would be

$$\$10,000 + \$600 = \$10,600$$

To develop an equation that can be used to determine the value in the account at the end of any year, let's define some variables:

P = present value = the amount of John's initial deposit

i = fractional interest rate (i.e., 0.06, not 6)

F = future value = the value at the end of any year

N = number of years since the initial deposit

After one year the amount in John's account can be computed as follows:

$$F_1 = \$10,000 + (0.06 \times \$10,000)$$
$$= P + i\,P$$
$$= P\,[1 + i]$$

After a second year, the amount in the account will be

$$F_2 = F_1 + i\,F_1$$

$$= \{P[1 + i]\} + i\,\{P[1 + i]\}$$

$$= P[1 + i]\,[1 + i]$$

$$= P[1 + i]^2$$

After N years, the amount in the account will be

$$F = P\,[1 + i]^N$$

The $[1 + i]^N$ is called the *single-payment compound amount factor*, and you can find tables of these factors for various interests rates in most economics texts, or you can easily create the table in Excel. A table created using Excel is shown here. (See Chapter 4 for more information on creating this table.)

Compound Amount Factors						
Interest Rate:	6%	7%	8%	9%	10%	11%
Fractional Rate:	0.06	0.07	0.08	0.09	0.1	0.11
Year						
0	1.0000	1.0000	1.0000	1.0000	1.0000	1.0000
10	1.7908	1.9672	2.1589	2.3674	2.5937	2.8394
20	3.2071	3.8697	4.6610	5.6044	6.7275	8.0623
30	5.7435	7.6123	10.0627	13.2677	17.4494	22.8923
40	10.2857	14.9745	21.7245	31.4094	45.2593	65.0009
50	18.4202	29.4570	46.9016	74.3575	117.3909	184.5648
60	32.9877	57.9464	101.2571	176.0313	304.4816	524.0572
70	59.0759	113.9894	218.6064	416.7301	789.7470	1488.0191
80	105.7960	224.2344	471.9548	986.5517	2048.4002	4225.1128

John calculated the future value of his money at 6% using the compound amount factors in the 6% column. After 10 years, the $10,000 John invested would be worth 1.7908 times his initial investment:

$$F_{10} = \$10,000 \times 1.7908 = \$17,908$$

After 20 years at 6%, the compound amount factor is 3.2071, so John's initial invest will have grown to

$$F_{20} = \$10,000 \times 3.2071 = \$32,071$$

Using the compound amount factors table, it was easy for John to calculate the future value of his money for each of the two possible interest rates.

How'd He Make His Table Look Like That?

The first step was to get the information into an Excel spreadsheet, like this:

	A	B	C	D
1	Accumulated Capital			
2	Age		6% Growth	11% Growth
3	18	10000	10000	
4	28	17908	28394	
5	38	32071	80623	
6	48	57435	228923	
7	58	102857	650009	
8	68	184202	1845648	
9				

The table could look better, so we will start modifying the formatting. The formatting changes required to create John's table are as follows:

1. Add dollar signs to the values in columns B and C.
2. Center the values in the Age column.
3. Bold the column headings in row 2.
4. Center the title over the entire table.
5. Add horizontal lines to the table.
6. Add a heavy border around the table.
7. Add a heavy border around the column headings.
8. Change the background and text colors of the title.

Step 1. Add dollar signs to the amounts in columns B and C.

Select the values in cells B3 through C8, then right-click to bring up the pop-up menu.

When you choose **Format Cells** the Format Cells dialog is displayed.

On the **Number** panel, select **Currency**, and set the number of displayed decimal places to 0. Click on the OK button to close the dialog.

When the currency format has been applied, column C is no longer wide enough to display the last value. To have Excel adjust the column width to fit the contents, use the **Format** menu, **Column**, and **Autofit Selection**

Step 2. Center the age values in column A.

Select the " Age " heading and the values in column A. Right-click on the selected region to bring up the pop-up menu. Select **Format Cells**

The Format Cells dialog is displayed. From the **Alignment** panel, set the horizontal alignment to **Center**. Click the **OK** button to close the dialog.

The Age heading and the age values should now be centered in column A.

	A	B	C	
1	Accumulated Capital			
2	Age	6% Growtl	11% Growth	
3	18	$10,000	$10,000	
4	28	$17,908	$28,394	
5	38	$32,071	$80,623	
6	48	$57,435	$228,923	
7	58	$102,857	$650,009	
8	68	$184,202	$1,845,648	
9				

Step 3. Bold the column headings in row 2.

Select the column headings in row 2 and press the **B** button on the toolbar.

This is also a good time to adjust the size of the columns to the contents of the table. Select the column headings in row 2, and then use **Format** on the main menu and **Column** and **Autofit Selection** to adjust the column widths.

	A	B	C	
1	Accumulated Capital			
2	**Age**	**6% Growth**	**11% Growth**	
3	18	$10,000	$10,000	
4	28	$17,908	$28,394	
5	38	$32,071	$80,623	
6	48	$57,435	$228,923	
7	58	$102,857	$650,009	
8	68	$184,202	$1,845,648	
9				

Step 4. Center the title over the entire table.

To center the title over the table, first merge cells A I through C 1, and format the merged cells to set the horizontal alignment to Center.

Select those three cells and right-click to bring up the pop-up menu. Select **Format Cells**

	A	B	C	D	
1	Accumulated Capital				
2	**Age**	**6% Growth**	**11% Gr**	✂ Cut	
3	18	$10,000	$1	Copy	
4	28	$17,908	$2	Paste	
5	38	$32,071	$8	Paste Special...	
6	48	$57,435	$22	Insert...	
7	58	$102,857	$65	Delete...	
8	68	$184,202	$1,84	Clear Contents	
9					
10				Insert Comment	
11				Format Cells...	
12				Pick From List...	
13				Hyperlink...	
14					

On the **Alignment** panel, set the horizontal alignment to **Center**, and put a check in the box before Merge Cells. Click **OK** to close the dialog.

Step 5. Add horizontal lines to each row of the table.

Select the entire table, right-click on the selected region, and choose **Format Cells**.

On the **Border** panel, first choose a **Line Style** and indicate which lines to draw. In the dialog box shown here, a narrow solid line at the top and bottom of the selected region has been requested, as well as horizontal lines between rows.

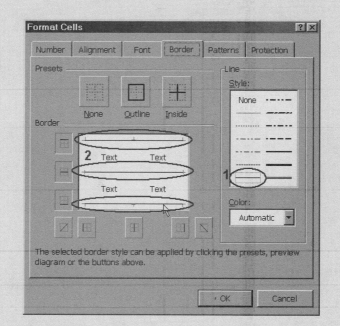

Step 6. Add a heavy border around the entire table.

Select the entire table, right-click, and choose **Format Cells** On the **Border** panel, first choose a line style and click on the **Outline** preset line configuration button.

Step 7. Add a heavy border around the column headings.

To add a heavy border around the title and column headings, select cells A1 through C3 and repeat the process described in step 6 above.

	A	B	C
1		Accumulated Capital	
2	Age	6% Growth	11% Growth
3	18	$10,000	$10,000
4	28	$17,908	$28,394
5	38	$32,071	$80,623
6	48	$57,435	$228,923
7	58	$102,857	$650,009
8	68	$184,202	$1,845,648
9			

Step 8. Change the background and text colors of the title.

Select the title (merged cells A1 through C1). Right-click and choose **Format Cells**. On the **Patterns** panel, choose a new background color (black was selected in this example).

On the **Font** panel, set the Font style to **Bold**, and the font color to white.

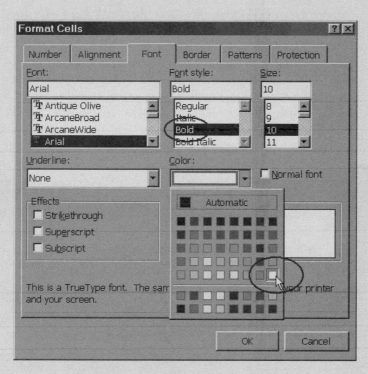

The completed table now looks like this:

	A	B	C
1		Accumulated Capital	
2	Age	6% Growth	11% Growth
3	18	$10,000	$10,000
4	28	$17,908	$28,394
5	38	$32,071	$80,623
6	48	$57,435	$228,923
7	58	$102,857	$650,009
8	68	$184,202	$1,845,648
9			

Chapter Summary

This chapter introduces the data types used in Excel and the methods for entering data into a worksheet. This chapter presents the commands for formatting cells, rows, columns, and worksheets. Also presented are the methods for conditional formatting of cells and sorting lists.

KEY TERMS

AutoFit	currency format	fill handle
conditional format	engineering economics	general format

Problems

1.   Open a worksheet and choose **Format** and **Cells** from the Menu bar. Note the first category in the format list named General. General format cells have no specific format. When you use the General format for a cell, the Excel application attempts to determine the numerical type from clues in the number. For example, if you type $3.56 into a cell, Excel guesses that you are representing money and changes the format type to Currency. What format type does Excel use if you enter a fraction such as 1/2 into a General format cell? What type does Excel use if you type?

2.   Have some fun with the cell formatting options. Play with the options under the **Font**, **Border**, **Alignment**, and **Patterns** tabs. If you get in trouble, learn to use the undo feature by choosing **Edit**, **Undo** from the Menu bar.

3.   Excel stores numbers with 15 digits of precision. Prove to yourself these limits of numerical precision. Select an empty cell and format the cell to the *Number* format with 20 decimal places. Select the equal sign on the Formula bar and type the following formula: =SQRT(2)

   Since the square root of 2 is an irrational number, the fractional part of its decimal representation has an unending number of nonrepeating digits. At what number of digits does Excel's accuracy stop?

4.   Create a worksheet that looks like Figure 3.14. Sort the data in your worksheet by station and then by date in ascending order. The results should look like Figure 3.15 (except for the shading).

	A	B	C
1	Station	Date	Temp (C)
2	A02	02/02/99	23.5
3	A07	01/23/99	72.6
4	A02	02/14/99	23.4
5	B05	03/01/99	34.6
6	B05	01/05/99	53.2
7	C12	02/12/99	12.5
8	A02	01/23/99	24.6
9	B05	02/05/99	23.2

Figure 3.14.   Temperature data

5.   Create conditional formatting that highlights temperatures between 15.0 and 24.0 degrees. The results should shade the same cells as Figure 3.15

	A	B	C
1	Station	Date	Temp (C)
2	A02	01/23/99	24.6
3	A02	02/02/99	**23.5**
4	A02	02/14/99	**23.4**
5	A07	01/23/99	72.6
6	B05	01/05/99	53.2
7	B05	02/05/99	**23.2**
8	B05	03/01/99	34.6
9	C12	02/12/99	12.5

Figure 3.15.   Sorted temperature data with conditional formatting

4

Engineering Computation

4.1 INTRODUCTION

The ability to manipulate formulas, arrays, and mathematical functions is the most important feature of Excel for engineers. A common scenario is for an engineer to test and refine potential solutions to a problem using Excel. After the engineer has been satisfied that the solution works for small data sets, the solution may be translated to a programming language such a C or FORTRAN. The resulting program can then be executed on a powerful workstation or supercomputer using large data sets. This use of a worksheet is called building a *prototype*. A spreadsheet package such as Excel is useful for building prototypes because solutions can be developed quickly and modified easily.

In the following sections, formulas and functions will be used to solve two problems that should be familiar to engineering students: (1) finding the solutions to a quadratic equation and (2) matrix multiplication. These examples will be used to demonstrate many of the features of Excel that are related to engineering computation.

In addition, you will be introduced to Excel macros — a method for recording and executing a series of actions. The use of macros can be a time-saving feature as you learn to solve problems that require a series of computations.

4.2 CREATING AND USING FORMULAS

A formula in Excel consists of a mathematical expression. The cell containing the formula can display either the formula definition or the results of applying the formula.

The default is to display the results in the cell. This is usually preferable since the formula definition for the currently

After reading this chapter, you should be able to

- Create mathematical formulas in a worksheet
- Use Excel's predefined functions
- Debug worksheet formulas with errors
- Perform simple matrix operations with Excel
- Record and run a macro
- Access the Visual Basic Editor

active cell is displayed in the Formula bar. Figure 4.1 shows cell D1 to be the currently active cell. The Formula bar shows the formula definition of D1 to be **=(A1*B1)/C1**. The result of applying this expression is displayed in cell D1 as **1.746296**. In the following paragraphs we will show how to build and debug formula definitions.

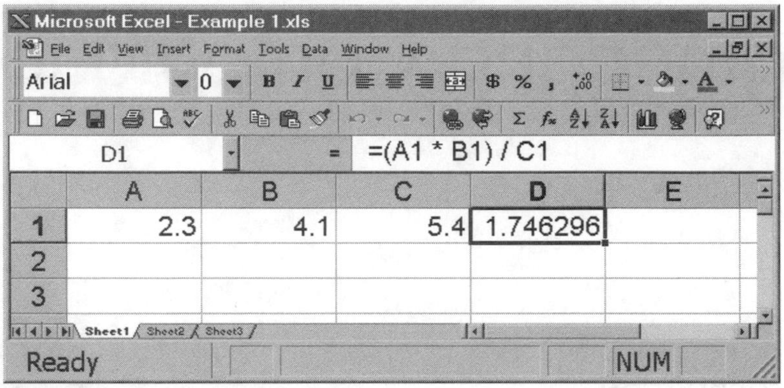

Figure 4.1. An example of a formula

4.2.1 Formula Syntax

An Excel formula has strict syntax. A formula can consist of operators, cell references, cell names, and function names. The use of each of these syntactic groups will be covered in this chapter.

A formula always begins with an equal sign (=). This symbol is an indicator for Excel to evaluate the following expression instead of simply placing the expression contents in the cell. (Try removing the equal sign and see what happens.) Since this is the most common error that users make when creating a formula, Microsoft has automated the placement of the equal sign when using the Formula Editor. The Formula Editor can be accessed by clicking the **=** button at the left end of the formula bar. We recommend the use of the Formula Editor because the user is given immediate feedback about syntax and execution errors. A variety of predefined functions may be selected directly from the Formula Editor (see Section 4.3). Table 4-1 displays the available arithmetic *operators*:

TABLE 4-1 Arithmetic operators

OPERATOR	OPERATION
%	Percentage
^	Exponentiation
*,/	Multiplication, Division
+/–	Addition, Subtraction

The operators are listed in order of precedence. For example, exponentiation will be calculated before addition. If a different precedence is desired, parentheses must be used. There are other operators for the manipulation of text and for Boolean comparison that will not be covered here. Please use the on-line help for further information about these operators.

Cell References can be entered in two ways. A cell location can be typed into the formula editor or the cell can be selected using the mouse. Let's walk through an example that uses both methods of referencing cells.

1. Enter the values 7.5 and 6.2 into cells A3 and B3, respectively.

2. Select cell C3.

3. Choose the **=** button. The Formula Editor will appear and an equal sign will automatically be entered as the first character in the formula.

4. Select cell A3 by clicking on it with the left mouse button. A3 will be added to the formula in the Formula Editor.

5. Move the cursor to the formula in the Formula Editor and type the rest of the following expression:A3 ***** B3 + A3^2

6. The screen should resemble Figure 4.2. Note that the results of evaluating the formula are displayed immediately in the Formula Editor as you build the formula.

7. Click on **OK** and the Formula Editor will disappear. The formula result of **102.75** will now be displayed in cell C3.

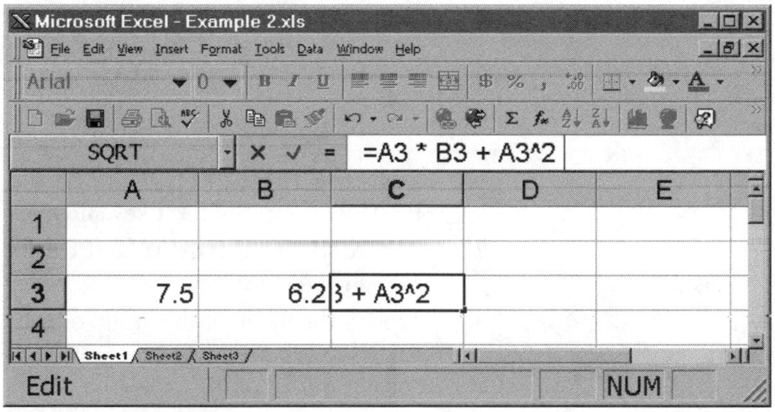

Figure 4.2. Creating a formula

4.2.2 Selecting Ranges

In the previous example single cells were selected (or typed) into the formula definition. A range of cells can also be used in a formula. A range of cells can be entered by dragging the mouse across the cells. Be careful not to insert a range into an expression that doesn't make sense mathematically. For example, the following formula

$$\textbf{=SUM(D4:D8)}$$

will sum cells D4 to D8. But, the following formula

$$\textbf{=SQRT(D4:D8)}$$

makes no sense since you can't take the square root of a range of numbers. When an invalid range is entered, Excel responds by placing the following error message in the target cell:

$$\textbf{\#VALUE}$$

4.2.3 Cell and Range Names

A group of cells can be named and the name added to a stored list. The name can then be used to reference the group of cells in a formula. Consider a range of cells that represents the following matrix:

$$A = \begin{bmatrix} 1 & -1 & 2 \\ 4 & 0 & -1 \\ -8 & 2 & 2 \end{bmatrix}$$

This matrix can be represented in a worksheet as depicted in Figure 4.3. Assume you want to perform operations on the diagonal of the matrix in a formula. For example, the following formula will sum the diagonal elements:

= SUM(A1,B2,C3)

	A	B	C
1	1	-1	2
2	4	0	-1
3	-8	2	-2

Figure 4.3. A 3 × 3 matrix

The following steps demonstrate how to name the diagonal elements:

1. Select the diagonal cells. Click on A1. Hold down the **Ctrl** key and click on B2. Hold down the **Ctrl** key and click on C3.
2. Choose **Insert**, **Name**, and **Define**. A drop-down menu titled Define Name should appear.
3. Type in the name of the group of cells (e.g., **Diagonal**). Your screen should resemble Figure 4.4.
4. Click **OK** to finish the operation

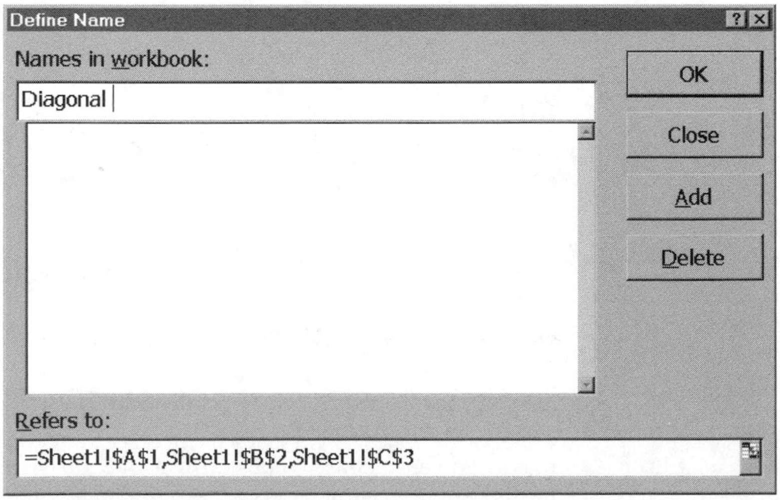

Define Name   ? X

Names in workbook:

Diagonal

OK

Close

Add

Delete

Refers to:

=Sheet1!$A$1,Sheet1!$B$2,Sheet1!$C$3

Figure 4.4. Naming a region of cells

The name Diagonal is now associated with the cell range (A1, B2, C3) and can be used anywhere the range is referenced. To use a name in a formula, first place the cursor at the insertion point, choose **Insert**, **Name** and then **Paste**. A drop-down box with the list of names will be displayed. Names can also be typed directly into formulas.

For example, a formula that sums the diagonal elements of the matrix can now be stated as

$$\textsf{=SUM(Diagonal)}$$

This is more readable and less prone to typographical errors than the original version of the formula. The importance of using names will become clear as you begin to build more complex formulas (and attempt to debug errors in them).

4.2.4 Absolute and Relative References

Formulas may be copied from one location to another in a worksheet. Usually, you will want the referenced cells to follow the formula. For example, you may want to copy a formula that sums a row of numbers. In Figure 4.5 notice that cell E4 contains a formula that sums the range A4:C4. If cell E4 is copied to cell E5 by using the **Edit**, **Copy**, and **Paste** selections, cell E5 will contain a copy of the formula. Note that the range of cells that are summed in Figure 4.5 has *followed* the formula. The formula in E5 sums A5:C5, not A4:C4!

E5		=	=SUM(A5:C5)	
	A	**B**	**C**	**D**	**E**
1					
2					
3					
4	3	4	7	Sum=	14
5	5	12	2	Sum=	19

Figure 4.5. A relative reference

This is called *relative referencing*. The range in the formula **=SUM(A4:C4)** is by default a relative reference. There are times when you may wish to copy a formula and not have the references follow the formula. This is called *absolute referencing*. A cell or range is denoted as an absolute reference by placing a dollar sign ($) in front of the row or column to be locked.

In Figure 4.5, change the formula in E4 to read **=SUM($A44:$C$4)**. Now copy the formula to cell E5. Notice that the cell references have not followed the formula and the resulting sum in cell E5 is still **14**.

PRACTICE!

There are times when you may want to make a relative reference to some cells and keep other references fixed. For example, a formula may use a constant and several variables. Place the following formula in cell C7 to compute the circumference of a circle: **=$C$3*B7^2** and create a worksheet that resembles Figure 4.6. Copy the formula to cells C8, C9, and C10. The reference to C3 (pi) should remain fixed since it is an absolute reference and the reference to B7 (radius) should follow the formula since it is a relative reference. Create a formula that computes the area of a circle and add it to your worksheet. Use an absolute reference for the constant *pi*. Use a relative reference for the variable *radius*

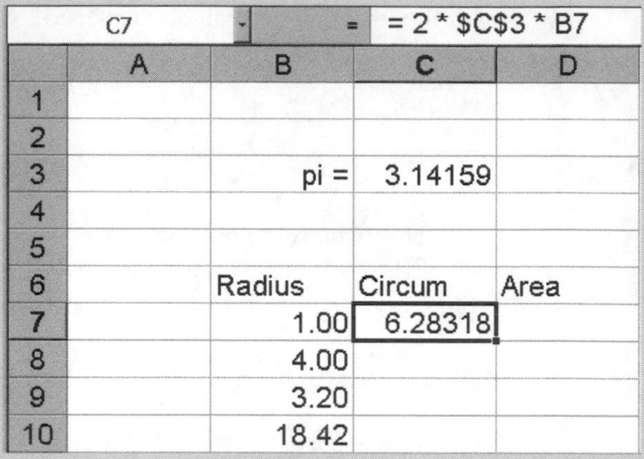

C7 = 2 * $C$3 * B7

	A	B	C	D
1				
2				
3		pi =	3.14159	
4				
5				
6		Radius	Circum	Area
7		1.00	6.28318	
8		4.00		
9		3.20		
10		18.42		

Figure 4.6. Mixed relative and absolute references

Example: Solution of Quadratic Equations

An example of a slightly more complex use of formulas is the solution of quadratic equations. You may recall from high school algebra that if a quadratic equation is expressed in the following form

$$ax^2 + bx + c = 0$$

then the solutions for x are

$$x = -b \pm \frac{\sqrt{b^2 - 4ac}}{2a}, \quad (2a \neq 0)$$

Since Excel does not directly recognize imaginary numbers, we must make the further restriction that

$$b^2 - 4ac \geq 0$$

Assume that a, b, and c are stored in cells A2, B2, and C2, respectively. We will place the formulas for the two solutions in D2 and E2, respectively. The Excel formula for the first solution is

```
=(-B2+SQRT(B2^2-4*A2*C2))/(2*A2)
```

and the formula for the second solution is:

```
=(-B2-SQRT(B2^2-4*A2*C2))/(2*A2)
```

PRACTICE!

Use the quadratic solutions given above to practice entering and using formulas in Excel. Label the columns so your worksheet resembles Figure 4.7. Copy the formulas so you can enter up to five sets of coefficients. (Don't type them five times.) Notice how the row numbers in the formulas change since you are using relative references. Also, notice that an error is displayed for the solutions on row 5 since one of our assumptions is violated (2a = 0).

D6	▾	=	= (-B6 + SQRT(B6^2 - 4 * A6 * C6)) / (2 * A6)	
	A	**B**	**C**	**D**	**E**

	A	B	C	D	E
1	Coefficient A	Coefficient B	Coefficient C	Root 1	Root 2
2	1	2	1	-1.0000	-1.0000
3	1	16	1	-0.0627	-15.9373
4	-4	-8	24	-3.6458	1.6458
5	0	18	24	#DIV/0!	#DIV/0!
6	-4	-8	4	-2.4142	0.4142

Figure 4.7. Computing solutions to a quadratic equation

Electric Circuit Analysis

A general expression for the current I in a DC transient circuit is

$$I(t) = I_\infty + (I_0 - I_\infty)e^{-t/T}$$

where

I_0 is the current at time zero (the moment the switch is moved)

I_∞ is the current at time $t = \infty$

$T = RC$ is the time constant for a series R–C (resistance - capacitance) circuit

$T = L/R$ is the time constant for a series R–L (resistance - inductance) circuit.

The engineer designing the circuit needs to know how long it will take the circuit to respond after the switch is closed. You can see from the general expression that the current will change from the initial value (I_0) to the final value (I_∞) following an exponential curve. Because the current asymptotically approaches the final value, the answer to the question, How long does it take for the circuit to respond when the switch closes? is infinite time. But, for practical purposes, the current gets very close to I_∞ fairly rapidly. We need a way to quantify how quickly the current gets close to the final value.

In the figure below, the current has been plotted as a percentage of the final value, and the time has been plotted as t/T.

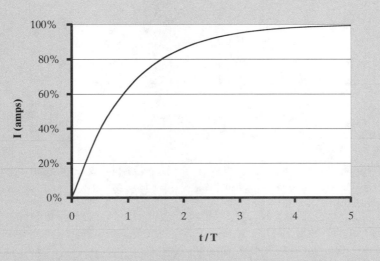

When $t = 1\ T$ (or $t/T = 1$), the current in the circuit will be approximately 63% of the final value. That is, after a period of time equal to one time constant, the current will have risen to 63% of the final value.

When $t = 2\ T$ ($t/T = 2$), the current will be about 86% of the final value. When $t = 3\ T$ ($t/T = 3$), the current is 95% of the final value.

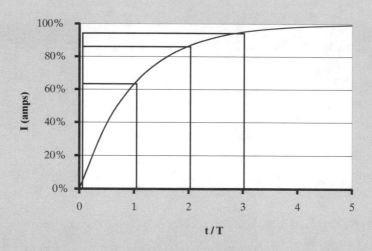

The time required for the current in the circuit to reach 95% of the final value is a commonly used approximation of the time required for the circuit to respond when the switch is closed. The time required for the current in a series R–C or R–L circuit to reach 95% of the final value is $3T$ (a time equal to three time constants for the circuit).

The equations in cells B7, B9 and B11 are

Cell B7:   = B5/B4

Cell B9:   = B3/B4

Cell B11:   = 3*B7

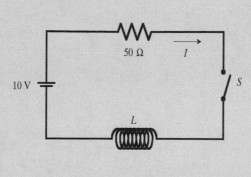

	A	B	C	
1	Transient DC Circuit			
2				
3	V:	10	volts	
4	R:	50	ohm	
5	L:	20	henry	
6				
7	T:	0.4	seconds	
8	I(0):	0	amp	
9	I(inf):	0.2	amp	
10				
11	3T:	1.2	seconds	
12				

For the circuit shown here, the initial current (the instant the switch is closed) is zero amps, and the final current can be determined from the voltage and resistance shown using Ohm's Law ($V = IR$). The time constant for this series R–L circuit is $T = L/R$, where L is an inductance with a value of 50 Henrys. Using Excel, you can calculate the time required for the current in the circuit to reach 95% of the final value and plot the current as a function of time.

To create a plot of current versus time

1. Create a column of time value from 0 seconds to something larger than $3T$ (1.2 seconds in this example).

2. Solve for the current at the first time value using the equationCell B16:

=$B$9+($B$8−$B$9)*EXP(−A16/$B$7)

Note that absolute cell references (dollar signs) were used for all of the constants in the general expression. Only the reference to the time should be changed when cell B16 is copied.

3. Copy the equation in cell B16 down to have Excel calculate the current at each time.

4. Use the Chart Wizard to create a plot of current versus time.

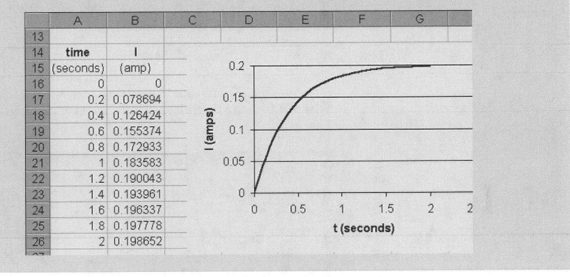

4.2.5 Error Messages

The formulas we have presented so far are relatively simple. If you make an error when typing one of the example formulas, the location of the error is relatively easy to spot. As you begin to develop more complex formulas, locating and debugging errors become more difficult. When a syntactic error occurs in a formula, Excel will attempt to catch the error immediately and display an error box that explains the error. However, formulas can be syntactically correct but still produce errors when the formula is executed. If an expression cannot be evaluated, Excel will denote the error by placing one of eight error messages in the target cell. These are listed in Table 4-2.

TABLE 4-2 Excel error messages

######	The value is too wide to fit in the cell, or an attempt was made to display a negative date or time.
#VALUE	The wrong type of argument was used in a formula (for example, text was entered when an array argument was expected).
#DIV/0	An attempt was made to divide by zero (see the quadratic equation example in Figure 4.7).
#NAME	A name is not recognized. Usually the function or defined name was misspelled. Note that named ranges or functions may not contain spaces.
#N/A	This error means not available. It occurs most often when a function has been given an incorrect number of arguments or, in the case of matrix functions, the argument matrix size does not correspond to the actual matrix size. Figure 4.8 demonstrates an attempt to place the inverse of a (2×2) matrix into a (3×3) matrix.
#REF	A referenced cell is not valid. This usually occurs when a cell is referenced in a formula and that cell is then deleted. It also occurs if an attempt is made to paste a cell over a referenced cell.
#NUM	The expression produces a numeric value that is out of range or invalid. Examples are extremely small or large numbers, or imaginary numbers. Try the formula **=SQRT(−1)**.
#NULL	An attempt was made to reference the intersection of two areas that don't intersect.

	A	B	C	D	E
				{=MINVERSE(A2:B3)}	
1					
2	3	4		-3	2
3	5	6		2.5	-1.5
4				#N/A	#N/A

Figure 4.8. Example of a #N/A (not available) error

4.2.6 Debugging Errors Using Cell Selection

Debugging errors in a worksheet is made much easier by the use of the special cell selection option. To view the special cell selection menu, first select a range of cells to view and click **Edit**, **Go To**, and **Special**. The Go To Special dialog box should appear as depicted in Figure 4.9.

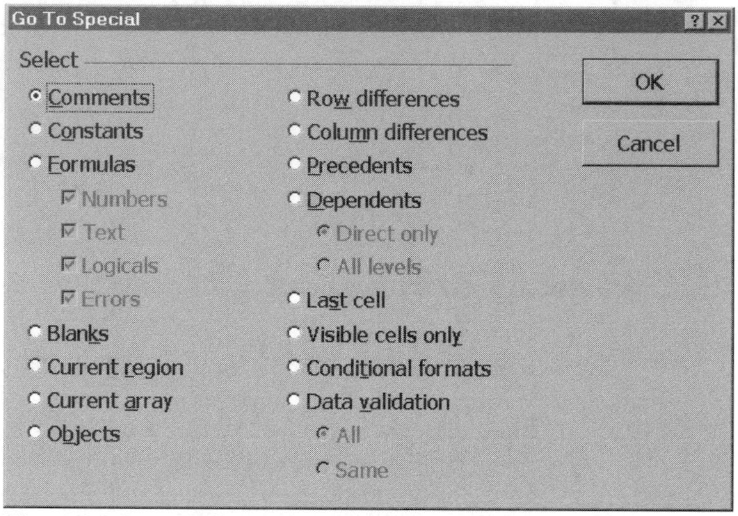

Figure 4.9. The Go To Special dialog box

From this menu, a variety of options may be used to assist in the debugging process. We will discuss several of the options that are most relevant to debugging mathematical formulas.

Formulas.

A common worksheet error is the accidental replacement of a formula with a constant. The selection of the **Formula** option will highlight all cells that contain formulas. You can further refine this option by selecting formulas that result in numerical, text, logical, or error values.

Precedents.

This option displays cells that precede the selected cell(s). The displayed cells are all necessary for the computation of the selected cell(s). For example if cell D4 contains the formula **=A3*B3**, cells A3 and B3 precede D4. This option may be refined by choosing either **Direct Only** or **All Levels**. The Direct Only option will display the immediate precedents. The All Levels option will recursively display precedents (precedents of precedents). If cell A3 contained the formula **=SUM(A1:A2)**, A1 and A2 (as well as A3 and B3) will show up as precedents of D4 if the All Levels option is selected.

Dependents.

This option displays cells that depend on the selected cell(s). For example, if you select cell B3 and choose the **Dependents** option, cell D4 will be displayed. This is because the formula in cell D4 depends on B3 for its computation.

Column (or Row) Differences.

This option highlights cells in a column or row that have a different *reference pattern* from the other cells. For example, if all of the selected cells in a column contain formulas except one cell (which contains a constant), the odd cell will be displayed.

The following example demonstrates the use of the cell selection technique. Figure 4.10 illustrates a worksheet that computes the standard deviation of the numbers in column A. The difference between a data value and the mean value is computed in column B using the formula **=A1-$E$2**. This difference is squared in column C using the formula **=B1^2**. The problem is that the answer is incorrect! The standard deviation should be 13.67 not 13.02. The error was found by using the following steps:

1. Select column B by clicking on the column label.
2. Choose **Edit**, **Go To**, and **Special**.
3. Choose **Column Differences** and click **OK**.

The result is that cell B5 is highlighted. By looking in the Formula bar you can see that B5 incorrectly contains a constant value instead of a formula. The debugging tools prove their worth as the worksheet gets larger and more complex. (Consider trying to find the same error without the debugging tool if column A contained 3,000 rows.)

B5		=	-8.54				
	A	B	C	D	E	F	G
						Sum of Differences Squared	Standard Deviation
1	32	0.7143	0.5102		Mean		
2	14	-17.2857	298.7959		31.2857	1017.8500	13.02466
3	52	20.7143	429.0816				
4	26	-5.2857	27.9388				
5	18	-8.5400	72.9316				
6	45	13.7143	188.0816				
7	32	0.7143	0.5102				

Figure 4.10. Using cell selection to debug a formula

4.2.7 Debugging Errors Using Tracing

Excel also provides a visual method for tracing precedents, dependents, and cells with errors. The auditing tool may be accessed by choosing **Tools** and **Auditing**. The easiest way to manipulate the visual tool is to select ***Show Auditing Toolbar***. The Auditing toolbar contains buttons for tracing precedents, dependents, and cells with errors. The tool draws blue arrows showing the direction of precedence. Cells with arrows are boxed in red. Figure 4.11 demonstrates the effect of choosing **Trace Precedents** from the Auditing Toolbar when cell F2 is selected. Every cell in column C is a precedent of the formula in cell F2 **=SUM(C1:C7)**.

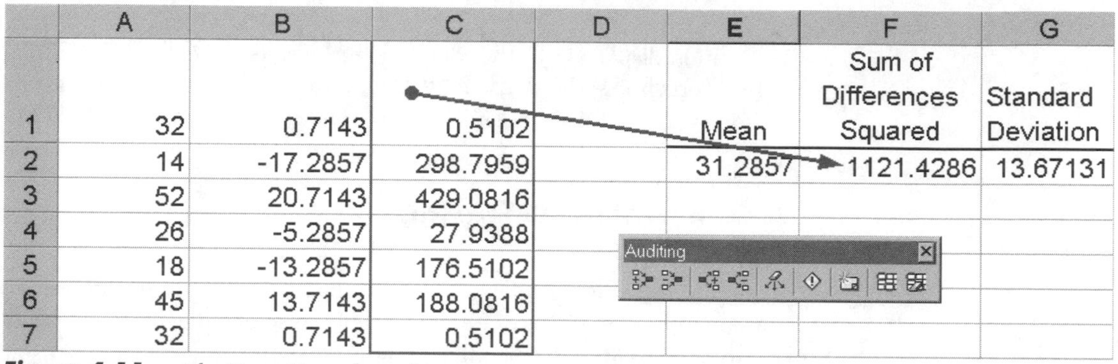

	A	B	C	D	E	F	G
1	32	0.7143	0.5102		Mean	Sum of Differences Squared	Standard Deviation
2	14	-17.2857	298.7959		31.2857	1121.4286	13.67131
3	52	20.7143	429.0816				
4	26	-5.2857	27.9388				
5	18	-13.2857	176.5102				
6	45	13.7143	188.0816				
7	32	0.7143	0.5102				

Figure 4.11.   The Trace Precedents feature

4.3   MATHEMATICAL FUNCTIONS

Excel has a large number of built-in functions that are similar to functions in a programming language. A function takes a specified number of arguments as input and returns a value. Excel functions are organized into function groups. The groups include database functions, financial functions, text functions, and date/time functions. Three groups that are of the most interest to engineers are the mathematical functions, the logical functions, and the statistical functions. We will focus on the use of these three function groups.

To browse the available functions, click the **ƒₓ** Paste Function button on the Standard toolbar. The Paste Function dialog box will appear as depicted in Figure 4.12. You can use this dialog box to select and paste functions into a formula or merely to browse and learn about the available functions and their syntax.

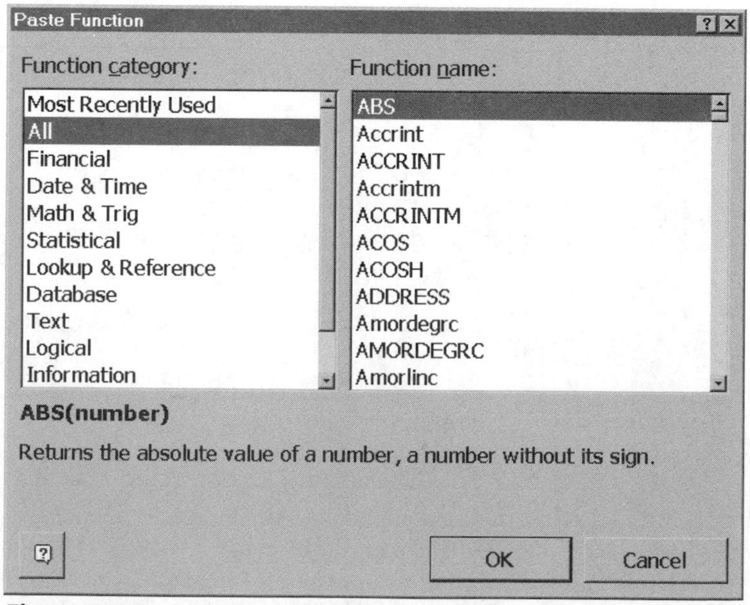

Figure 4.12.   The Paste Function dialog box

The following steps will walk you through the use of two simple statistical functions that compute the mean and median of a list of numbers.

1. Enter Seven midterm grades into the range A1:A7 (you can use the numbers from the example in Section 4.2.7.) Format the cells to be numbers with one digit to the right of the decimal point.

2. Name the cell range (e.g., **MidTerm**) by selecting the region, then choose **Insert**, **Name**, **Define** from the Menu bar.

3. Select a cell to hold the mean (average) of the midterm grades; then select the Paste Function key f_x .

4. The Paste Function dialog box will appear. Select **Statistical** from the Function Category list and select **Average** from the Function Name list. Click **OK**.

5. The Formula Editor should now appear. Erase whatever is labeled Number 1 on the line and type **MidTerm**. The Formula Editor should resemble Figure 4.13. (Note that cell A7 = 32 doesn't appear in Figure 4.13 since it extends beyond the extent of the box.)

6. Click OK to finish the operation.

```
┌─ AVERAGE ─────────────────────────────────────────────────┐
│                                                            │
│   Number1  Midterm                          = {32;14;52;26;18;45
│   Number2                                   = number       │
│                                                            │
│                                             = 31.28571429  │
│   Returns the average (arithmetic mean) of its arguments, which can be numbers or names,
│   arrays, or references that contain numbers.              │
│        Number1: number1,number2,... are 1 to 30 numeric arguments for which you want
│                 the average.                               │
│                                                            │
│   [?]     Formula result = 31.2857          [  OK  ] [ Cancel ]
└────────────────────────────────────────────────────────────┘
```

Figure 4.13. The Formula Editor

PRACTICE!

Perform steps 1 to 6 above, except choose Median from the function Name list instead of Average.

4.4 MATRIX OPERATIONS

Matrices or arrays are frequently used in the formulation and solution of engineering problems. A *matrix* is defined to be a rectangular array of elements. Elements are referenced by row and column number. A spreadsheet is a natural application to represent and manipulate matrices. Excel has a number of built-in matrix operations that are called *array functions*. These include

MDETERM(array)—returns the matrix determinant for the named array;

MINVERSE(array)—returns the inverse of the named array;

MMULT(array1, array2)—performs matrix multiplication on the two named arrays.

There are also several predefined functions that compute sums or differences of products on matrices. In addition, many other functions take ranges as arguments and can be used to evaluate a matrix. For demonstration purposes we'll use the two following matrices which are entered in ranges A3:B4 and D3:E4, respectively (see Figure 4.14).

$$A = \begin{bmatrix} 3 & 1 \\ 4 & 3 \end{bmatrix} \qquad\qquad B = \begin{bmatrix} 3 & -5 \\ 1 & 0 \end{bmatrix}$$

The following steps will guide you through performing matrix addition. Recall that matrix addition is performed by adding each of the corresponding cells of two matrices. The two matrices must be of the same *order*, which means they both have the same number of rows and same number of columns. The order of a matrix is often described as the number of rows by the number of columns (rows x columns). The example matrices above are of order (2×2).

1. Name matrices *A* and *B* by choosing **Insert**, **Name**, **Define** from the Menu bar.

2. Select the range G3:H4 by clicking and dragging the mouse over these cells.

3. Type the following formula into the formula bar:

   =A+B

4. Simultaneously press the following keys: **Ctrl**, **Shift**, and **Enter**. Curly braces will appear enclosing the formula. (*Note*: You cannot type the curly braces; the **Ctrl**, **Shift**, and **Enter** key sequence must be used.) The range G3:H4 will now display the matrix sum of *A* and *B*. Your screen should be identical to Figure 4.14.

G3		= {=A + B}					
A	B	C	D	E	F	G	H
1							
2							
3	3	1		3	-5		6	-4
4	4	3		1	0		5	3

Figure 4.14.   Example of matrix addition

As a second example, we will walk you through the execution of the *transpose* operation. The transpose of a matrix is the matrix that is formed by interchanging the rows and columns of the original matrix. To find the transpose of *B*;

1. Select a range of empty cells in which to store the results. The selected range must be of the same order as *B* (2×2).

2. Type the following into the formula bar:

   =TRANSPOSE(B)

3. Simultaneously press the following keys: **Ctrl**, **Shift**, and **Enter**. Curly braces will appear enclosing the formula. The result should be

$$B^T = \begin{bmatrix} 3 & 1 \\ -5 & 0 \end{bmatrix}$$

PRACTICE!

Matrix multiplication is defined as follows. If $A = [a_{ij}]$ is an $m \times n$ matrix and $B = [b_{ij}]$ is an $n \times p$ matrix, then the *product* $AB = C = [c_{ij}]$ is an $m \times p$ matrix defined by

$$c_{ij} = \sum_{k=1}^{n} a_{ij}b_{kj}, \quad i = 1,2,\dots,m, \quad j = 1,2,\dots,p,$$

From this example, the product of A and B is calculated to be

$$AB = \begin{bmatrix} 3 & 1 \\ 4 & 3 \end{bmatrix}\begin{bmatrix} 3 & -5 \\ 1 & 0 \end{bmatrix} = \begin{bmatrix} (3 \cdot 3) + (1 \cdot 1) & (3 \cdot -5) + (1 \cdot 0) \\ (4 \cdot 3) + (3 \cdot 1) & (4 \cdot -5) + (3 \cdot 0) \end{bmatrix} = \begin{bmatrix} 10 & -15 \\ 15 & -20 \end{bmatrix}$$

Excel has a built-in matrix multiplication function named MMULT(). Use this function to verify the above results. You can practice using this function even if you have not yet studied matrix multiplication.

4.5   USING MACROS TO AUTOMATE COMPUTATIONS

A macro is a stored collection of commands. If you repeat the same set of commands repeatedly, using a macro can be a convenient time saving feature.

A macro is stored internally in a Visual Basic module. It is not within the scope of this text to teach you the Visual Basic language. However, Excel supports recording and executing macros without knowing Visual Basic. In the following sections, you will be guided through recording and running a macro. Then you will be shown how to view the Visual Basic code that contains the macro commands. If you were to learn Visual Basic, you could edit the code directly or write your own macros in the Visual Basic language.

4.5.1   Recording a Macro

Before recording a macro, it is wise to carefully plan the steps that you will be taking. When in recording mode, everything you type is recorded — mistakes and all. In the following example, the majors steps for computing several statistics of a set of data are listed. It is assumed you are familiar with the use of Excel's built-in mathematical functions. If not, first review the previous sections in this chapter.

To record an example macro, perform the following steps:

1.   Create a new workbook and place the following numbers in cells A1:A10 10, 12, 45, 32, 23, 23, 76, 21, 32, 21.

2.   Turn on macro recording by selecting **Tools**, **Macro**, and **Record New Macro** from the Menu bar. The Record Macro dialog box will appear as depicted in Figure 4.15. Give your macro a name—the example uses MyFirstMacro. This dialog box also allows you to choose where to store the macro, and if you wish, to identify a shortcut key to execute the macro. Be careful: Any shortcut key you choose will overwrite the default Excel shortcut key. When you are finished, press **OK**. Note that everything you now type will be recorded in the macro until you stop the recording process! To assist you in stopping the recording process, the small Stop Recording box will appear as depicted in Figure 4.16.

3. Click on the top left-hand square on the border of the worksheet and choose **Format** and **Cells** from the Menu bar. Format the cells to be of type Number with two decimal points of accuracy.

4. Place the text Mean in cell B1 and place the formula AVERAGE(A1:A10) in cell B2.

5. Place the text Median in cell C1 and place the formula MEDIAN(A1:A10) in cell C2.

6. Place the text Max in cell D1 and place the formula MAX(A1:A10) in cell D2.

7. Place the text Min in cell E1 and place the formula MIN(A1:A10) in cell E2.

8. Center and format your column labels if you wish.

9. Now press the **Stop** button in the Stop Recording box.

Congratulations, you have recorded a macro! Your worksheet should resemble Figure 4.17. Save your worksheet.

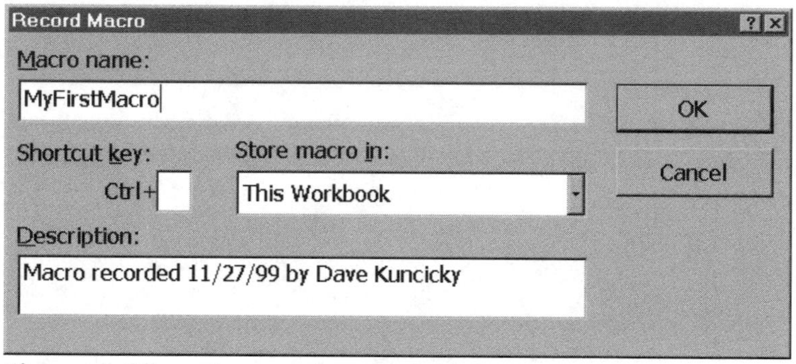

Figure 4.15. The Record Macro dialog box

Figure 4.16. The Stop Recording box

	A	B	C	D	E
1	10.00	Mean	Median	Max	Min
2	12.00	29.50	23.00	76.00	10.00
3	45.00				
4	32.00				
5	23.00				
6	23.00				
7	76.00				
8	21.00				
9	32.00				
10	21.00				

Figure 4.17. Sample worksheet after performing steps in Section 4.5.1

4.5.2   Executing a Macro

You can now retrieve and reuse your recorded macro at will. To see how powerful the use of macros can be, first clear the contents of all of the cells on your current worksheet. Then type in ten new numbers into cells A1:A10.

Execute the macro by choosing **Tools**, **Macro**, **Macros** from the Menu bar. The shortcut keys **ALT+F8** will perform the same action. The Macro dialog box will appear as depicted in Figure 4.18.

Select your macro's name from the list and choose **Run**. Voila! You worksheet should automatically perform all of the commands you typed previously.

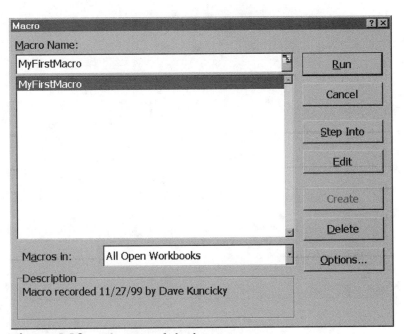

Figure 4.18.   The Macro dialog box

4.5.3   Editing a Macro

Several functions may be performed from the Macro dialog box. The macro may be deleted by choosing the **Delete** button. A shortcut key may still be added for a macro by choosing the **Options** button. The **Step Into** button allows you to debug a macro.

Choose the **Edit** button and the Microsoft Visual Basic Editor will appear as depicted in Figure 4.19. Inside the editor you can view and modify the Visual Basic code that was created when you recorded the macro.

For example, the line

```
ActiveCell.FormulaR1C1 = " Mean "
```

is the code that places the text Mean in cell B1.

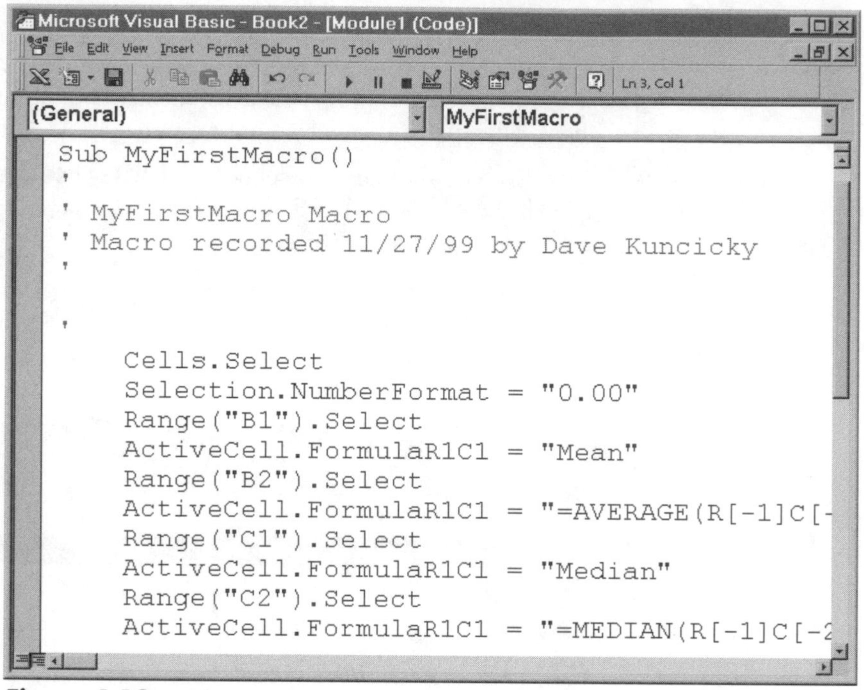

Figure 4.19. The Visual Basic Editor

PRACTICE!

Convince yourself that the code displayed in the visual Basic Editor is actually the same code contained in the macro. You can do this without knowing the Visual Basic language. Make several trivial changes such as changing the line

```
ActiveCell.FormulaR1C1 = "Mean"
```

to

```
ActiveCell.FormulaR1C1 = "Average"
```

Execute the modified macro by choosing the **Run** button ▶ on the Visual Basic Editor standard toolbar. Your worksheet should have changed to reflect your code change!

APPLICATION

Creating Tables—Compound Amount Factors

Excel is a great tool for creating and displaying tables of information based upon repetition of formulas. This example shows how to create a table, a compound amount factor table, that shows the power of compound interest. Using this table, an investor can see how the value of their initial investment will increase over time at different interest rates. For example, using the table below, a person who invests $ 1,000 at 6% interest for 20 years will have

$1,000 \times 3.2071$ or \$3,207. A person who invests \$1,000 at 11% interest for 20 years will have $1,000 \times 8.0623$ or \$8,062. Because investments with higher interest payments normally carry a higher degree of risk, this table helps one assess whether the potential increase in pay-off makes this risk acceptable. To create this table, follow the steps listed. We will assume you obtained the requisite formula from an economics textbook.

Compound Amount Factors						
Interest Rate:	6%	7%	8%	9%	10%	11%
Fractional Rate:	0.06	0.07	0.08	0.09	0.1	0.11
Year						
0	1.0000	1.0000	1.0000	1.0000	1.0000	1.0000
10	1.7908	1.9672	2.1589	2.3674	2.5937	2.8394
20	3.2071	3.8697	4.6610	5.6044	6.7275	8.0623
30	5.7435	7.6123	10.0627	13.2677	17.4494	22.8923
40	10.2857	14.9745	21.7245	31.4094	45.2593	65.0009
50	18.4202	29.4570	46.9016	74.3575	117.3909	184.5648
60	32.9877	57.9464	101.2571	176.0313	304.4816	524.0572
70	59.0759	113.9894	218.6064	416.7301	789.7470	1488.0191
80	105.7960	224.2344	471.9548	986.5517	2048.4002	4225.1128

Step 1. Add titles and headings

	A	B	C	D	E	F	G
1	Compound Amount Factors						
2	Interest Rate:	6%	7%	8%	9%	10%	11%
3	Fractional Rate:						
4	Year						
5							

Step 2. Enter the interest rates as fractional values in row C.

	A	B	C	D	E	F	G
1	Compound Amount Factors						
2	Interest Rate:	6%	7%	8%	9%	10%	11%
3	Fractional Rate:	0.06	0.07	0.08	0.09	0.1	0.11
4	Year						

Step 3. Create the column of Year values

First enter the 0 in cell A5 and a 10 in A6. Then select cells A5 and A6 and drag the fill handle down seven more rows.

	A	B	C	D	E	F	G
1	Compound Amount Factors						
2	Interest Rate:	6%	7%	8%	9%	10%	11%
3	Fractional Rate:	0.06	0.07	0.08	0.09	0.1	0.11
4	Year						
5	0						
6	10						
7	20						
8	30						
9	40						
10	50						
11	60						
12	70						
13	80						
14							

For appearance, center justify the year values.

Step 4. Enter a value of one in each column for year zero.

	A	B	C	D	E	F	G
1	**Compound Amount Factors**						
2	Interest Rate:	6%	7%	8%	9%	10%	11%
3	Fractional Rate:	0.06	0.07	0.08	0.09	0.1	0.11
4	Year						
5	0	1	1	1	1	1	1
6	10						

Step 5. Enter the formula for the single payment compound amount factor in cell B6.

$$=(1+B\$3)\textasciicircum\$A6$$

Notice that dollar signs have been included to indicate that the interest rate is always in row 3, and that the year is always in column A.

B6	▼	=	=(1+B$3)^$A6				
	A	B	C	D	E	F	G
1	**Compound Amount Factors**						
2	Interest Rate:	6%	7%	8%	9%	10%	11%
3	Fractional Rate:	0.06	0.07	0.08	0.09	0.1	0.11
4	Year						
5	0	1	1	1	1	1	1
6	10	1.7908477					
7	20						
8	30						

Step 6. Copy the formula in cell B6 to cells B7 through B13 using the fill handle.

B13	▼	=	=(1+B$3)^$A13				
	A	B	C	D	E	F	G
1	**Compound Amount Factors**						
2	Interest Rate:	6%	7%	8%	9%	10%	11%
3	Fractional Rate:	0.06	0.07	0.08	0.09	0.1	0.11
4	Year						
5	0	1	1	1	1	1	1
6	10	1.7908477					
7	20	3.2071355					
8	30	5.7434912					
9	40	10.285718					
10	50	18.420154					
11	60	32.987691					
12	70	59.07593					
13	80	105.79599					
14							

Note that these formulas would not have copied correctly if the dollar signs had not been included in the formula in cell B6.

Step 7. Copy the formulas in cells B6 through B13 to columns C through G using the fill handle.

	A	B	C	D	E	F	G
	G13		=	=(1+G$3)^$A13			
1	**Compound Amount Factors**						
2	Interest Rate:	6%	7%	8%	9%	10%	11%
3	Fractional Rate:	0.06	0.07	0.08	0.09	0.1	0.11
4	Year						
5	0	1	1	1	1	1	1
6	10	1.7908477	1.9671514	2.158925	2.3673637	2.5937425	2.839421
7	20	3.2071355	3.8696845	4.6609571	5.6044108	6.7274999	8.0623115
8	30	5.7434912	7.612255	10.062657	13.267678	17.449402	22.892297
9	40	10.285718	14.974458	21.724521	31.40942	45.259256	65.000867
10	50	18.420154	29.457025	46.901613	74.35752	117.39085	184.56483
11	60	32.987691	57.946427	101.25706	176.03129	304.48164	524.05724
12	70	59.07593	113.98939	218.60641	416.73009	789.74696	1488.0191
13	80	105.79599	224.23439	471.95483	986.55167	2048.4002	4225.1128
14							

Step 8. Format the values in the table to show four decimal places.

Select all of the compound amount factors in cells B5 through G13. Right-click on the selected region to bring up an option menu.

Insert...

Delete...

Clear Contents

Insert Comment

Format Cells...

Pick From List...

Set the type of format to "number" and the number of displayed decimal places to four. Click **OK** to apply the formatting to the selected cells.

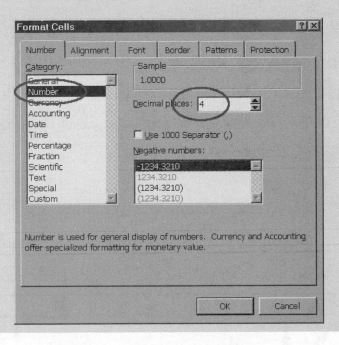

The single payment compound amount factor table has been completed. Notice that the equation for a compound amount factor was only entered once (in step 5).

All that was necessary to complete the rest of the table was copying the equation in cell B6 to the rest of the cells.

	A	B	C	D	E	F	G
1	**Compound Amount Factors**						
2	Interest Rate:	6%	7%	8%	9%	10%	11%
3	Fractional Rate:	0.06	0.07	0.08	0.09	0.1	0.11
4	Year						
5	0	1.0000	1.0000	1.0000	1.0000	1.0000	1.0000
6	10	1.7908	1.9672	2.1589	2.3674	2.5937	2.8394
7	20	3.2071	3.8697	4.6610	5.6044	6.7275	8.0623
8	30	5.7435	7.6123	10.0627	13.2677	17.4494	22.8923
9	40	10.2857	14.9745	21.7245	31.4094	45.2593	65.0009
10	50	18.4202	29.4570	46.9016	74.3575	117.3909	184.5648
11	60	32.9877	57.9464	101.2571	176.0313	304.4816	524.0572
12	70	59.0759	113.9894	218.6064	416.7301	789.7470	1488.0191
13	80	105.7960	224.2344	471.9548	986.5517	2048.4002	4225.1128
14							

APPLICATION - DC CIRCUITS

A general expression for the current I in a DC transient circuit is

$$I(t) = I_\infty + (I_0 - I_\infty)e^{-t/T}$$

where

I_0 is an initial value at the instant of sudden change,

I_∞ is the current at time $t = \infty$,

$T = RC$ is the time constant for a series R–C circuit, and

$T = L/R$ is the time constant for a series R–L circuit.

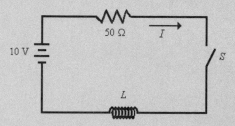

If the switch is closed at $t = 0$, we can calculate the current in the circuit after three time constants ($t = 3t$). Since $I_0 = 0$ and $I_\infty = V/R$, a worksheet can be set up that calculates $I(3T)$ for various values of V and R. If I_0, V, and R are placed into cells B5, C5, and D5, respectively, the Excel formula for I_∞ is

=C5/D5

and the Excel formula for $I(3T)$ is

=E5+(B5−E5)*EXP(F5)

If you enter the voltage (10 volts) and resistance (50 ohms) from the circuit displayed above, your results should resemble Figure 4.20. The current at three time constants after the switch is closed equals 0.190043 A. Try entering various values for V and R.

	A	B	C	D	E	F	G
1							
2							
3							
4		I(0)	V	R	I(infinity)	-t/T	I(3T)
5		0	10	50	0.2	-3	0.190043

Figure 4.20. Computing the current in a DC transient circuit

Chapter Summary

The use of mathematical formulas and functions is an important use of worksheets for engineers. This chapter introduces and demonstrates the use of formulas and functions in Excel. Mathematical and engineering functions are emphasized. You are also presented with methods for debugging and auditing worksheets. Matrix representation and manipulation are natural tasks for a spreadsheet application. Several matrix operations are demonstrated. Finally, the methods for recording, executing, and editing a macro are demonstrated.

KEY TERMS

absolute reference	matrix product	reference pattern
cell references	operators	relative reference
dependents	order	transient circuit
macro	precedents	transpose
matrix	prototype	Visual Basic Editor

Problems

1. Create an Excel formula that will compute $f(x)$ in the following equation for $x = 1,2,\dots,10$:

$$f(x) = \ln x + e^x \sin x$$

   Write the formula once and use the fill handle to drag the formula over the other nine cells.

2. The displacement of a structure is defined by the following equation for a damped oscillation as depicted in Figure 4.21. Create an Excel formula that will compute $f(x)$ for the equation

$$f(x) = 8 \cdot e^{-kt} \cdot \cos(\omega t)$$

   where $k = 0.5$ and the frequency $\omega = 3$. Compute $f(x)$ for $t = 0.0, 0.1, 0.2,\dots,4.0$ seconds. What is the value of $f(x)$ for $t = 3.6$?

3. The formula that calculates the number of combinations of r objects taken from a collection of n objects is

$$C(n,r) = \frac{n!}{(n-r)!r!}$$

   Thus the number of collections of eight people that can fit into a six-passenger vehicle is calculated as

$$C(8,6) = \frac{8!}{(8-6)!6!} = 28$$

   Write an Excel equation to calculate combinations.

4. Excel has a number of predefined logical functions. One of these, the IF() function has the following syntax:

IF(EXP,T,F)

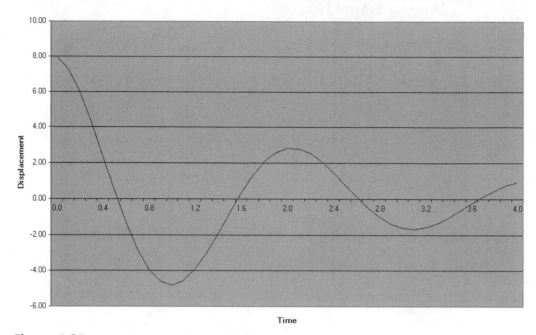

Figure 4.21.   Displacement of a structure

The effect of the function is to evaluate EXP, which must be a logical expression. If the expression is true, then T is returned. If the expression is false then F is returned. For example, the following function

IF(X[less]200,X,"Cholesterol is too high")

returns the value of X if X is less than 200. But, if X is greater than or equal to 200, the text statement " Cholesterol is too high " is placed in the selected cell.

Expand the quadratic equation example in this chapter to test for divide by zero. If the expression $2a = 0$ is true, display " Divide by Zero " ; otherwise return the value of $2a$.

Perform a similar test for $b^2 - 4ac \geq 0$; display " Requires Complex Number " if the test is false.

5.   The horizontal range of a projectile fired into the air at angle q degrees is given by

$$R = \frac{2V^2 \sin\theta \cos\theta}{g}$$

assuming no air resistance. Create a worksheet that computes R for a selected initial velocity V and firing angle θ. Use $g = 9.81$ meter/sec^2. Convert degrees to radians using the RADIANS() function. An initial velocity of 150 meter/sec and firing angle of 25° should result in R = 1756 meters.

6.   Two other frequently performed matrix operations are the calculation of the *determinant* of a matrix and the *inverse* of a matrix. Expand on the examples used in this chapter to find the determinant of matrix A and the inverse of matrix B.

7.   Create a macro that computes, labels, and displays the determinant and inverse of a 3 × 3 matrix that is typed into cells (A1:C3). Create a shortcut key to execute the macro.

5

Working with Charts

5.1   CREATING CHARTS

5.1.1   Using the Chart Wizard
to Create an XY Scatter Chart

The Chart Wizard guides you through the construction of a chart. Once the chart is built, its components may be modified. Before proceeding, create the worksheet depicted in Figure 5.1. These data were collected by measuring the current (I) across a resistor for eight measured voltages (V). Ohm's law, $V = IR$, states that the relationship between V and I is linear if temperature is kept relatively constant. An XY scatter plot of the data in Figure 5.1 can be used to visualize this relationship.

	A	B
1	Potential (V)	Current (A)
2	6.97	0.051
3	5.96	0.044
4	4.95	0.038
5	3.98	0.032
6	3.03	0.025
7	1.91	0.018
8	1.02	0.012
9	0.5	0.008

Figure 5.1.   Data collected by measuring current across a 150-Ω resistor

Before starting the Chart Wizard, select the region containing the data (A2:B9). Start the Chart Wizard by choosing the Chart Wizard button ⊞ from the Standard toolbar, or alternatively, choose **Insert**, **Chart** from the

OBJECTIVES

After reading this chapter, you should be able to

- Understand the principles used to build all of the different types of Excel charts
- Know the specific methods used to build line charts and XY scatter plots
- Understand the available options for editing and formatting chart legends, axes, and titles
- Scale axes and create error bars

Menu bar. The first Chart Wizard dialog box should appear as depicted in Figure 5.2. This dialog box prompts you to choose a chart type. Select **XY (Scatter)** from the list labeled *Chart type*. Select the top-left box from the area labeled *Chart sub-type* and choose the **Next >** button to proceed.

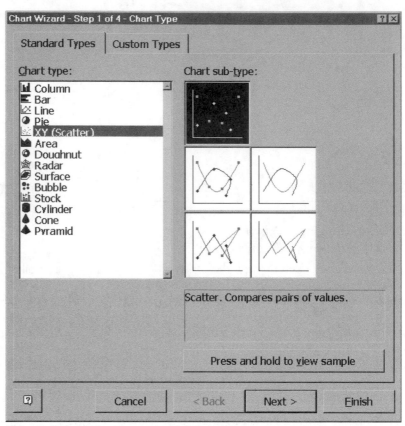

Figure 5.2. The Chart Wizard dialog box—step 1

The second Chart Wizard dialog box should now appear. Choose the **Series** tab as depicted in Figure 5.3. Excel has chosen, by default, to plot cells (A2:A9) on the *X*-axis, and cells (B2:B9) on the *Y*-axis.

You can modify the selected regions for the *X* values or the *Y* values by choosing the button on the right end of the boxes labeled *X Values* or *Y Values*. The Source Data dialog box will appear as depicted in Figure 5.4. The currently selected region will be surrounded by a dashed line. If you wish to change the *X* values, use the mouse to select a region and then choose the button from the Source Data dialog box to return to the Chart Wizard. For our current example, the *X* values do not need to be modified. Choose **Next >** to proceed.

The third Chart Wizard dialog box should appear as depicted in Figure 5.5. This dialog box guides you through the chart formatting options. From this dialog box you can create and modify the chart titles, axes, gridlines, data labels, and the legend. Choose the **Titles** tab; then type the chart title and *X* axis and *Y* axis titles as depicted in Figure 5.5. Remove the legend by choosing the **Legend** tab. Make sure that the box titled Show Legend is not checked. Choose [Next >] to proceed to the fourth and final step.

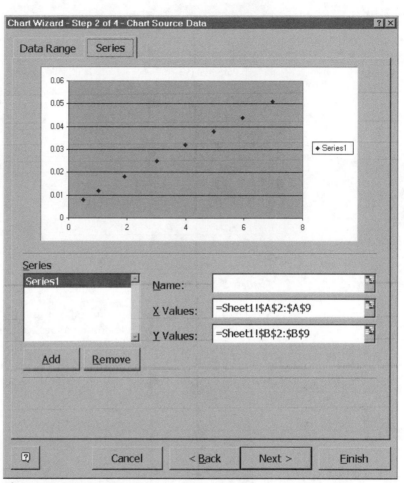

Figure 5.3. The Chart Wizard dialog box—step 2

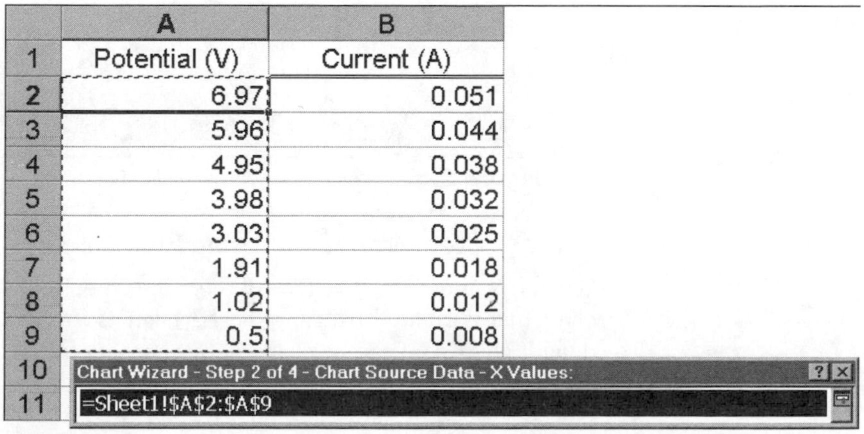

	A	B
1	Potential (V)	Current (A)
2	6.97	0.051
3	5.96	0.044
4	4.95	0.038
5	3.98	0.032
6	3.03	0.025
7	1.91	0.018
8	1.02	0.012
9	0.5	0.008

Chart Wizard - Step 2 of 4 - Chart Source Data - X Values: ? ✕

=Sheet1!$A$2:$A$9

Figure 5.4. Choosing a region for *X* values in a chart

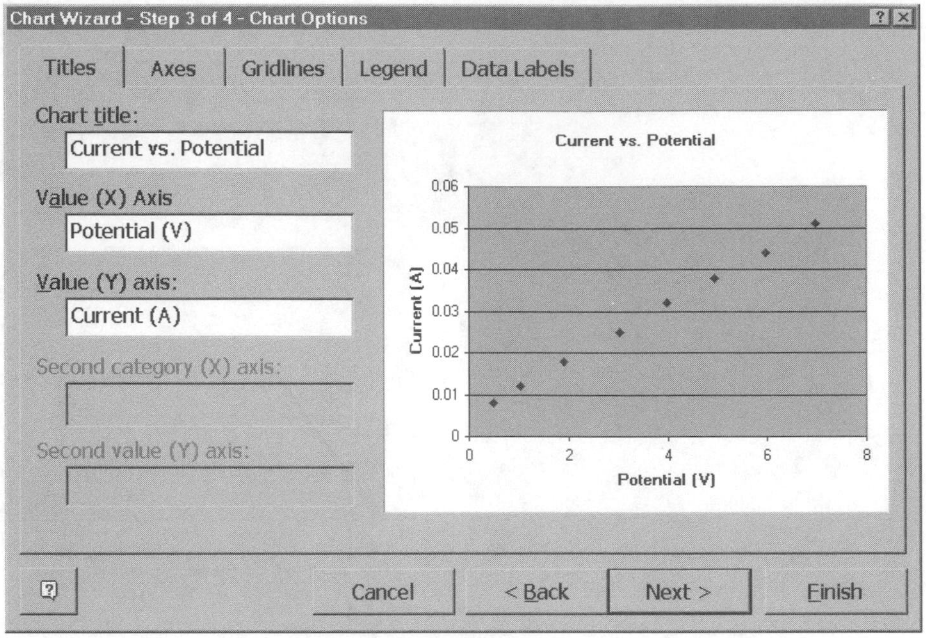

Figure 5.5.   The Chart Wizard dialog box—step 3

The fourth Chart Wizard dialog box should now appear as depicted in Figure 5.6. This dialog box prompts you to choose a location for the chart. There are two choices.

The first choice, titled *As new sheet*, will place the chart as a separate worksheet in the current workbook. If a name is not typed, Excel provides a default name of Chart 1, Chart 2, and so on. The second choice, titled *As object in*, will place the chart as an object in the selected worksheet. Choose a location for the chart and click the Finish button. The finished *XY* Scatter chart should appear as depicted in Figure 5.7.

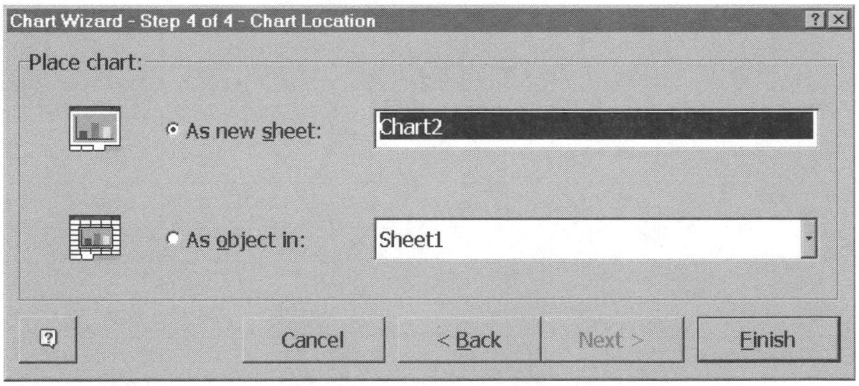

Figure 5.6.   The Chart Wizard dialog box—step 4

5.1.2   Creating a Chart Using Shortcut Keys

If you frequently create charts of the same type, the **F11** shortcut key may be helpful. A chart that is created by using the **F11** key is formatted in the default chart type. The default chart type can be changed by choosing **Chart**, **Chart Type** from the Menu bar. The Chart Type dialog box will appear as depicted in Figure 5.8. Choose a chart type and subtype and click on **Set as default chart**. Finally, choose **Cancel** instead of **OK** to exit the dialog box.

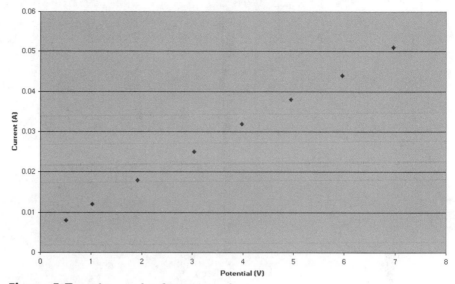

Figure 5.7. The completed XY Scatter chart

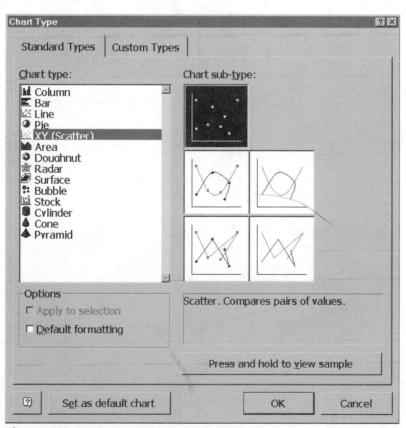

Figure 5.8. The Chart Type dialog box

PRACTICE!

Practice creating a chart using the Chart Wizard by following the above steps. Afterwards, practice creating a chart using the **F11** key. First, set the default chart type to *XY scatter* and select the data and headings from Figure 5.1. If you press the **F11** key, a chart should appear as depicted in Figure 5.9. Note that the chart title and labels could use improvement.

Fortunately, chart elements can easily be modified. In Section 5.3, you will be shown how to modify and format charts

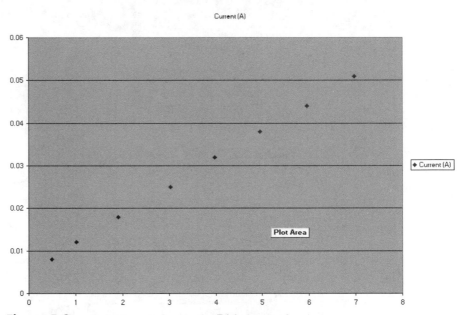

Figure 5.9.   A chart created using the **F11** shortcut key

Excel makes several assumptions when creating a chart automatically. If the data do not follow Excel's conventions, surprising results can sometimes occur. If the chart does not turn out as expected, the chart can always be reformatted as described in Section 5.3.

- Excel orients the chart so that the data for the *X* category are taken from the longest side of the selected region. In our example (from Figure 5.1), the longest side of the selected region is vertical.

- If the contents of the cells along the short side of the selected region contain text, they are used as labels for the data series in the legend. In our example, the label *Current (A)* is taken from the top cell of the short (horizontal) side of the selected region. If the cells contain numbers, the default data series names are used (Series 1, Series 2, etc.).

- If the contents of the cells along the long side of the selected region contain text, they are used as *X* category labels. If the cells contain numbers, Excel assumes that the cells contain a data series.

5.1.3   Previewing and Printing Charts

To preview a chart before printing, either choose **File**, **Print Preview** from the Menu bar or choose the  button from the Standard toolbar. A chart that is embedded within a worksheet will print with the worksheet by default. If the chart is selected before choosing print preview, the embedded chart can be printed separately. A chart that is formatted as a separate worksheet will, by default, be printed separately.

As an example, select the sheet containing the example *XY* Scatter chart in Figure 5.7 and choose  from the Standard toolbar. The Print Preview dialog box should appear. Select the **Margins** button and the margin lines will appear as depicted in Figure 5.10. The margin lines can be dragged to resize and reshape the chart. The **Zoom** button can be used to focus on chart detail.

Choose the **Setup** button to select more print formatting options. The Page Setup dialog box will appear as depicted in Figure 5.11. From the tabs on this dialog box, you may select portrait or landscape mode, select the chart size, select the printing quality, specify margins manually, and insert headers or footers.

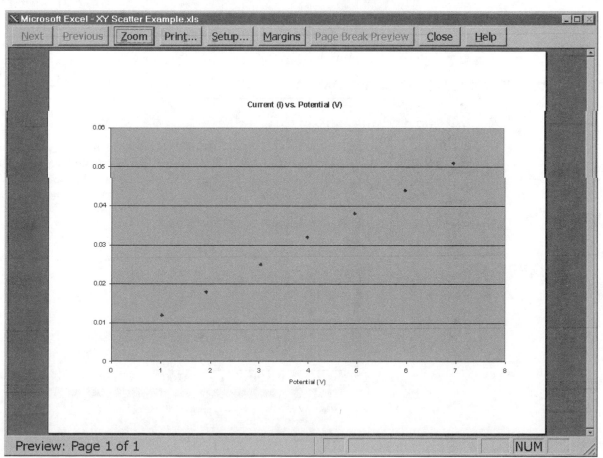

Figure 5.10.   Print Preview options

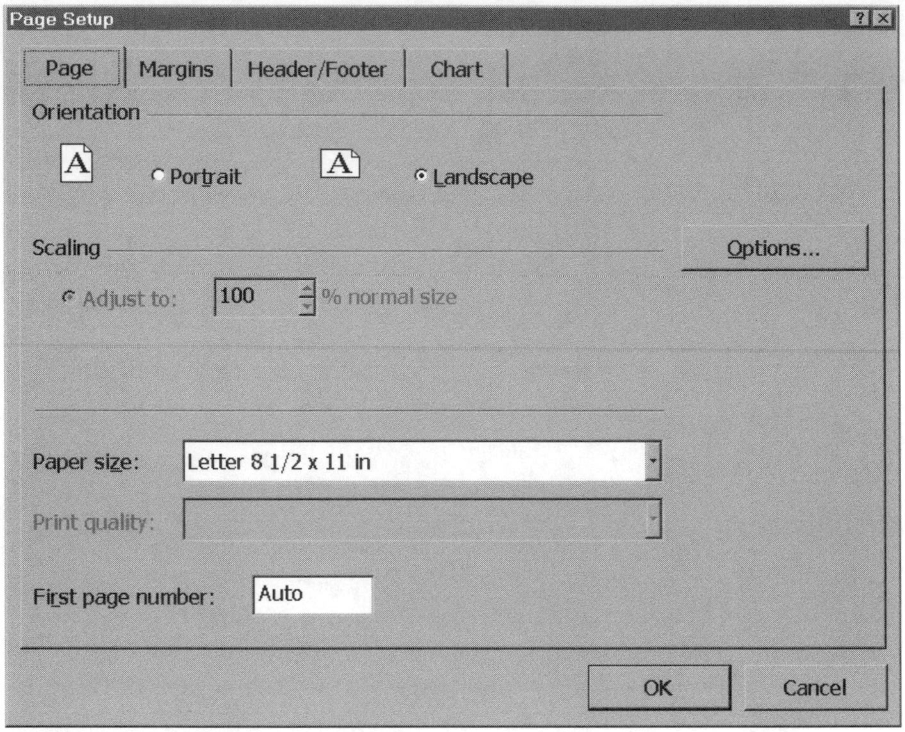

Figure 5.11. The Page Setup dialog box

5.2 ADDING AND EDITING CHART DATA

5.2.1 Adding Data Points

Data can be added or removed from a chart by activating the relevant chart by choosing **Chart**, **Add Data** from the Menu bar. The Add Data dialog box will appear as depicted in Figure 5.12. As shown in Figure 5.12, we have added another data point in the experiment with Ohm's law.

	A	B
1	Potential (V)	Current (A)
2	6.97	0.051
3	5.96	0.044
4	4.95	0.038
5	3.98	0.032
6	3.03	0.025
7	1.91	0.018
8	1.02	0.012
9	0.5	0.008
10	0.2	0.001

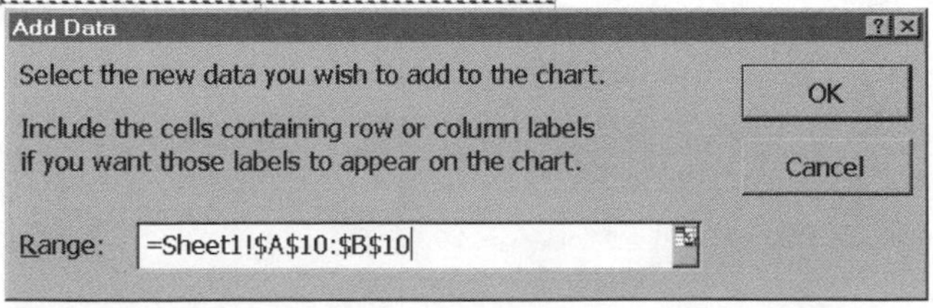

Figure 5.12. Adding data to a chart

After selecting the new data range, the Paste Special dialog box will appear as depicted in Figure 5.13. Check the box labeled *New point(s)*, since we want to add a new data point to the existing data series. Check the box labeled *Columns* since, in our example, the Y values (Current) are listed in columns. Check the box labeled *Categories (X Values) in First Column* since our X values (Potential) are listed in the first column. Click **OK** and the new data point will be added to the chart.

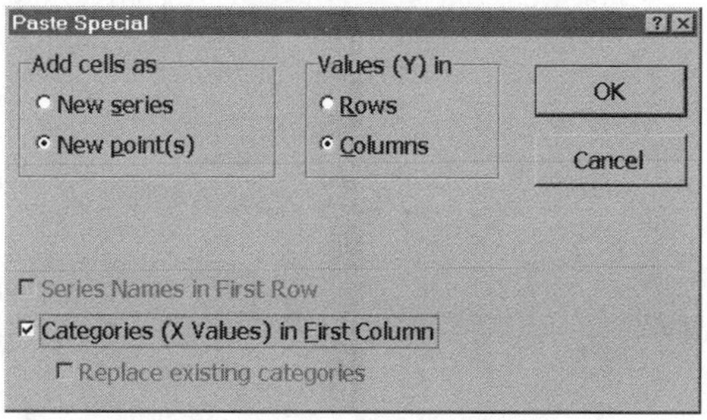

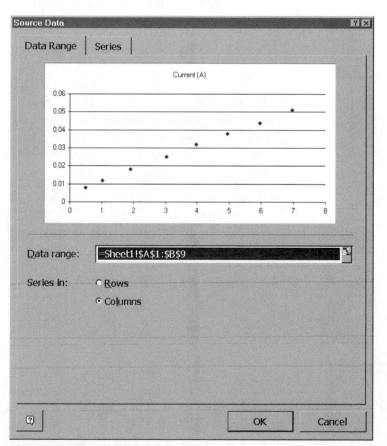

Figure 5.13. The Paste Special dialog box

Another method for adding (or deleting) data points is to modify the source data definition. Activate the chart by clicking once on the chart and then choose **Chart**, **Source Data** from the Menu bar. The Source Data dialog box will appear as depicted in Figure 5.14. Choose the **Data Range** tab and modify the contents of the box labeled Data range to add, modify, or delete source data points.

Figure 5.14. The Data Range tab of Source Data dialog box

5.2.2   Multiple Data Series

In the examples of charts so far, we have used a single *data series*. A data series is a collection of related data points that are to be represented as a unit. For example, the points in a data series are connected by a single line in a line chart. The data for a series would likely be represented by a separate row or column in the worksheet.

Table 5-1 shows data representing the flow rate for two tributaries of a river. The lowest one-day flow rate (in cubic feet per second) per year is shown. Create a worksheet that contains the data in Table 5-1 and use it for the rest of the examples in this chapter.

TABLE 5-1   Annual flow rate of two river branches

YEAR	EAST BRANCH FLOW (CFS)	WEST BRANCH FLOW (CFS)
87	221	222
88	354	315
89	200	175
90	373	400
91	248	204
92	323	325
93	216	188
94	195	202
95	266	254
96	182	176

Once you have created a worksheet containing the data and titles in Table 5-1, select the region and choose **Insert**, **Chart** from the Menu bar, or choose the button from the Standard toolbar. Follow the Chart Wizard instructions. Select **Line Chart** for a chart type and select the first line chart subtype. The second Chart Wizard box will appear. Select the **Series** tab. The results should resemble Figure 5.15.

The Chart Wizard has created three data series, one for each column in the selected region of the worksheet. Since we would like the first column (Year) to be the X-axis data labels, remove the series titled *Year* from the Series box by selecting **Year** and clicking the **Remove** button. Add the range for the *Year* column to the box titled *Category (X) axis labels*. Complete the Chart Wizard. The resulting chart (without chart titles and axis titles) is depicted in Figure 5.16. Save this chart and use it as an example in the next section on chart formatting.

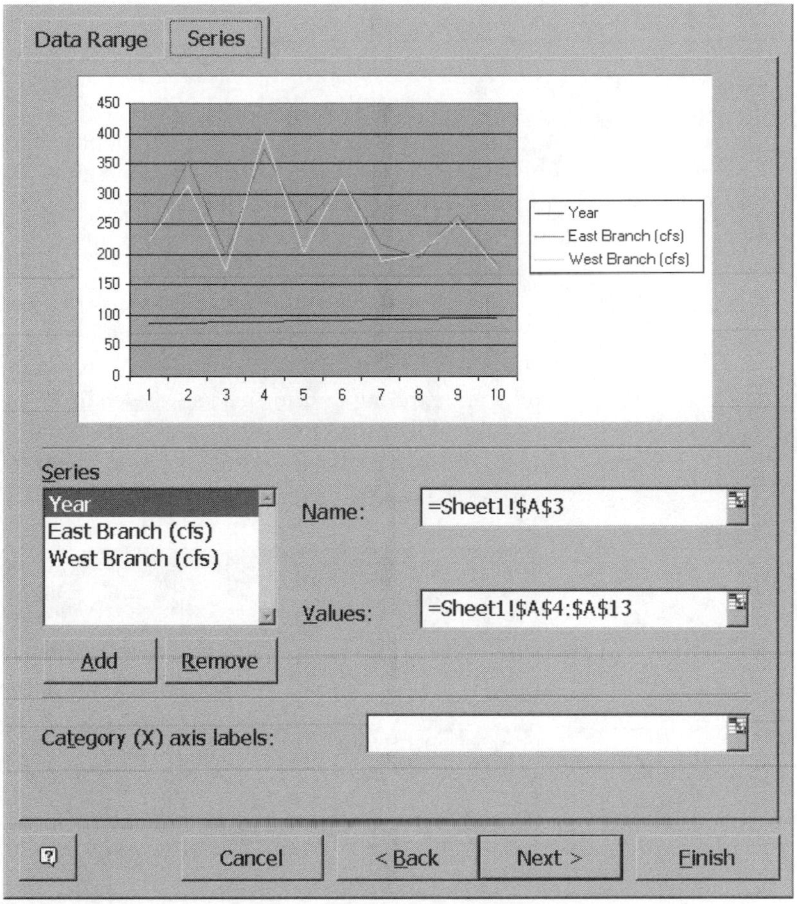

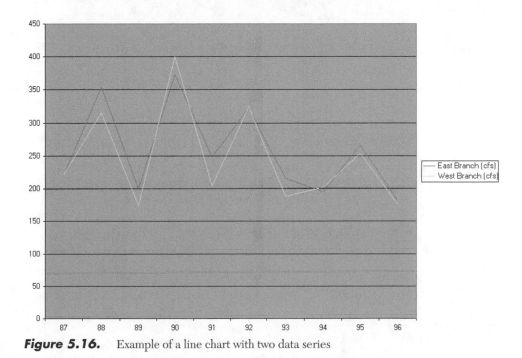

Figure 5.15. Selection of multiple data series

Figure 5.16. Example of a line chart with two data series

5.3 FORMATTING CHARTS

5.3.1 Creating Chart Objects

A chart consists of a number of elements called *chart objects*. Examples of chart objects are the chart legend and the chart title. Each object can be formatted and customized separately. It is usually faster to create the chart objects with the default formatting first. This will give you the general look of the chart. You can then customize each object separately.

To create and enter data into chart objects, choose **Chart**, **Chart Options** from the Menu bar. The Chart Options dialog box will appear as depicted in Figure 5.17. The Chart Options dialog box contains seven tabs that are used respectively, for entering and formatting the chart titles, axes, gridlines, legend, data labels, and data table, respectively. Use these tabs to edit your chart to improve its appearance and clarity. Carefully chosen titles, labels, legends, and appropriate choice of axes will increase the quality of your chart.

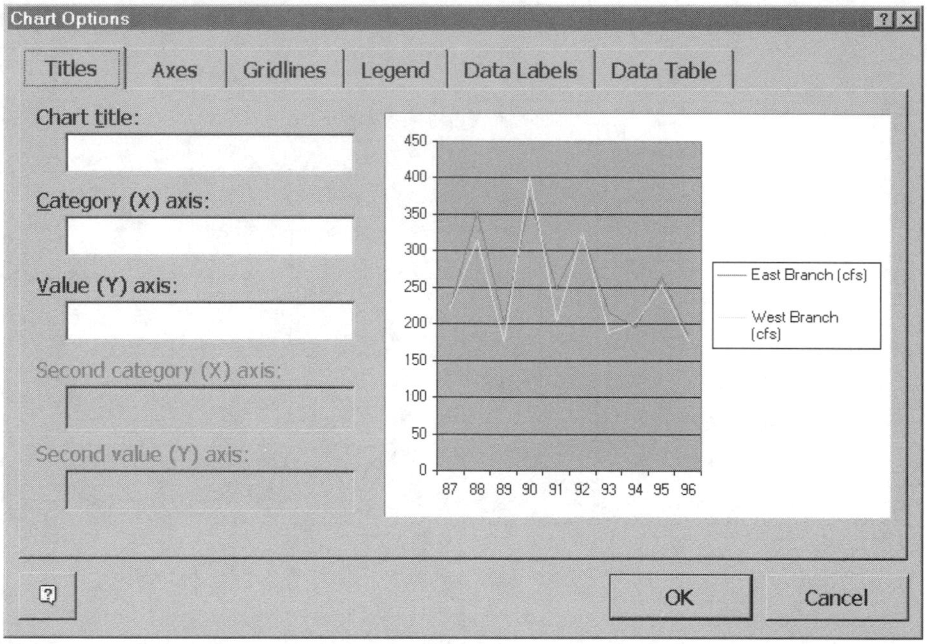

Figure 5.17. The Chart Options dialog box

5.3.2 Formatting Chart Objects

Any chart object can be formatted by selecting the object with the left mouse button. When selected, an object is surrounded by a gray box. If the mouse cursor is positioned over the object, the name of the object, is displayed. Figure 5.18 depicts the selected legend from Figure 5.16.

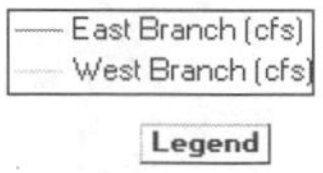

Figure 5.18. A selected chart object (Legend)

To format the selected object, click the right mouse button and choose **Format Legend Entry**. The Format Legend dialog box will appear as depicted in

Figure 5.19. From the Format Legend dialog box the border patterns, colors, font characteristics, and object placement can be customized. Another method for placing an object in the chart is to drag the object to the desired location.

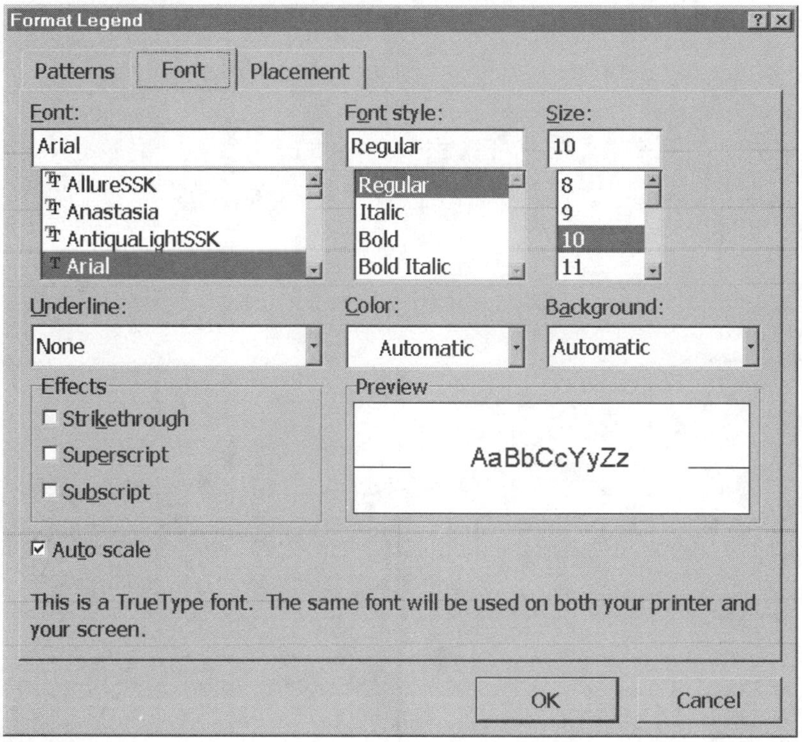

Figure 5.19. The Format Legend dialog box

This general method of selecting and formatting will work for any chart object. Experiment by selecting, in turn, the *X*-axis, the *Y*-axis, and each of the data series. View the formatting dialog boxes for each object. The entire chart can be selected by clicking near the edge of the chart area. The plot area can be formatted by clicking in the rectangular plot area.

PROFESSIONAL SUCCESS — FORMATTING CHARTS

The appearance of a chart in a document is important. A chart can make a lasting visual impression that summarizes or exemplifies the main points of your presentation or document. The following formatting guidelines will help you create a professional looking chart.

1. A chart title should contain a clear, concise description of the chart contents.

2. Create a label for each axis that contains, at a minimum, the name of the variable and the units of measurement that were used.

3. Create a label for each data series. The labels can be consolidated in a legend if each data series is represented by a distinct color or texture.

4. Scale graduations should be included for each axis. The graduation marks may take the form of gridlines or tick marks. The choice of scale graduations can be manipulated somewhat by selecting the **Scale** tab from the Format Axis dialog box.

5. Ideally, scale graduations should follow the *1, 2, 5 rule*. The 1, 2, 5 rule states that one should select scale graduations so the smallest division of the axis is a positive or negative integer power of 10 times 1, 2, or 5–For example, a scale graduation of 0.33 does not follow the rule.

PRACTICE!

Experiment with the chart in Figure 5.16.

- Add a chart title and titles for each axis.
- Format and move the legend.
- Change the plot background color.

After you have experimented with the chart in Figure 5.16, try to format your chart so it resembles Figure 5.20 as closely as possible.

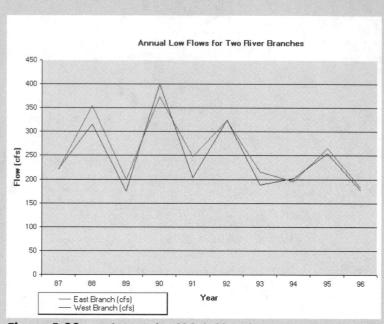

Figure 5.20.   A formatted and labeled line chart

5.3.3   Changing Chart Types

The type of chart displayed can be changed after a chart has been created. The same data are used for the new chart type. Not all types of charts are appropriate for some data sets. For example, a pie chart is not appropriate for the data in Table 5-1. A bar chart **is** an acceptable chart type for the data in Table 5-1. To change the chart type for the chart in Figure 5.20, select the chart and choose **Chart**, **Chart Type** from the Menu bar. Select **Column** from the box labeled *Chart Type* and select the first style from the box labeled *Chart sub-type*. The resulting chart should resemble Figure 5.21. Note that the chart in your worksheet has been replaced and that the line chart is gone.

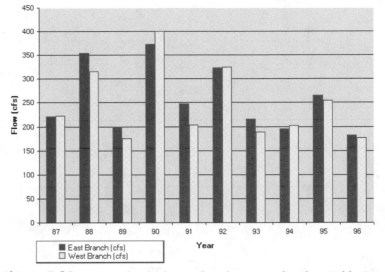

Figure 5.21. Example of columnar bar chart using data from Table 5-1

5.3.4 Inserting Text

The text for titles and axis labels can be added or modified by selecting and formatting chart objects. This is described in Section 5.3.2. Formatting Chart Objects. At times, you may wish to add free-floating text to a chart. Free-floating text can be used to highlight or explain a specific data point. The functions on the Drawing toolbar may be used to create arrows or other free-floating shapes.

As an example, we will add text and an arrow to the chart in Figure 5.20 to emphasize that 1989 was a low flow year for both river branches. To create the free-floating text,

1. Select any nontext object in the chart (e.g., the outside border);
2. Type the text and press the **Enter** key. In our example, we typed *1989 was a low flow year.*

The text should appear inside a small gray box. The font may be modified by choosing **Format**, **Text Box** from the Menu bar. If you are increasing the font size, the text box must be large enough to hold the new font. The box may be moved or resized with the mouse. The text can be edited directly on the chart simply by selecting the text box and then typing.

An arrow can be added by using the Drawing toolbar. If the Drawing toolbar does not appear on your screen, choose **View**, **Toolbars** from the Menu bar and check the box titled *Drawing*. Practice creating a text box and arrow that resemble Figure 5.22.

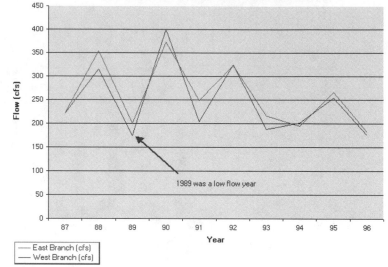

Figure 5.22. Chart with free-floating text and arrow

5.4 CHARTING FEATURES USEFUL TO ENGINEERS

Excel has many advanced features for formatting charts. Some of the features are particularly useful for engineering applications. These include the use of trendlines, error bars, what-if analysis, axis scaling, and the use of secondary axes.

5.4.1 Scaling an Axis

The scale of an axis is used to delimit the range of the axis as well as the intervals between axis markers called *ticks*. Large tick marks are specified in *major units*, and small tick marks are specified in *minor units*.

To change the axis formatting, click the left mouse button on the axis until the axis is highlighted, then choose **Format**, **Selected Axis** from the Menu bar. The Format Axis dialog box will appear as depicted in Figure 5.23. Select the **Scale** tab.

By checking the boxes labeled **Minimum**, **Maximum**, **Major unit**, and **Minor unit**, Excel will automatically choose appropriate values for the items. If you uncheck the boxes, then you can customize the items.

Of particular interest to engineers is the logarithmic scale. If you select this box the values of the **Minimum**, **Maximum**, **Major unit**, and **Minor unit** boxes will be recalculated to be powers of 10. A logarithmic axis cannot contain values that are less than or equal to zero. Illegal values will produce an error message.

5.4.2 Error Bars

Error bars represent the range of statistical error in a data series. Error bars should not be used unless you understand their purpose. To add error bars to a data series, first select the series by clicking on the series once with the left mouse button. Choose **Format**, and then **Selected Data Series** from the Menu bar. Select the **Y Error Bars** tab. The Format Data Series dialog box will appear as depicted in Figure 5.24.

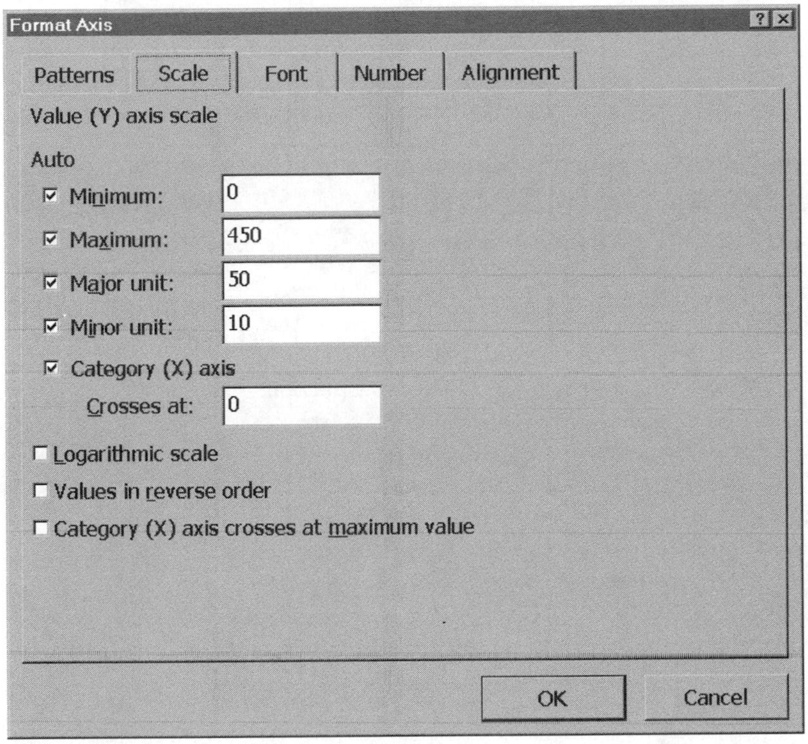

Figure 5.23. The Format Axis dialog box

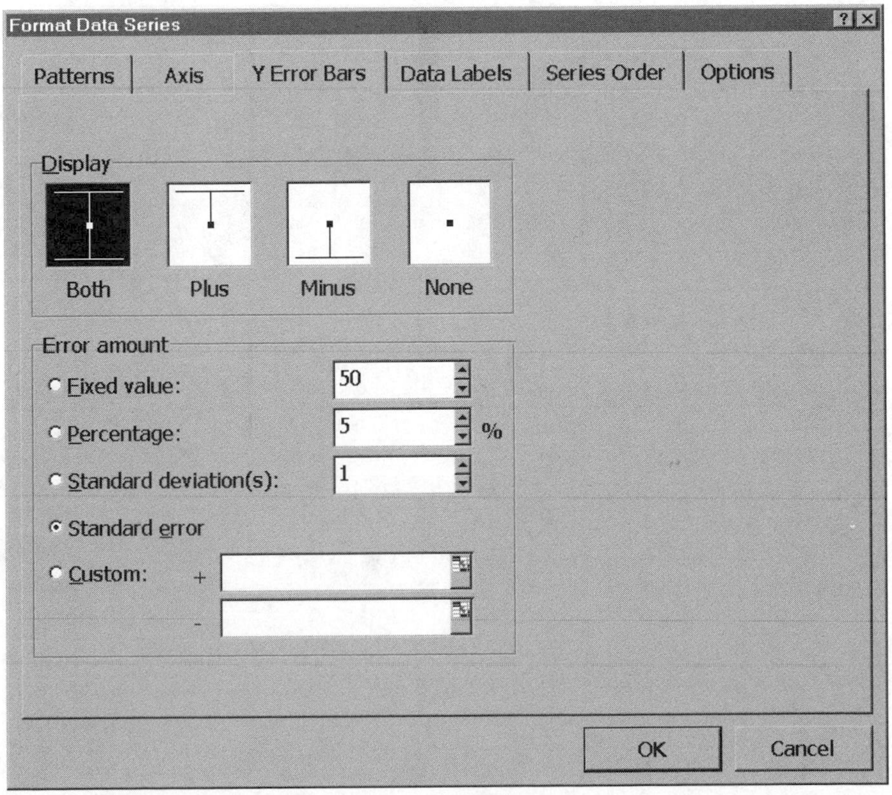

Figure 5.24. The Format Data Series dialog box

Choose a display type and an error amount. You can set a fixed or percentage amount if you have information about the error in the data series. Alternatively, you can let Excel calculate the standard deviation or standard error of the series for you. After you have created error bars, they will automatically be updated if the values in the data series change.

Graphing to Evaluate a Function

Visualization can be a big help in trying to understand what your data mean, or how a function works. Excel can help with this by allowing you to quickly and easily graph data or data you create by evaluating a function. For example, exponentials and hyperbolic sines are commonly used functions for solving differential equations. When solving these equations, you select the appropriate function based on its characteristics. Being able to see a graph of a function is a big help in understanding how the function behaves.

B2			=	=SINH(A2)	
	A	B	C	D	E
1	x	sinh(x)			
2	-10	-11013			
3	-9	-4052			
4	-8	-1490			
5	-7	-548			
6	-6	-202			
7	-5	-74			
8	-4	-27			
9	-3	-10			
10	-2	-4			
11	-1	-1			
12	0	0			
13	1	1			
14	2	4			
15	3	10			
16	4	27			
17	5	74			
18	6	202			
19	7	548			
20	8	1490			
21	9	4052			
22	10	11013			
23					

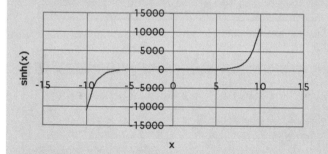

The other step is simply to graph the x and $\sinh(x)$ values. To do that, select the two columns of values and

How'd You Do That?

To help visualize a function you first evaluate the function over a range of values. In the spreadsheet shown below, the function $\sinh(x)$ was evaluated over the range −10 to 10. To create the column of x values, the first two values were entered and selected; then, using the right mouse button, the fill handle was dragged down the column to create the series. When the right mouse button was released, **Fill Series** was selected from the pop-up menu. The equation for hyperbolic sine of x was entered into cell B2 as **=SINH(A2)**. Cell B2 was then copied down the colunm to complete the table.

	A	B	C	D
1	x	sinh(x)		
2	−10	−11013		
3	−9	−4052		
4	−8	−1490		
5	−7	−548		
6	−6	−202		
7	−5	−74		
8	−4	−27		
9	−3	−10		
10	−2	−4		
11	−1	−1		
12	0	0		
13	1	1		
14	2	4		
15	3	10		
16	4	27		
17	5	74		
18	6	202		
19	7	548		
20	8	1490		
21	9	4052		
22	10	11013		
23				

click the **Chart Wizard button**, on the toolbar.

Select an *XY* (Scatter) chart type, with smoothed curves and no data point markers. Click **Next >** to continue.

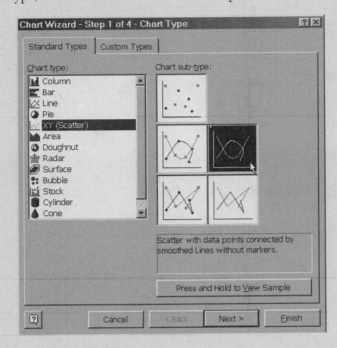

A preview of the graph is displayed. Step 2 of the Chart Wizard provides an opportunity to make changes to the displayed data. Since we don't need to do that, click on **Next >** to continue to step 3.

Step 3 is where you can begin adding formatting features to the graph. On the **Titles** panel, axis labels have been added.

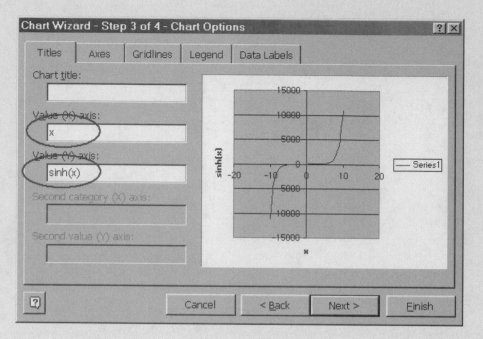

On the **Gridlines** panel, major gridlines on the x-axis were added. (Major gridlines on the y-axis are standard, so they did not need to be added.)

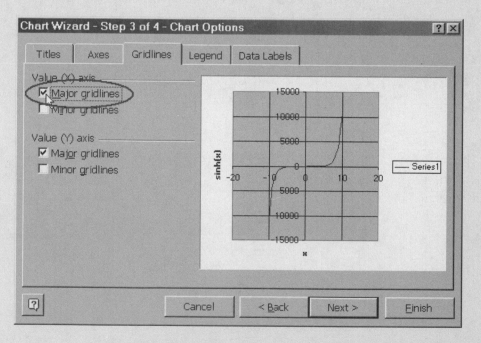

When the chart shows only a single curve, the legend doesn't tell you very much, so it was turned off on the **Legend** panel.

The last step of the Chart Wizard is to indicate where the new chart should be placed. If you select **As** object in Sheet 1, the graph is placed on the same worksheet page as the data.

At this point the completed chart is displayed on the spreadsheet, although it does not look quite like the version shown at the beginning of the chapter.

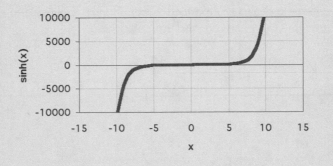

The following formatting changes are necessary to recreate the original chart:

1. Set the y-axis limits to $-10{,}000$ and $10{,}000$. (Double-click on the y-axis to make this change.)
2. Have the y-axis cross the x-axis at $x = -15$ (Moves the y-axis to the left edge of the chart. Double-click on the y-axis.)
3. Remove the gray background. (Double-click on the background away from any lines. Set the Area to **none**.)
4. Display the curve with a heavier line. (Double-click on the curve.)
5. Display the gridlines in gray rather than black. (Double-click on an x gridline and set the line color to light gray. Repeat for the y gridlines.)

After making these formatting changes, the chart looks like the original.

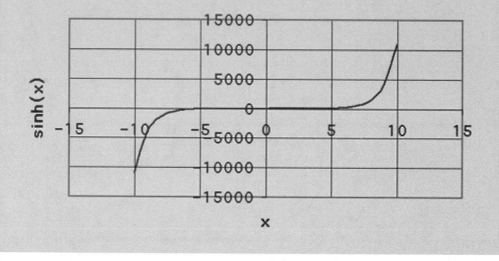

Chapter Summary

In this chapter, the methods for creating and formatting charts are described. We emphasize line charts and *XY* scatter plots, since these types of charts are frequently used in scientific and engineering applications. The available options for formatting chart elements are described. Several topics applicable to engineering, scaling axes and creating error bars, are also presented.

KEY TERMS

1, 2, 5 rule	error bars	Ohm's law
chart objects	major units	ticks
data series	minor units	

Problems

1. Generate data points for the function

$$y = 4\sin(x) - x^2$$

for $x = -5.0, -4.5, ..., 4.5, 5.0$. Chart the results using an XY scatterplot.

2. Add appropriate title and axis labels for the chart in Problem 1. Try changing chart types. Experiment with line charts and 3D views.

3. A graph that uses logarithmic scales on both axes is called a log-log graph. A log-log graph is useful for plotting power equations since they appear as straight lines. A power equation has the form

$$y = ax^b$$

Table 5-2 presents data that are collected from an experiment that measured the resistance of a conductor for a number of sizes. The size (cross-sectional area) was measured in millimeters squared and the resistance was measured in milliohms per meter. Create a scatter plot of these data.

4. Modify both the X- and Y-axes of the chart created in the previous problem to use a logarithmic scale. What can you infer about the relationship between resistance and size of a conductor in this experiment from viewing the resulting scatter plot?

TABLE 5-2 Resistance versus area of a conductor

AREA A (mm²)	RESISTANCE (milliohms per meter)
0.009	2000.0
0.021	1010.0
0.063	364.0
0.202	110.0
0.523	44.0
1.008	20.0
3.310	8.0
7.290	3.5
20.520	1.2

6

Performing Data Analysis and Optimization

6.1 USING THE ANALYSIS TOOLPAK

An add-in package is available for Excel that includes a number of statistical and engineering tools. This package, called the *Analysis ToolPak*, can be used to shorten the time that it usually takes to perform a complex analysis.

The Analysis ToolPak is installed as a separate add-in to Excel. To determine whether the ToolPak is installed on your system, choose **Tools** from the Menu bar. If the Data Analysis command does not appear on the Tools menu, the Analysis ToolPak has not been installed or it has not been configured correctly. To install the Analysis ToolPak, run the Setup program on your Microsoft Office or Excel CD. After you have installed the ToolPak with the Setup program, load the add-in into Excel by choosing **Tools**, **Add-Ins** from the Menu bar. Check the box labeled *Analysis ToolPak* and click **OK**.

Once the ToolPak has been successfully installed, choose **Tools**, and **Data Analysis** from the Menu bar. The Data Analysis dialog box will appear as depicted in Figure 6.1. Browse through the list labeled *Analysis Tools*. Each tool requires a set of input parameters in a specific format. These usually consist of an input range, an output range, and varying options. The results of the analysis are displayed in an output table. Additionally, some tools will generate a chart.

In this chapter, we will describe how to use several of these tools to create a histogram and provide descriptive statistics, correlation, and a regression analysis of several data series. It is beyond the scope of this text to interpret

OBJECTIVES

After reading this chapter, you should be able to

- Access and use the Analysis ToolPak
- Calculate descriptive statistics for a data series
- Calculate the correlation between two data series
- Perform a regression analysis on a set of data
- Calculate linear and exponential trends for data series
- Project trendlines onto charts
- Perform visual interactive analysis using pivot tables
- Undertake the iterative solution of equations using the Goal Seeker
- Perform constrained linear and nonlinear optimization using the Solver tool

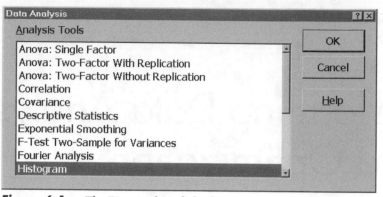

Figure 6.1.   The Data Analysis dialog box

the results of these statistical analyses or explain the meaning of statistical terms such as confidence interval, residuals, R square, standard error, and so on. To effectively use these tools, you should already be familiar with the area of statistics terms that will be used.

We will demonstrate the use of the Analysis ToolPak with the creation of a *histogram*. A histogram is a graph of the frequency distribution of a set of data. The data are aggregated into classes and the classes are graphed in a bar chart. The width of each bar represents the range of a class and the height of each bar represents the frequency of data within a particular range. A class range is sometimes called a *bin* since the histogram effectively places each data point into a bucket or bin.

An example of the use of a histogram is to graph the distribution of a set of student test scores for a course. A glance at the histogram can tell the instructor if the test results are normally distributed or skewed. The two input ranges that are required for a histogram are a data set and a set of bin ranges.

The bin ranges are defined by listing the ascending boundary values. A data point is determined to be in a particular bin if the value of the data point is less than or equal to the bin number and greater than the previous bin number. You can choose to omit the bin range, in which case a set of evenly distributed bins between the data's minimum and maximum values is created.

This will be made clearer with an example. Figure 6.2 shows a worksheet that contains the midterm grades of 20 students (B6:B25) and a set of boundary values for the classes or bins (D6:D13).

To create a histogram using the Analysis ToolPak, select **Histogram** from the Data Analysis dialog box. The Histogram dialog box will appear as depicted in Figure 6.3. Select the input range containing the test scores (B6:B25) and the bin range containing the bin boundaries (D6:D13). The output can be directed to a specified range, to a new worksheet, or a new workbook.

Several optional features are available. These include sorting the histogram (*Pareto*), display a cumulative percentage (*Cumulative Percentage*), and charting the histogram (*Chart Output*). In the example, *Chart Output* is selected. The resulting frequency distribution table and chart are displayed in Figure 6.4.

The Help button on the Histogram dialog box displays detailed information about the input parameters and options for the Histogram tool. The Help button can be used to access unique help for each of the analysis tools.

	A	B	C	D
5	Student#	Mid Term		Classes
6	1	45		30
7	2	89		40
8	3	90		50
9	4	67		60
10	5	88		70
11	6	93		80
12	7	32		90
13	8	85		100
14	9	68		
15	10	52		
16	11	77		
17	12	96		
18	13	54		
19	14	78		
20	15	83		
21	16	89		
22	17	79		
23	18	83		
24	19	72		
25	20	91		

Figure 6.2. A group of student test scores and bin ranges

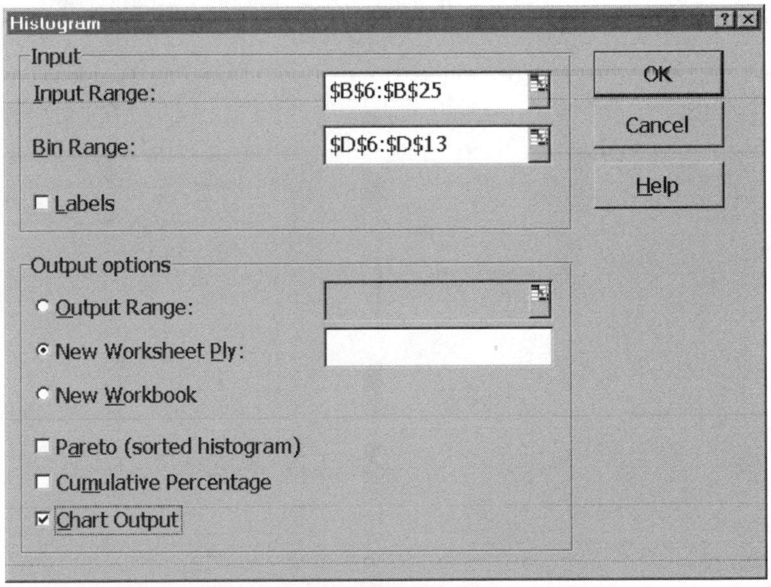

Figure 6.3. The Histogram dialog box

6.2   DESCRIPTIVE STATISTICS

Excel provides a tool for computing common descriptive statistics for sets of data. You could calculate each of these values by using individual formulas from the formula menu. The data analysis tool conveniently aggregates the most common computations for you in a table.

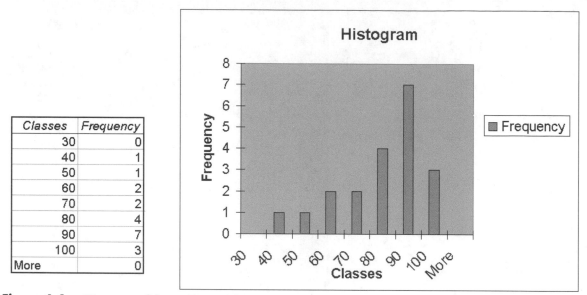

Classes	Frequency
30	0
40	1
50	1
60	2
70	2
80	4
90	7
100	3
More	0

Figure 6.4. Histogram of data in Figure 6.2

For the next several sections, we will use a set of data from 11 students. The data consist of each of the student's Grade Point Averages (GPAs) for their high school career and for their first year of college. To follow the text's examples, first create a worksheet with the data in Figure 6.5.

	A	B
3	**1st YR College GPA**	**HS GPA**
4	3.8	3.5
5	1.4	3.0
6	1.4	2.6
7	3.1	3.1
8	2.5	3.8
9	3.8	3.7
10	3.5	2.0
11	2.0	2.5
12	2.7	3.9
13	3.8	3.7
14	2.8	2.5

Figure 6.5. Eleven student GPAs

Choose **Tools**, and then **Data Analysis** from the Menu bar. The Data Analysis dialog box will appear as depicted in Figure 6.1. Choose **Descriptive Statistics** from the Data Analysis dialog box. The Descriptive Statistics dialog box will appear as depicted in Figure 6.6.

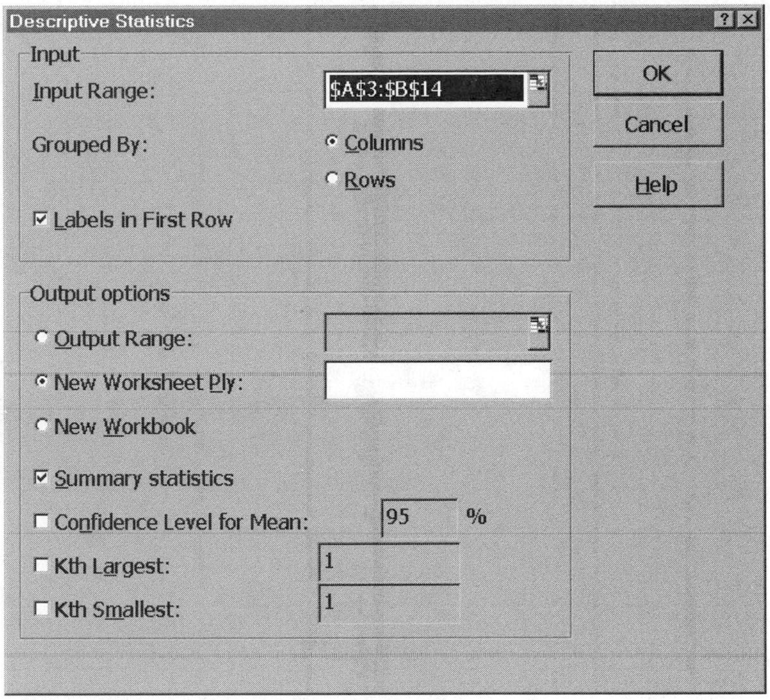

Figure 6.6.   The Descriptive Statistics dialog box

Select the input range to include both columns of data from Figure 6.5 and include the header columns. You can direct the output to a specified range, to a new worksheet, or a new workbook. Check the output option labeled *Summary Statistics* and press **OK**. The results are depicted in Figure 6.7. Note that the mean GPA dropped between high school and the first year of college.

	A	B	C	D	E
1	*1st YR College GPA*			*HS GPA*	
2					
3	Mean	2.8000		Mean	3.1182
4	Standard Error	0.2737		Standard Error	0.1953
5	Median	2.8000		Median	3.1000
6	Mode	3.8000		Mode	3.7000
7	Standard Deviation	0.9077		Standard Deviation	0.6478
8	Sample Variance	0.8240		Sample Variance	0.4196
9	Kurtosis	-1.1022		Kurtosis	-1.2850
10	Skewness	-0.4343		Skewness	-0.3448
11	Range	2.4000		Range	1.9000
12	Minimum	1.4000		Minimum	2.0000
13	Maximum	3.8000		Maximum	3.9000
14	Sum	30.8000		Sum	34.3000
15	Count	11.0000		Count	11.0000

Figure 6.7.   Descriptive statistics for student GPAs

6.3   CORRELATION

The correlation of two data sets is a measure of whether two ranges of data move together. If large values of one set are associated with large values of the other, a positive correlation exists. If small values of one set are associated with large values of the other, a negative correlation exists. If the correlation is near zero, the values in both sets are unrelated.

To calculate the correlation between the student's high school GPAs and first-year college GPAs, choose **Correlation** from the Data Analysis dialog box. The Correlation dialog box will appear as depicted in Figure 6.8.

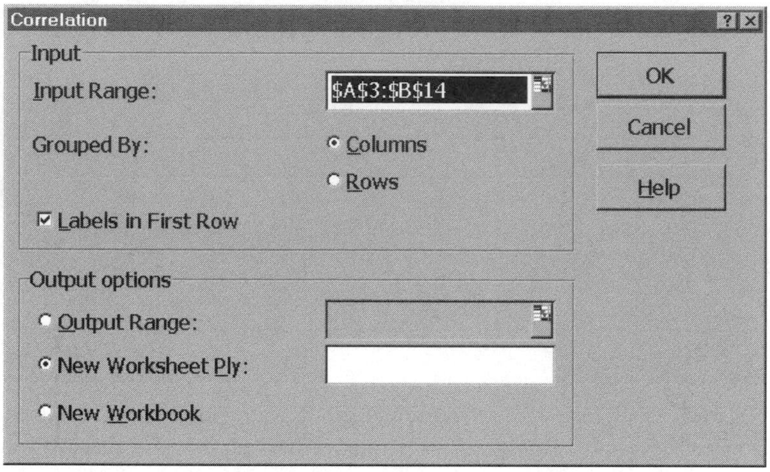

Figure 6.8.   The Correlation dialog box

Select the input range to include both columns of data from Figure 6.5 grouped by columns and include the header columns. You can direct the output to a specified range, to a new worksheet, or a new workbook. Check the output option labeled *Labels in First Row* and press **OK**. The results are depicted in Figure 6.9. Note that the correlation $r = 0.316$. If we square the correlation, we can state that $r^2 = 0.100$ or only 10% of the first-year GPA can be predicted by knowing the high school GPA.

	A	B	C
1		*1st YR College GPA*	*HS GPA*
2	1st YR College GPA	1.000	
3	HS GPA	0.316	1.000

Figure 6.9.   The correlation between high school and college GPA

6.4   LINEAR REGRESSION

The Excel Regression Analysis tool performs linear regression analysis by using the *least squares* method to fit a line through a set of observations. In this section, we will show

how to perform a regression that analyzes how a single dependent variable is affected by a single independent variable.

If the regression is a good fit to the data, the regression allows us to make predictions of future performance. For example, we might make a prediction about a student's first-year college Grade Point Average (GPA) based on the high school GPA. After having computed the relationship between a representative sample of previous students' high school GPAs and their first-year college GPAs, we would use the regression equation to predict how students will do in their first year in college.

If more than one independent variable is considered, the analysis technique is called *multiple regression*. For example, the student's SAT score and IQ may both be considered as predictors in addition to the high school GPA.

To compute a regression analysis for the students GPAs, choose **Regression** from the Data Analysis dialog box. The regression dialog box will appear as depicted in Figure 6.10.

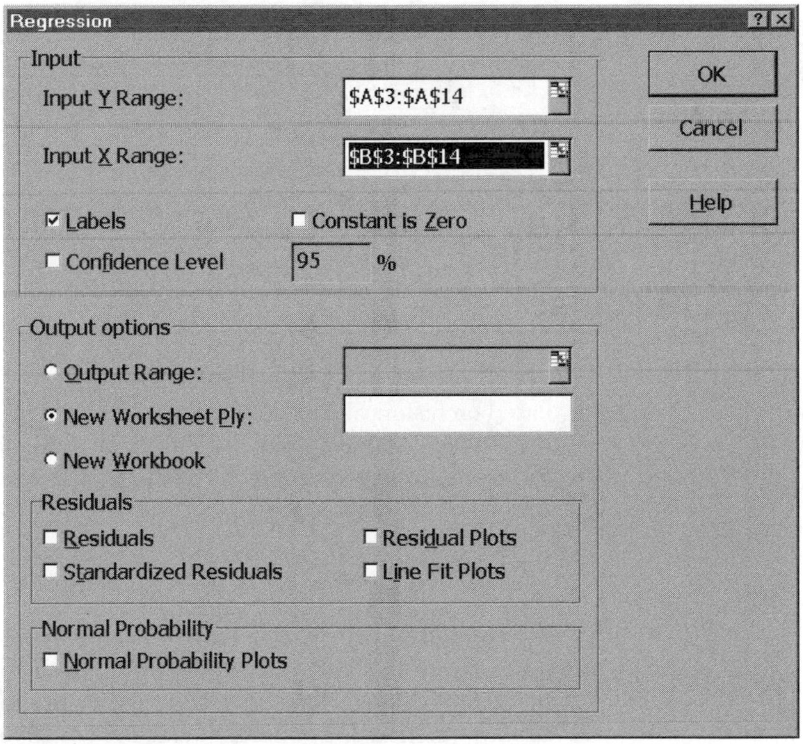

Figure 6.10. The Regression dialog box

Select the input range to include both columns of data from Figure 6.5 grouped by columns and include the header columns. You can direct the output to a specified range, to a new worksheet, or a new workbook. Check the output option labeled *Labels* and press **OK**. The results are depicted in Figure 6.11. Since the significance of F is greater than 0.05, we can assume the regression equation is not significant. That is, the use of high school GPA alone to predict first-year college success is no better than a chance prediction.

	A	B	C	D	E	F
1	SUMMARY OUTPUT					
2						
3	*Regression Statistics*					
4	Multiple R	0.316				
5	R Square	0.100				
6	Adjusted R^2	0.000				
7	Standard Error	0.908				
8	Observations	11.000				
9						
10	ANOVA					
11		*df*	*SS*	*MS*	*F*	*Sig F*
12	Regression	1	0.824	0.824	1.001	0.343
13	Residual	9	7.416	0.824		
14	Total	10	8.240			
15						
16		*Coeff*	*Std Error*	*t Stat*	*P-value*	
17	Intercept	1.418	1.409	1.007	0.340	
18	HS GPA	0.443	0.443	1.000	0.343	

Figure 6.11.   A regression analysis of student GPAs

6.5   TREND ANALYSIS

Trend analysis is the science of forecasting or predicting future elements of a data series based on historical data. Trend analysis is used in many areas such as financial forecasting, epidemiology, capacity planning, and criminology. Excel has the ability to calculate linear and exponential growth trends for data series. Excel can also calculate and display various trendlines for charts.

6.5.1   Trend Analysis with Data Series

A trend analysis can either extend or replace a series of data elements. The simplest method for extending a data series with a linear regression is to drag the fill handle past the end of the data series. For example, Figure 6.12 shows the number of occurrences of a hypothetical disease for the years 1993 to 1996. Assuming a linear rate of increase in the disease, the number of occurrences can be estimated for 1997, 1998, and 1999.

To calculate the linear trend, select the known data (A4:D4) and drag the fill handle to the right so the fill box covers cells (E4:G4). When you release the mouse, cells (E4:G4) will contain the data elements predicted by a linear regression of the original data (see Figure 6.12).

The Fill Series command can be used for somewhat more sophisticated trend analysis. To extend or replace a data series using the Fill Series command, first select the region of data over which the analysis is to occur. This includes the original data and the new cells that are to hold the predicted data. Using the example in Figure 6.12, first clear cells (E4:G4) and then select cells (A4:G4). Choose **Edit**, **Fill**, and **Series** from the Menu bar. The Series dialog box will appear as depicted in Figure 6.13.

	A	B	C	D	E	F	G
1	Occurrence of Disease X (in thousands)						
2							
3	1993	1994	1995	1996	(1997)	(1998)	(1999)
4	1.1	1.9	3.0	3.8			

	A	B	C	D	E	F	G
1	Occurrence of Disease X (in thousands)						
2							
3	1993	1994	1995	1996	(1997)	(1998)	(1999)
4	1.1	1.9	3.0	3.8	4.8	5.7	6.6

Figure 6.12.   A sample set of disease data and the projected disease occurrences for 1997–1999 using linear best fit by dragging the fill handle

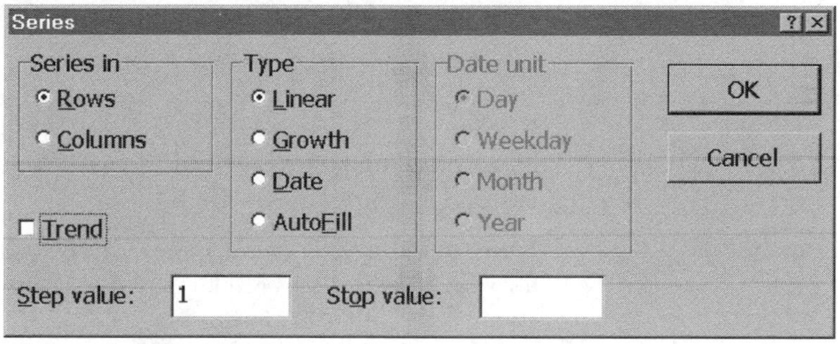

Figure 6.13.   The Series dialog box

Note that a *step value* of 1 has been calculated by Excel. The step value can be modified manually to set the increment value for x in the linear equation $y = mx + b$. A *stop value* may be entered if you want to set an upper limit to the trend.

To extend the known values with a linear regression and leave the original values unchanged, check the box labeled *AutoFill* and uncheck the box labeled *Trend*. The results from the example are depicted in Row 6 (labeled Linear Extension) in Figure 6.14. Note that these results are identical to the results obtained by dragging the fill handle in Figure 6.12.

To calculate a linear trend line and replace the original data values with best fit data, check the box labeled *Linear* and check the labeled *Trend*. The trend line is no longer forced to pass through any of the original data points. The results are depicted in Row 8 (labeled Linear Replacement) in Figure 6.14.

A trend line using exponential growth can be calculated by checking the box labeled *Growth* and checking the box labeled *Trend*. The original data values are replaced and the trend line is not forced pass through any of the original data points. The results are depicted in Row 10 (labeled Exponential Replacement) in Figure 6.14.

6.5.2   Trend Analysis Functions

Excel provides two trend analysis functions; one for linear trend calculation and another for calculating exponential trends. These are useful if the known dependent data may change and the trend line must be recalculated frequently. The linear trend function TREND uses the least squares method for its calculation. The syntax for TREND is:

```
TREND (known_y's, known_x's, new_x's, const)
```

	A	B	C	D	E	F	G	H
1		Occurrence of disease X (in thousands of cases)						
2								
3		1993	1994	1995	1996	1997	1998	1999
4	Original Known Values	1.1	1.9	3.0	3.8			
5								
6	Linear Extension	1.1	1.9	3.0	3.8	4.8	5.7	6.6
7								
8	Linear Replacement	1.1	2.0	2.9	3.8	4.8	5.7	6.6
9								
10	Exponential Replacement	1.2	1.8	2.7	4.1	6.3	9.5	14.5
11								
12	TREND() function	1.1	2.0	2.9	3.8	4.8	5.7	6.6

Figure 6.14. Examples of trend analysis options

The arguments are described below.

Known_y's. The known y values are the known dependent values in the linear equation $y = mx + b$. In Figure 6.14, the known y values are 1.1, 1.9, 3.0, and 3.8 in the range (B4:E4).

Known_x's. The known x values are the values of the independent variable for which the y values are known. In Figure 6.14, these are the values 1993, 1994, 1995, and 1996 in the range (B3:E3). If the known x values are omitted, the argument is assumed to be {1,2,3,4, ... }.

New_x's. The new x values are the values of the independent variable for which you want new y values to be calculated. If you want the predictions for years 1997 to 1999, select the range (F3:H3). If you want to calculate the linear trend for the whole time span (1993–1999), select the range (B3:H3).

Const. If the *const* argument is set to FALSE, b is set to zero, so the equation describing the relationship between y and x becomes $y = mx$. If the const argument is set to TRUE or omitted, b is computed.

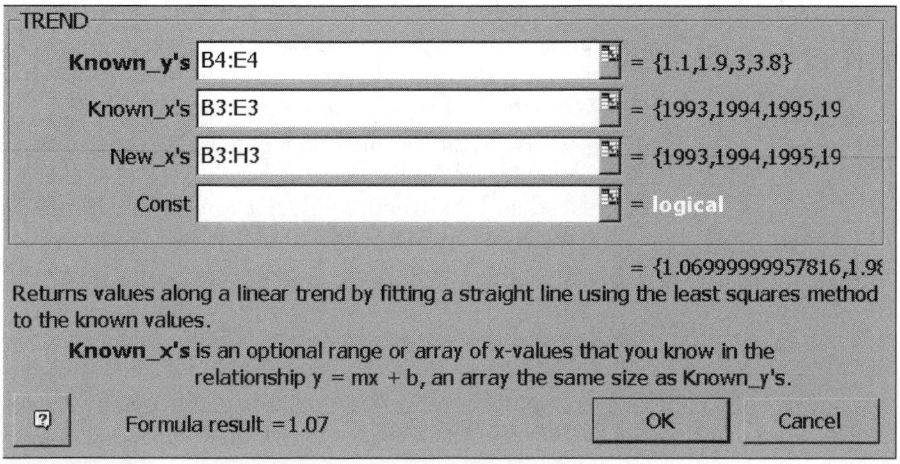

Figure 6.15. The TREND function dialog box

To use the TREND function with our example, first select a region in which to place the results. The region should be the same size as the number of *new_x's* to be calculated. Choose the **Edit Formula** button ▪ and select the TREND function from the function list.

The TREND function dialog box will appear as depicted in Figure 6.15. Select or type the ranges described in Figure 6.15. Since in this example the arguments to TREND are arrays rather than single values, press **Shift** + **Ctrl** + **Enter**. The results are depicted in Row 12 (labeled *TREND() function*) of Figure 6.14. Since we selected the entire range of years for our *new_x's*, the results are identical to the results for linear replacement. The *known_x's* values can now be modified and the trend results will immediately be recalculated.

There is a corresponding Excel function for predicting exponential trend named GROWTH. The arguments to the GROWTH function are similar to the arguments for TREND.

6.5.3   Trend Analysis for Charts

Excel will calculate and display trendlines on a chart. Five types of regression lines can be added or a moving average can be calculated. Each type of trend line is described in Table 6-1. Trendlines cannot be added to all types of charts. For example, trendlines cannot be added to data series in pie charts, 3D charts, stacked charts, or doughnut charts. Trendlines can be added to bar charts, XY scatter plots, and line charts. If a trendline is added to a chart and the chart type is subsequently changed to one of the exempted types, the trendline is lost.

TABLE 6-1   Formulas used to calculate chart trendlines

TRENDLINE TYPE	FORMULA
Linear	The least squares fit is calculated using $y = mx + b$. (m is the slope and b is a constant.)
Logarithmic	Calculates least squares using $y = c \cdot \ln(x) + b$ (c and b are constants.)
Polynomial	Calculates least squares for a line using $$y = b + c_1 x + c_2 x^2 + \dots + c_n x^n$$ ($b, c_1, c_2, \dots, c_n$ are constants; the order can be set in the Add Trendline dialog box, and the maximum order is 6.)
Exponential	Calculates least squares using $$y = ce^{bx}$$ (c and b are constants.)
Power	Calculates least squares using $$y = cx^b$$ (c and b are constants.)
Moving Average	Each data point in a moving average is the average of a specified number of previous data points. The series is calculated using $$F_{(t+1)} = \frac{1}{N} \sum_{1}^{N} A_{t-j+1}$$ (N is the number of prior periods to average, A_t is value at time t, F_t is the forecasted value at time t.)

To create a trendline, first create a chart of an acceptable type. As an example, create an XY chart using the exponential growth data in Row 10 of Figure 6.14. Choose **Chart**, **Add Trendline** from the Menu bar. The Add Trendline dialog box will appear as depicted in Figure 6.16. Choose the **Type** tab. Since we know the data represent exponential growth, first choose **Linear** from the box labeled *Trend/Regression type*. A linear trendline will not fit the data and will show maximum contrast for the example. Choose **Series1** from the list labeled *Based on Series*.

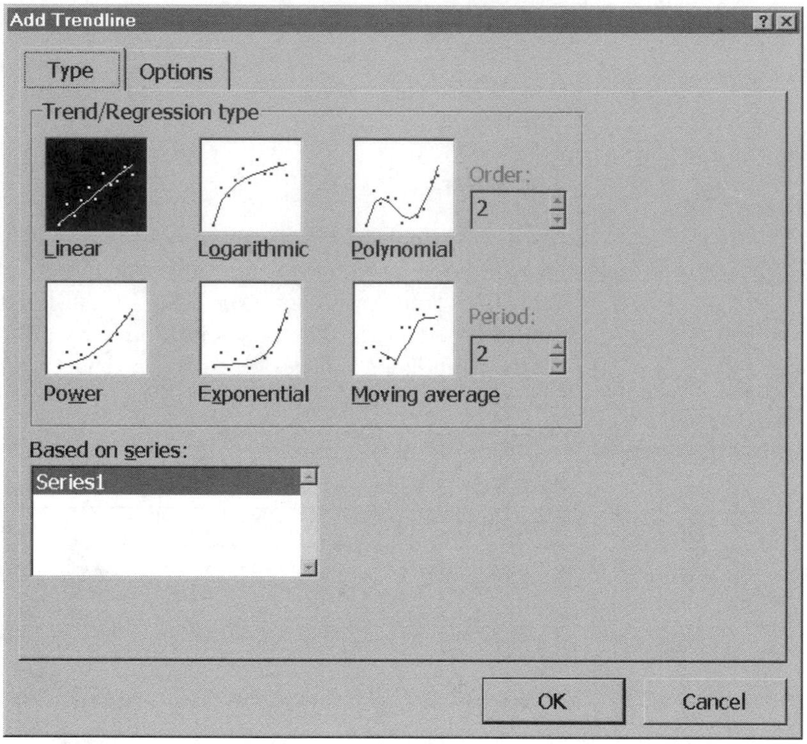

Figure 6.16. The Type tab on the Add Trendline dialog box

Now choose the **Options** tab on the Add Trendline dialog box as depicted in Figure 6.17. The first box under the Options tab gives the option of naming of the trendline. The second box can be set to forecast data points prior to or after the input data. The next item allows you to set the *y*-intercept to a constant value. If the box labeled *Set intercept* is not checked, the intercept is calculated. Check the box labeled *Display equation on chart* and click **OK**. The resulting chart and trendline should resemble Figure 6.18. If you add a trendline of exponential type, the data and trendline will match exactly. Try this yourself to verify that the chart data points and trendline match each other.

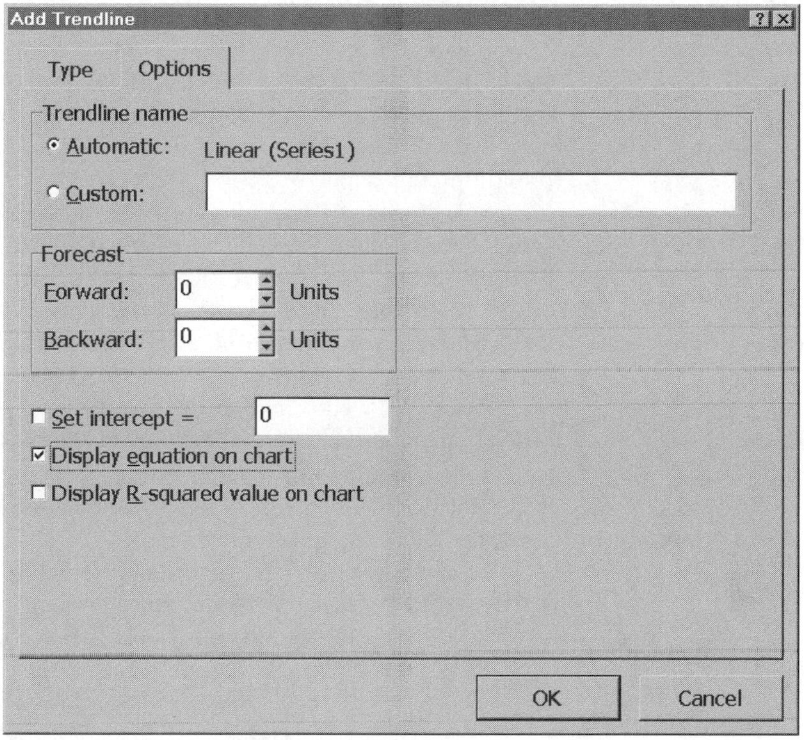

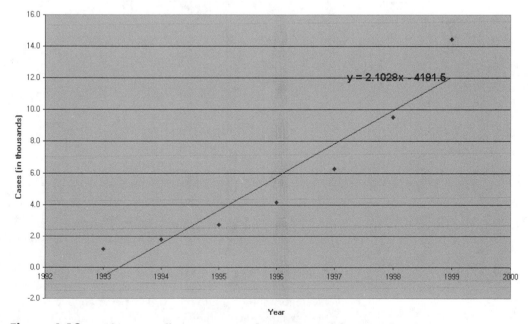

Figure 6.17. The Options tab on the Add Trendline dialog box

Figure 6.18. A linear trendline superimposed on exponential data

6.6 PIVOT TABLES FOR INTERACTIVE ANALYSIS

A *pivot table* is a table that summarizes data and that can be interactively manipulated. This frequently involves rotating or pivoting rows and columns, hence the name pivot table. The advantage of using a pivot table is the ease with which the data can be viewed from different perspectives.

A pivot table is a type of report. The data presented in the table cannot be manipulated directly. The underlying list can be modified and the pivot table can be refreshed to display any resulting changes.

A pivot table is created from a list or database. The list can be an Excel worksheet or the list can be imported from an external source. The external source can be a database application such as Access, dBase, or Oracle. The external source can also be the World Wide Web. The data for the example used in this chapter was obtained by using the Web query for Dow Jones Stocks by PC Quotes, Inc.

Before creating a pivot table, create or obtain a list of data to analyze. If you would like to practice the following example, create a worksheet that resembles Figure 6.19 or obtain the data using a Web query.

To create a pivot table, use the PivotTable Wizard by choosing **Data**, **Pivot Table Report** from the Menu bar. Step 1 of the Pivot Table Wizard asks for the source of the data. Choose the box labeled *Microsoft Excel list or database*.

	A	B
	Category	**Net Change**
1		
2	TRANSPORTATION	-1 3/4
3	TRANSPORTATION	-1 1/4
4	INDUSTRIALS	-1
5	INDUSTRIALS	- 5/8
6	TRANSPORTATION	- 9/16
7	INDUSTRIALS	- 3/8
8	INDUSTRIALS	- 3/8
9	UTILITIES	- 3/16
10	UTILITIES	- 3/16
11	UTILITIES	1/8
12	UTILITIES	1/4
13	INDUSTRIALS	5/8
14	INDUSTRIALS	2 1/2
15	TRANSPORTATION	3 7/16
16	INDUSTRIALS	6 5/8

Figure 6.19. Sample data for the PivotTable example

A portion of the stock quote data that we downloaded over the Web is depicted in Figure 6.20. In the following example, we are going to summarize the number of stocks in each category and compute the average net change for each category.

Step 2 of the PivotTable Wizard asks for a range of data to summarize. Select the range of the sample worksheet that you created or, if you used a Web query, select the resulting worksheet.

Step 3 asks you to construct the table by dragging *field buttons* into the report. The field buttons represent the field names of the database. In this example, drag the

	A	B	C	D	E	F	G
1	Company Name & Symbol	Category	Last Price	Net Change	Open	High	Lov
4	AMERICAN EXPRESS COMPANY (AXP)	INDUSTRIALS	85 15/16	15/16	85 5/8	86 5/8	85 5
9	WALT DISNEY CO. (DIS)	INDUSTRIALS	93 9/16	-1 5/8	93 9/16	93 15/16	93
15	INTERNATIONAL BUSINESS MACHINES (IBM)	INDUSTRIALS	109 1/4	-1 1/8	110 5/8	111 5/16	108
18	J. P. MORGAN & CO., INC. (JPM)	INDUSTRIALS	122 3/4	2 1/2	120 1/4	124 1/4	119

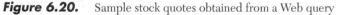

Figure 6.20.   Sample stock quotes obtained from a Web query

Category button into the box labeled *Row*. Then drag the **Category** button into the box labeled *Data*. The button will change its name to read **Count of Category**. Finally, drag the **Net Change** button into the data area. The name is automatically changed to **Sum of Net Change**. This is depicted in Figure 6.21.

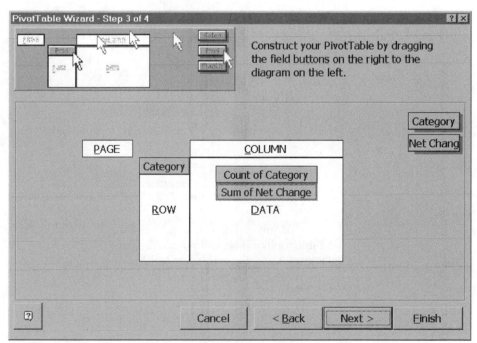

Figure 6.21.   The PivotTable Wizard—step 3

Step 4 of the Pivot Table Wizard asks you where to place the results. Choose the box labeled *New Worksheet*. Choose the **Finish** button. The completed pivot table and the Pivot Table toolbar will appear as depicted in Figure 6.22.

	A	B	C
1	Category	Data	Total
2	INDUSTRIALS	Count of Category	7
3		Sum of Net Change	7.375
4	TRANSPORTATION	Count of Category	4
5		Sum of Net Change	-0.125
6	UTILITIES	Count of Category	4
7		Sum of Net Change	0
8	Total Count of Category		15
9	Total Sum of Net Change		7.25
10			
11			
12			

Figure 6.22.   Example pivot table

Now, the benefits of using a pivot table will become apparent. Recall that we want to compute the average of the stock's net change (not the sum). Select one of the cells labeled *Sum of Net Change* and choose the Pivot Table Field button from the Pivot Table toolbar. The Pivot Table Field dialog box will appear as depicted in Figure 6.23.

Select **Average** from the list labeled *Summarize by* and choose **OK**. The resulting pivot table will now show the average of the net stock changes for each category.

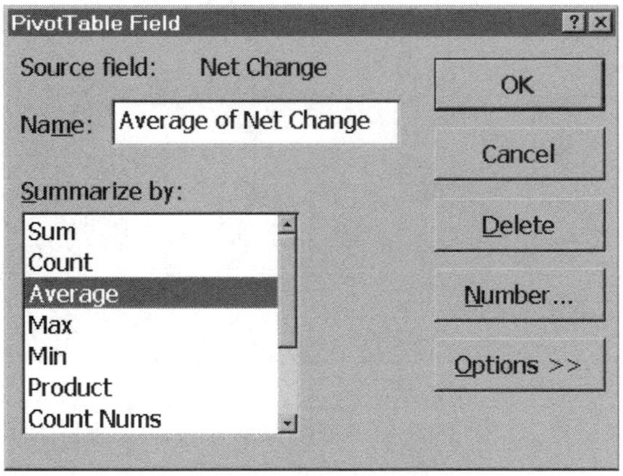

Figure 6.23.   The PivotTable Field dialog box

At any point, you may select the Pivot Table Wizard button from the Pivot Table toolbar. This will immediately return you to step 3 of the Pivot Table Wizard (see Figure 6.21). From this box you can drag the field buttons to new locations and quickly rearrange the pivot table report.

6.7   USING THE GOAL SEEKER FOR WHAT-IF ANALYSIS

The *Goal Seeker* is used to find the input values of a formula when the results are known. The Goal Seeker takes an initial guess for an input value and uses iterative refinement to attempt to locate the real input value.

An example of the use of the Goal Seeker is the solution of a polynomial equation, for example,

$$f(x) = 3x^3 + 2x^2 + 4 = 0$$

The equation $f(x)$ has a real solution that is approximately -1.3. We can use the initial guess of -1.3 as a seed for the Goal Seeker. The Goal Seeker will then attempt to converge on a more accurate value for x. The Goal Seeker does not always converge. With some functions, the initial guess must approximate the solution.

To see how the Goal Seeker works, create a worksheet that resembles Figure 6.24. Note the coding for $f(x)$ in the formula box. The formula should be placed in cell C3. The initial guess for $x = 1$ should be placed in cell C5. This results in $f(x) = 9$.

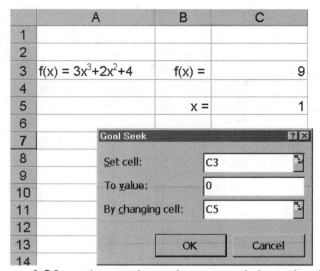

Figure 6.24. Solving a polynomial equation with the Goal Seeker

Choose **Tools**, and then **Goal Seek** from the Menu bar. The Goal Seek dialog box will appear as depicted in Figure 6.24.

Place the solution cell (C3), which contains the formula, in the box labeled *Set cell*. Place the desired solution (0) in the box labeled *To value*. Place the cell containing the initial guess (C5) in the box labeled *By changing cell*. Choose **OK**. The resulting value of $x = -1.373468173$ produces a solution for $f(x) = 0.0000375$, which is close to zero.

6.8 USING SOLVER FOR OPTIMIZATION PROBLEMS

Many engineering problems have more than one solution. Engineers choose among a range of possible solutions by applying limits to the input parameters of the problem. The problem becomes one of finding a minimum (or maximum) solution given the limitations. For example, you may want to minimize the cost of production of widgets given the limitations of staff hours, availability of raw materials, power consumption, and so on.

The equation that is to be maximized (or minimized) is called the *objective function*. The limitations to the input parameters of the objective function are called *constraints*. Problems of this type, finding a minimum or maximum given multiple constraints, are called *optimization* problems.

6.8.1 Introduction to Microsoft Excel Solver

Microsoft Excel provides a tool for solving such problems called Solver. Microsoft Excel Solver uses a methodology called Generalized Reduced Gradient (GRG2) for nonlinear optimization. The GRG2 code was developed by Leon Lasdon, University of Texas at Austin, and Allan Waren, Cleveland State University. John Watson and Dan Fylstra of Frontline Systems, Inc. implemented the methods used for linear and integer problems. Linear problems are solved using the simplex method with bounds on the variables, and integer problems are solved using the branch-and-bound method.

Solver must be installed as an add-in. To see if Solver is installed on your system, choose **Tools**, from the Menu bar and look for the **Solver** menu item. If it is not present, choose **Tools** and then **Add-Ins** from the Menu bar. Choose **Solver** from the Add-Ins dialog box and click **OK**. If Solver does not appear on the list, it should be installed from the Microsoft Excel or Microsoft Office installation CD.

6.8.2　Setting Up an Optimization Problem in Excel

The most difficult part of solving an optimization problem is setting up the objective function and identifying the constraints. An objective function takes the form

$$y = f(x_1, x_2, \ldots, x_n)$$

The independent variables are limited by m constraints, which take the form

$$c_i(x_1, x_2, \ldots, x_n) = \text{ for } i = 1, 2, \ldots, m$$

The constraints may also be expressed as inequalities. Excel Solver can handle both linear and nonlinear constraints. However, nonlinear constraints must be continuous functions. Although the constraints are expressed as functions, they are always evaluated within a range of precision called the *tolerance*. A constraint such as $x_1 < 0$ may be evaluated as TRUE when $x_1 = 0.0000003$ if the tolerance is large enough.

Nonlinear optimization problems may have multiple minima or maxima. In a minimization problem, all solutions except the absolute minimum are called *local minima*. The solution that is chosen by Solver is dependent on the initial starting point for the solution. The initial guess should be as close to the real solution as possible. These are problems with optimization in general, not with Excel Solver. For the rest of the examples in this section, it is assumed that you have some familiarity with optimization.

6.8.3　Linear Optimization Example

Assume that you wish to maximize the profit for producing widgets. The widgets come in two models: economy and deluxe. The economy model sells for $49.00 and the deluxe model sells for $79.00. The cost of production is determined primarily by labor costs, which are $14.00 per hour. The union limits the workers to a total of 2,000 hours per month. The economy widget can be built in three people-hours and the deluxe widget can be built in four people-hours. The management believes that it can sell up to 600 deluxe widgets per month and up to 1,200 economy widgets. Since you have a limited work force, the main variable under your control is the ability to balance the number of economy versus deluxe units that are built. Your job is to determine how many economy widgets and how many deluxe widgets should be built to maximize the company's profit.

The independent variables are

$$w_1 = \text{the number of economy widgets produced each month}$$

$$w_2 = \text{the number of deluxe widgets produced each month}$$

The target that you wish to maximize is the profit p. It is described mathematically by the objective function

$$p = (49 - (3 \cdot 14))w_1 + (79 - (4 \cdot 14))w_2 = 7w_1 + 23w_2$$

The constraints can be expressed mathematically as limitations on w_1 and w_2. The maximum number of widgets to be produced is limited by both sales and labor availability. The sales limitations can be expressed as

$$w_1 \leq 1200 \text{ widgets}$$

and

$$w_2 \leq 600 \text{ widgets}$$

The limitation impose by the availability of labor can be expressed as

$$3w_1 + 4w_2 \leq 2000$$

Finally, the general constraint of nonnegativity is imposed on w_1 and w_2 since you cannot produce a negative number of widgets:

$$w_1, w_2 \geq 0$$

Figure 6.25 shows how to set up the widget problem in a worksheet. Cells D5 and D6 have been named w_1 and w_2, respectively, to make the formulas more readable. Note the underlines in the names. The names w1 and w2 cannot be used since these are reserved for cell identifiers. The formulas are displayed in the cells for readability. To display formulas instead of their results choose **Tools**, **Options**, and then **View** from the Menu bar. Check the box labeled *Formulas*.

	A	B	C	D	E
1		Widget Profit Optimization Worksheet			
2					
3					
4		Independent variables			
5	Ecomony widgets/month w1=			0	
6	Deluxe widgets/month w2=			0	
7					
8		Objective function			
9		Profit(p)		=7*w_1 + 23*w_2	
10					
11					
12		Constraints			
13		Labor constraint		=3*w_1 + 4*w_2	

Figure 6.25. Worksheet for linear optimization example

Choose **Tools** and then **Solver** from the Menu bar. The Solver Parameters dialog box will appear as depicted in Figure 6.26. The box labeled *Set Target Cell* should contain the cell holding the objective function (the profit function). Check the box labeled *Max* since you want to maximize profit. The box labeled *By changing Cells* should contain the input parameters w_1 and w_2. Add each of the constraints as depicted in Figure 6.26 and choose **Options**.

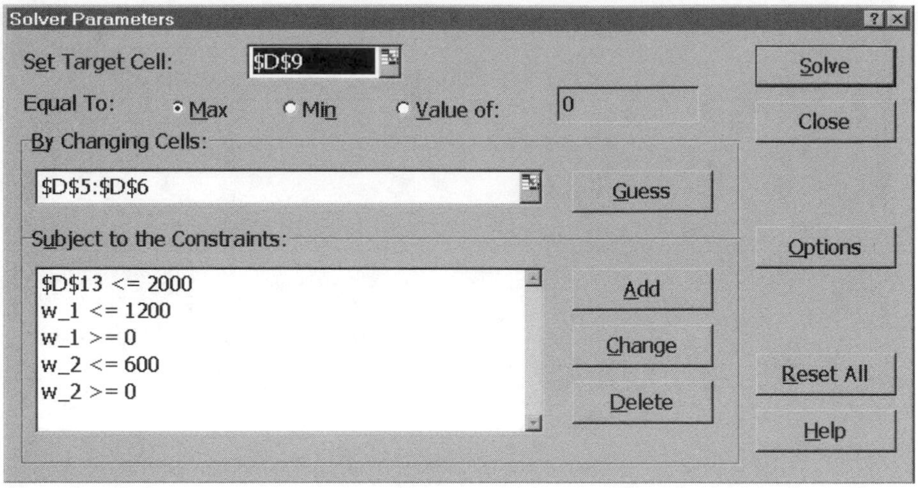

Figure 6.26. The Solver Parameters dialog box

The Solver Options dialog box will appear as depicted in Figure 6.27. Accept most of the options in the Solver Options dialog box. These should not be changed unless you understand the GRG2 and simplex methods used to implement solver. Since this is a linear problem, check the box labeled *Assume Linear Model* and choose **OK** to return to the Solver Parameters dialog box. Choose **Solve** to begin the computation.

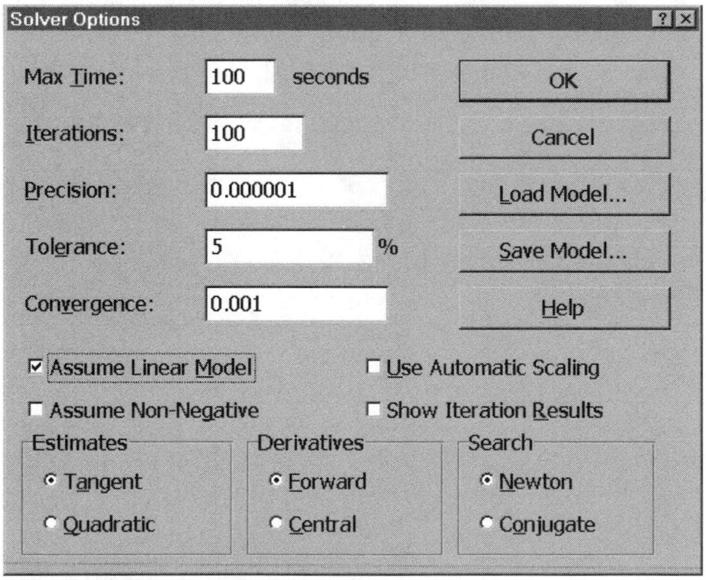

Figure 6.27. The Solver Options dialog box

The Solver Results dialog box will appear as depicted in Figure 6.28. It should state that Solver has found a solution. There are three types of reports available from solver. Select all three: **Answer**, **Sensitivity**, and **Limits**. Check the box labeled *Keep Solver Solution* and press **OK**.

The worksheet you created will now contain modified values for the input parameters and objective function. In addition, three new worksheets will be created for the Answer, Sensitivity, and Limits Reports.

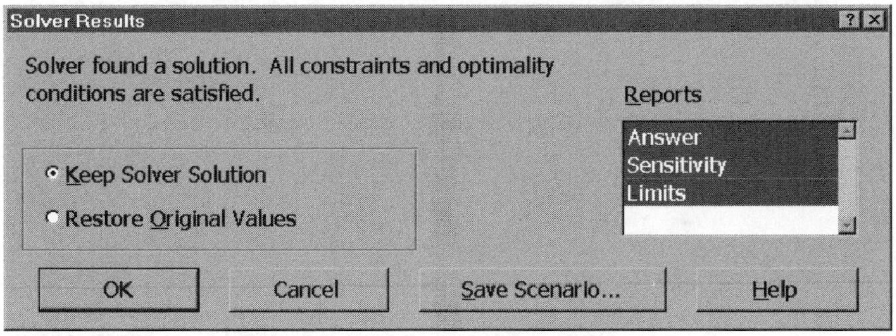

Figure 6.28. The Solver Results dialog box

The Answer report summarizes the initial and final values of the input parameters and the optimized variable. The Sensitivity report describes information about marginal effects of making small changes in the constraints. Sometimes, a small constraint change can make a large difference in the output. For nonlinear models, these are called Lagrange multipliers. For linear models, these are sometimes called dual values or shadow prices. The Limits report shows the effect on the solution as each input parameter is set to its minimum and maximum limit.

The resulting spreadsheet from our example is show in Figure 6.29. A brief look at this worksheet shows that the maximum profit of $11,500 per month is achieved by producing only deluxe widgets. Only 500 deluxe widgets can be produced per month but the company can sell 600 per month, thus a limiting constraint is the available labor pool. As manager, you can easily modify the constraints and rerun Solver to see the effect. You could rapidly view the effect on profit of hiring more laborers, modifying prices, or adjusting the widget mix.

	A	B	C	D	E
1	Widget Profit Optimization Worksheet				
2					
3					
4	Independent variables				
5	Ecomony widgets/month w1=			0	
6	Deluxe widgets/month w2=			500	
7					
8	Objective function				
9	Profit(p)			11500	
10					
11					
12	Constraints				
13	Labor constraint			2000	

Figure 6.29. Results of linear optimization

6.8.4 Non-Linear Optimization Example

As an example of nonlinear optimization, we will use an optimization problem for which the solution is obvious. This will familiarize you with the process of setting up a nonlinear optimization problem and convince you that the results are correct.

The objective function that we wish to minimize is

$$y = 100(x_2 - x_1^2)^2 + (1 - x_1)^2$$

with the nonnegativity constraints

$$x_1 \geq 0$$

and

$$x_2 \geq 0$$

Since the terms $(x_2 - x_1^2)^2$ and $(1 - x_1)^2$ must be positive for real numbers x_1 and x_2, the minimum y is zero with $x_1 = 1$ and $x_2 = 1$. The worksheet for this example is shown in Figure 6.30.

	A	B	C	D	E
1		Example of non-linear optimization			
2					
3		Input Parameters			
4		x1=	0		
5		x2=	0		
6					
7		Objective Function			
8		y=	=100*(x_2 - x_1^2)^2 + (1-x_1)^2		

Figure 6.30.   Worksheet for nonlinear optimization example

Follow the steps described for linear optimization, but make the following changes:

- Check the box labeled *Min*.
- Set the constraints to be $x\_1 \geq 0$ and $x\_2 \geq 0$.
- Do **not** check the box labeled *Assume Linear Model*.

The results produced by Solver are good approximations of the true minimum:

$$x_1 = 0.999977$$

$$x_2 = 0.999962$$

$$y = 6.49784E - 09$$

There are other local minima for this objective function. Try setting the initial parameters to $x_1 = 3$ and $x_2 = 5$. The results produced by Solver show that the algorithm is stuck in a local minimum:

$$x_1 = 1.639202$$

$$x_2 = 2.668455$$

$$y = 0.44290084$$

Materials science is an important field of study for engineers that covers the electronic, optical, mechanical, chemical, and magnetic properties of metals, polymers, composite materials, and ceramics.

Crystalline materials are subject to *slip deformation* when a shear stress is applied to the material. The deformation occurs when atomic planes slide along the directions of densest atomic packing.

When crystalline materials such as metals and alloys are formed by cooling molten metal, separate crystals form in the melt and grow together. The boundaries between the growing crystals form barriers to slip deformation, increasing the observed *yield strength* of the metal. The relationship between grain size (i.e., the size of the individual crystals in the metal) and observed yield strength, σ_y, is described by the Hall-Petch equation:

$$\sigma_y = \sigma_o + k_y \frac{1}{\sqrt{d}}$$

where σ_o is the yield strength of the pure metal (i.e., single crystal, $d = \infty$). The value of the proportionality factor, k_y, depends on the material and can be obtained by regression analysis from experimental data.

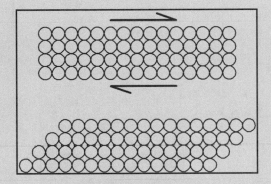

Grain Size	Yield Strength		
d	σ_y		
(μm)	(MN/m²)		
284	86	0.059318	86
92	127	0.104257	127
60	152	0.129099	152
37	182	0.165408	182
25	210	0.2	210
15	247	0.256495	247

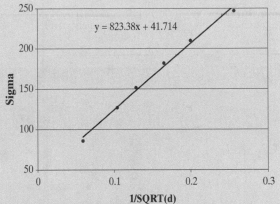

For the data shown here, the coefficients for the Hall-Petch equation can be found using Excel:

$$\sigma_y = 41.714 \frac{MN}{m^2} + 823.38 \frac{MN\,\mu m^{0.5}}{m^2} \frac{1}{\sqrt{d}}$$

The k_y value would typically be reported as

$$k_y = 0.823 \frac{MN}{m^{3/2}} .$$

How'd They Do That?

The Hall-Petch equation is an example of an equation that can be written in linear form:

$$y = ax + b$$

where a is the slope of the line through the data values, and b is the y-intercept. Comparing terms with the Hall-Petch equation, you see that:

$$\sigma_y = y$$

$$\sigma_o = b$$

$$\frac{1}{\sqrt{d}} = x$$

A plot of $\dfrac{1}{\sqrt{d}}$ on the x-axis against σ_y on the y-axis

shows the desired linear relationship.

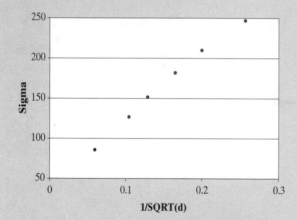

Excel can calculate the equation of the line through the data points (called a *trendline*) automatically. Once the graph has been created, just right-click on one of the data points. A menu will pop up. Select **Add Trendline**... from the menu.

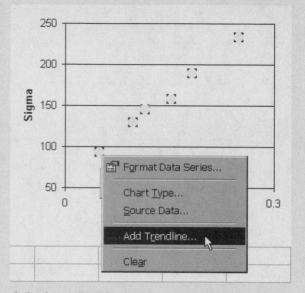

A dialog box will be displayed that allows you to set options for the trendline. On the Type panel, choose **Linear** to have Excel put a straight line through the data points.

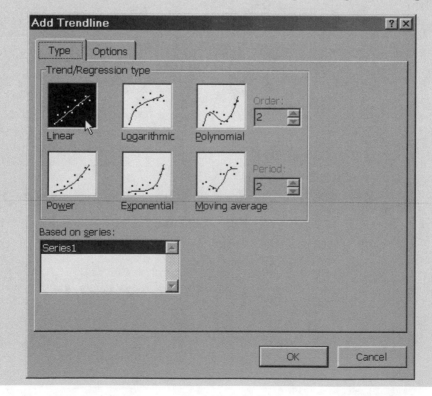

On the Options panel, ask Excel to show the equation by clicking on the checkbox by **Display equation on chart**. Then click on the **OK** button to close the dialog.

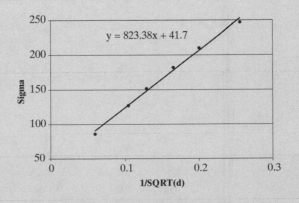

Excels finds the "best" equation through the data points using linear regression (see Section 6.4) and displays the result on the graph.

Chapter Summary

This chapter introduced many of the powerful data analysis tools offered by Excel. The tools presented in this chapter can be used to solve problems in your engineering courses. These include a large number of statistical and engineering functions in the Analysis ToolPak, a method for solving equations using the Goal Seeker, and methods for solving optimization problems using the Solver feature.

KEY TERMS

Analysis ToolPak	field button	regression
bin	Goal Seeker	step value
correlation	histogram	stop value
descriptive statistics	optimization	trend analysis
Fast Fourier Transform	pivot table	

Problems

1. Use the Analysis ToolPak Histogram feature and the data in Figure 6.3 to create a graph of the cumulative percent of students in each bin. What percent of the students earned a score of 80 or less on the midterm exam?

2. Use the Descriptive Statistics selection from the Analysis ToolPak to find the mean and standard deviation for the student data in Figure 6.3. How many midterm grades lie more than two standard deviations from the mean?

3. Collect the high school GPAs and first-year college GPAs (or cumulative college GPAs) of your classmates. Perform the correlation and regression analysis described in Sections 6.3 and 6.4. How well does the high GPA predict college success for your sample group?

4. Generate the values for $f(x) = 2.5\ln(x) + 1.34$ for $x = 1, 2, \ldots, 10$. Chart the results using an XY scatter plot. Create a logarithmic trendline for the data series. How well does the trendline match the data? Choose the options box on the Format Trendline dialog box, forecast forward four units, and display the equation on the chart. How closely does the equation match the original function?

5. Generate data points for the function

$$y(x) = 4\sin(x) - x^2$$

for $x = -5.0, -4.5, \ldots, 4.5, 5.0$. Chart the results using a line chart. Add a trendline to the chart. Display the equation on the chart. Does a fifth-order polynomial closely match data?

6. Use the same method described in Problem 5 to find the solution to

$$f(x) = x^3 + \sin(x/2) + 2x^2 - 4 = 0 \text{ for } -1.0 \leq x \leq 2.0$$

7. Compute the values of

$$f(x) = x^3 - 12x^2 - 9$$

for $x = -4.0, -3.5, -3.0, \ldots, 3.5, 4.0$. Chart the results using an XY scatterplot. Note that in this range $f(x)$ crosses the X-axis three times near $x = -3.0, -0.8$, and 3.8. Use the Goal Seeker to find more accurate solutions for

$$x^3 - 12x^2 - 9 = 0$$

8. Use the Solver to minimize the objective function

$$f(x) = (x_1 + 2x_2 - 7)^2 + (2x_1 + x_2 - 5)^2$$

for $-10 \leq x_i \leq 10$.

9. A cylindrical chemical petroleum tank is to be built to hold 6.8 m³ of hazardous waste. Your task is to design the tank in a cost-effective manner by designing the tank to minimize its surface area. Ignore the thickness of the walls in your design. Recall that the surface area S of a right-angled cylinder is

$$S = 2\pi r^2 + 2\pi rh \text{ square meters}$$

and the volume V of a cylinder is

$$V = \pi r^2 h \text{ cubic meters.}$$

Use the Solver to minimize r and h.

7

Database Management within Excel

7.1 INTRODUCTION

Microsoft Excel implements a rudimentary database management system by treating lists in a worksheet as database records. This is helpful for organizing, sorting, and searching through worksheets that contain many related items. You can import complete databases from external *Database Management Systems (DBMS)* such as Microsoft Access, Oracle, dBase, Microsoft FoxPro, and text files. You can create structured queries using Microsoft Query that will retrieve selected information from external sources.

If you require a relational DBMS, you are encouraged to use another, more complete software application such as Microsoft Access. However, the database functions within Excel are adequate for many problems. An example of one way an engineer might use this functionality is to import experimental data that have been stored in a relational DBMS in order to perform analysis on the data using Excel's built-in functions.

7.2 CREATING DATABASES

7.2.1 Database Terminology

A database within Excel is sometimes called a *list*. The two terms will be treated synonymously in this book. A *database* can be thought of as an electronic file cabinet that contains a number of folders. Each folder contains similar information for different objects. For example, each folder might contain the information about a student at a college of engineering. The database is the collection of all student folders. The data in each folder is organized in a similar fashion. For

After reading this chapter, you should be able to

- Create a database within Excel
- Enter data into a database
- Sort a database on one or more keys
- Use filters to search or collapse databases
- Use Microsoft Query to access external databases

example, each folder includes a student's first name, last name, social security number, address, department, class, and so on.

Using database terminology, each folder is called a *record*. Each data item, such as first name, is stored within a *field* or *row*. The title for each data item is called a *field name*.

Any region in an Excel worksheet can be defined to be a database. Excel represents each record as a separate row. Each cell within the row is a field. The heading for each column is the field name.

Figure 7.1 depicts a small student database. Rows 2 through 7 each represent a student record. Each record has five fields. The field names are the column headings, (e.g., *Last Name*).

	A	B	C	D	E
1	**Last Name**	**First Name**	**SSN**	**Department**	**Class**
2	Clinton	Willie	243-65-7666	Electrical	Junior
3	Smith	Randolph	245-54-3223	Chemical	Senior
4	Simpson	Susie	268-22-5365	Electrical	Senior
5	Smith	Christine	287-56-4532	Civil	Junior
6	Washington	Frank	532-45-3343	Mechanical	Junior
7	Granger	Linda	576-43-5455	Chemical	Senior

Figure 7.1.   Example of a student database

7.2.2   Database Creation Tips

Most database management systems store records in one or more files. The file delimits the boundaries of the database. Excel, however, stores a database as a region in a worksheet.

Excel must have some way of knowing where the database begins and ends in the worksheet. There are two methods for associating a region with a database. One method is to leave a perimeter of blank cells around the database region. The second is to name the region explicitly. Because of the unique way that Excel delimits a database, the following tips are recommended.

- Maintain only one database per worksheet. This will speed up access to the sorting and filtering functions, and you will not need to name the database regions.

- Each column heading in the database must be unique. If there were two headings for *Last Name*, for example, a logical query such as *Find all records with last name equal to Smith* would not make sense.

- Create an empty column to the right of the database and an empty row at the bottom of the database. Excel uses the empty row and column to mark the edge of the database. An alternate method is to assign a name to the region of the database. A disadvantage of assigning a name is that the allocated region may have to be redefined when records are added or deleted.

- Do not use cells to the right of the database for other purposes. Filtered rows may inadvertently hide these cells.

7.2.3   Entering Data

Once the field names for the database have been created in the column headings, data may be entered using several methods. One method of data entry is to enter data directly into a cell. A database field may have any legitimate Excel value, including numerical, date, text, or formula. For example, you might add a column to the database in Figure 7.1 that is titled *Full Name*. Instead of copying or retyping the first and last names of each student, the new field could concatenate *First Name* and *Last Name* using the following formula:

```
=CONCATENATE(B2, " " ,A2)
```

A second method for entering data is to use a form. To access the data entry form, first click on any data cell in the database. Choose **Data**, then **Form** from the Menu bar. The Data Entry form will appear as depicted in Figure 7.2. The title of the Data Entry form will be the same as the name of the current worksheet.

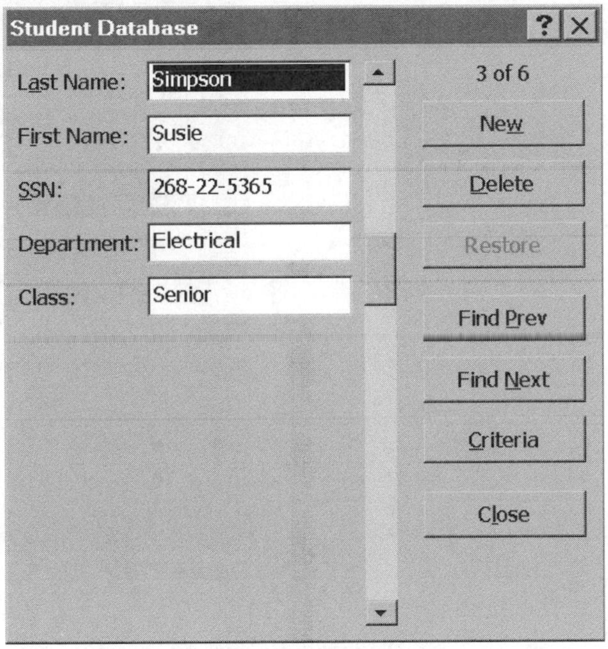

Figure 7.2. The Data Entry form

From the Data Entry form, a new record can be created by clicking the **New** button. From this form, you can also scroll through the database, delete records, and modify existing records. The Data Entry form can also be used to filter data. This feature is explained in the next section.

PRACTICE!

Before proceeding, it would be helpful if you created the database depicted in Figure 7.2. This database will be used for the examples in Section 7.2.

Enter some of the data using the Data Entry form. Enter some of the data by typing directly into the worksheet. Which method is less prone to typing errors?

7.3   SORTING, SEARCHING, AND FILTERING

The power of a database management system lies in its ability to search for information, rearrange data, and filter information.

7.3.1   Sorting a Database

To sort a database, first select any cell within the database and choose **Data**, **Sort** from the Menu bar. The Sort dialog box will appear as depicted in Figure 7.3. The field on which the sort is made is called the *sort key*. Excel allows you to sort on multiple keys. For example, choose **Last Name** in ascending order as the first key. Choose **First Name** in ascending order as the second key. Make sure that the box labeled Header Row is checked and click **OK**. The result is an alphabetical listing of the student database.

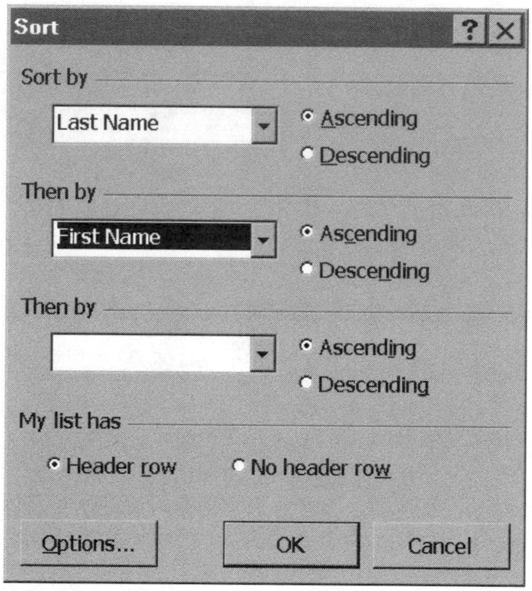

Figure 7.3.   The Sort dialog box

Warning: Be sure to select the entire database before sorting. If some columns are left out of the sort, the database may become scrambled. If you accidentally scramble the database, immediately choose **Edit**, **Undo Sort** from the Menu bar. The easiest way to select the entire database is to click on a single cell before performing any database operations. The entire database will be highlighted.

7.3.2   Searching and Filtering

Excel has several mechanisms for locating records that match specified criteria. For example, you may be interested in reviewing the students with chemical engineering majors. After you specify the criterion of department to be Chemical, Excel displays only those records with the Department field equal to Chemical. The process of limiting the visible records based on some criterion is called *filtering*. There are three general methods for filtering a database in Excel. The easiest methods are the use of the Data Entry form and the AutoFilter function. The Advance Filter function allows you to search using more logically sophisticated search criteria.

Filtering with the Data Entry Form.

To use the Data Entry form to filter and search a database, first select a cell within the database and choose **Data**, **Form** from the Menu bar. Select the Criteria button on the Data Entry form. A blank record will appear. As an example, type **Smith** in the Last Name field. Now repeatedly click the **Find Next** and **Find Prev** buttons and note that only students with a last name of Smith appear.

To clear the filter, choose **Criteria**, **Clear**, and **Form** from the Data Entry form. Now if you click the **Find Next** and **Find Prev** buttons, all of the students will appear.

Using the AutoFilter Function.

The AutoFilter function allows you to filter records while viewing the database as a worksheet. To turn on the AutoFilter function, first select a cell within the database and choose **Data**, **Filter**, and **AutoFilter** from the Menu bar. A small arrow will appear in the heading of each column. When you click on one of the arrows, a small drop-down menu will appear that contains the possible choices for that field. Figure 7.4 depicts the drop-down menu for the Department field.

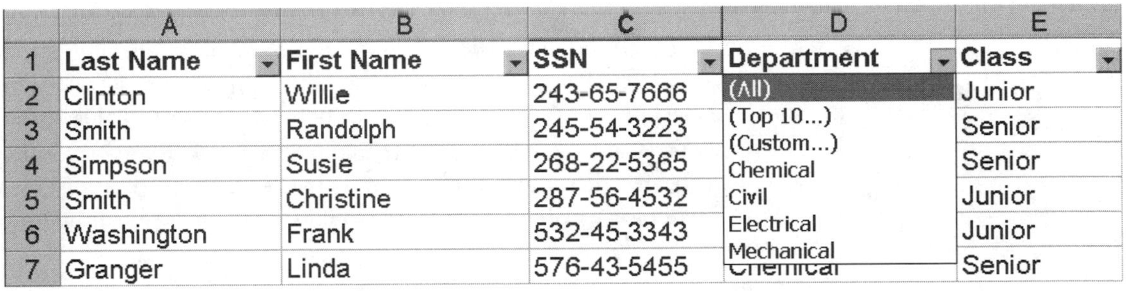

	A	B	C	D	E
1	Last Name ▾	First Name ▾	SSN ▾	Department ▾	Class ▾
2	Clinton	Willie	243-65-7666	(All)	Junior
3	Smith	Randolph	245-54-3223	(Top 10...) (Custom...)	Senior
4	Simpson	Susie	268-22-5365	Chemical	Senior
5	Smith	Christine	287-56-4532	Civil	Junior
6	Washington	Frank	532-45-3343	Electrical	Junior
7	Granger	Linda	576-43-5455	Mechanical Chemical	Senior

Figure 7.4. An example AutoFilter menu

PRACTICE!

Practice using the AutoFilter function and you will see how easy it is to define a filter and modify the filter. First, select the arrow in the Class field and choose **Senior**. The database will immediately hide all the records except the seniors. Now select the arrow in the Department field and select **Electrical**. The result is a filter that displays all of the students who are seniors and are also in electrical engineering. The two criteria are treated as if connected with a logical AND.

Note that the arrows for the Department and Class fields have changed color. This alerts you that a filter has been applied on these fields. To remove the filters, choose each colored arrow and select **(ALL)** from the drop-down menu. The arrow will return to its original color and all of the database records will reappear.

You can specify criteria that are more complex by selecting a field and choosing **(Custom)**. Try this by selecting the arrow in the **Department** field and choosing **(Custom)**. The Custom AutoFilter dialog box will appear as depicted in Figure 7.5.

Experiment with the criteria. The selections in Figure 7.5 will create a filter that displays students whose department begins with a **C** or equals **Mechanical**. Try experimenting with the **?** and ***** wildcards. For example, try a custom filter using the criterion:

```
SSN equals *45*
```

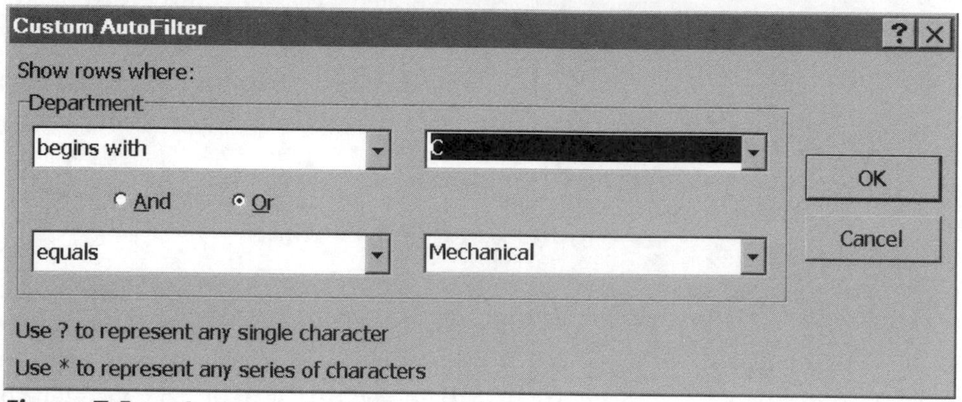

Figure 7.5.   The Custom AutoFilter dialog box

Using the Advanced Filter Function.

The Advanced Filter function is useful if you have a complex set of criteria or you want to filter on calculated cells. Before creating a complex set of criteria, you must first set up a criteria table. Do this by copying the field names to another location in the worksheet. Leave at least one blank row of cells between the criteria table and the database.

A criteria table may have more than one active row. Every criterion within a single row must be met for a match to occur. This is equivalent to a logical AND operator. Figure 7.6 depicts a criteria table and a database. The first row of the criteria table (Row 5) is equivalent to the English statement

Select the students whose GPA is greater than 3.5 AND who are seniors.

The second row of the criteria table (Row 6) is equivalent to the English statement

```
Select the students whose GPA is greater than 3.1 AND who are
in the Electrical Engineering Department.
```

The Advanced Filter accepts matches from either criterion. This is equivalent to a logical OR operator. The AND operator has precedence over the OR operator. The effect of both rows is equivalent to the English statement

```
Select the students
whose GPA is greater than 3.5 AND who are seniors,
OR,
whose GPA is greater than 3.1 AND are in the Electrical
Engineering Department.
```

	A	B	C	D	E
1	Criteria				
3	**Last Name**	**First Name**	**GPA**	**Department**	**Class**
5			>3.50		Senior
6			>3.10	Electrical	
7					
8	Database				
9	**Last Name**	**First Name**	**GPA**	**Department**	**Class**
10	Clinton	Willie	3.51	Electrical	Junior
11	Smith	Randolph	2.98	Chemical	Senior
12	Simpson	Susie	3.92	Electrical	Senior
13	Smith	Christine	3.65	Civil	Junior
14	Washington	Frank	3.41	Mechanical	Junior
15	Granger	Linda	2.78	Chemical	Senior
16					
17					
18	Query Results				
19	**Last Name**	**First Name**	**GPA**	**Department**	**Class**
20	Clinton	Willie	3.51	Electrical	Junior
21	Simpson	Susie	3.92	Electrical	Senior

Figure 7.6. A criteria table used with the Advanced Filter

7.3.3   External Data Retrieval Using Microsoft Query

A stand-alone program called Microsoft Query is capable of retrieving data from other types of databases into your worksheet. Though Microsoft Query is included with the Excel package, it is not part of the default installation. If you have a version of Excel prior to Excel, Microsoft Query must be installed as an add-in. In addition, each type of database that can be accessed has a separate driver, called an ODBC driver. These include drivers for Paradox, dBase, Access, and so on. If Microsoft Query does not work, run the Excel or Microsoft Office Setup program and install Query and an ODBC driver for each type of database you wish to access.

For the following examples, we have created a small dBase database with four fields and four records. This database is depicted in Figure 7.7.

Record#	NAME	SSN	PHONE	AGE
1	Dave Kuncicky	267863456	(850)487-6431	48
2	Steffie Grow	254534321	(850)421-3013	41
3	Helen Alice	564324543	(850)385-4960	34
4	Cliff Browning	342546543	(850)421-5465	46

Figure 7.7. An example dBase database

After you have installed Microsoft Query, select a cell; then choose **Data**, **Get External Data**, and **Create New Query**. The Choose Data Source dialog box will appear as depicted in Figure 7.8. If the box labeled *Use the Query Wizard* is checked, remove the check. Select the database type from the list under the **Databases** tab. For this example, choose **dBase Files** from the list and choose **OK**.

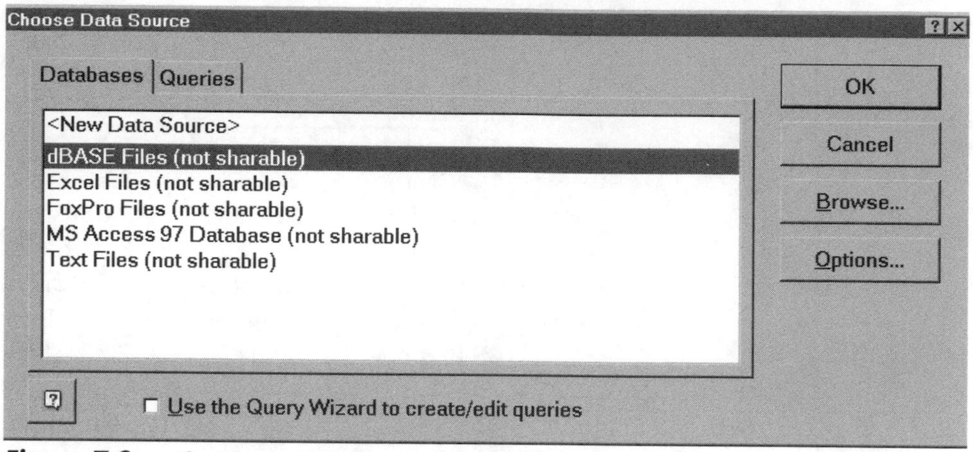

Figure 7.8. The Choose Data Source dialog box

The Add Tables dialog box will appear as depicted in Figure 7.9. Locate the database from which you wish to import data and click **Add**. The Microsoft Query program will then execute and the database name and field names should appear in the MS Query window. Part of the MS Query window is depicted in Figure 7.10.

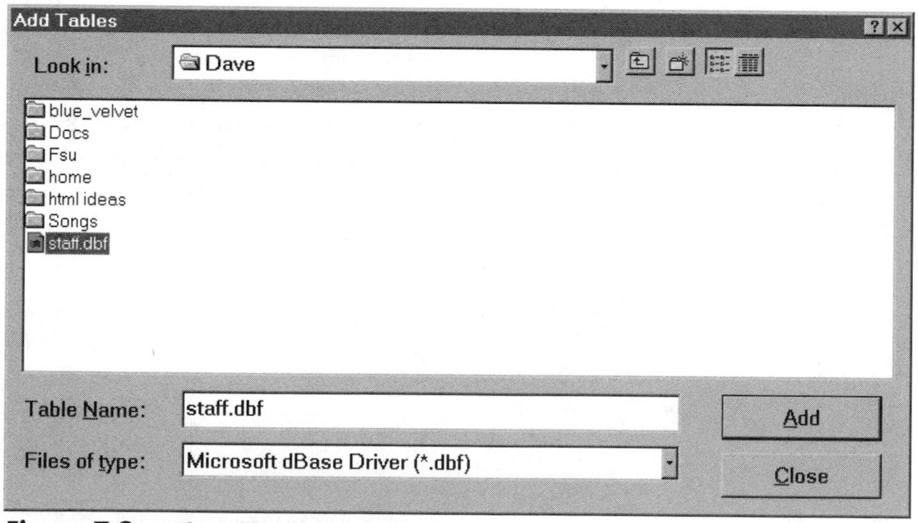

Figure 7.9. The Add Tables dialog box

Note that the four fields in the dBase file (depicted in Figure 7.7) appear in the top pane of the MS Query window. You can select the fields of interest by clicking on the field names. The result will appear at the bottom of the window. In the example, the fields AGE and NAME were selected (see Figure 7.10).

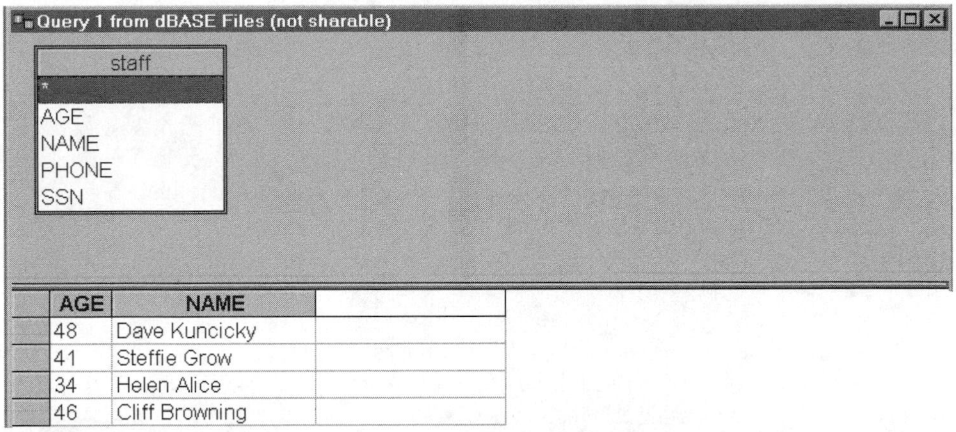

Figure 7.10.   Selecting fields from the external database

Once the fields have been selected, the database may be filtered to limit the records that are displayed. If the Criteria pane does not appear in the MS Query window, choose **View**, and then **Query** from the MS Query Menu bar. In Figure 7.11, the criterion

$$AGE > \text{'45'}$$

has been selected. The results of the filter are immediately displayed in the bottom pane of the MS Query window.

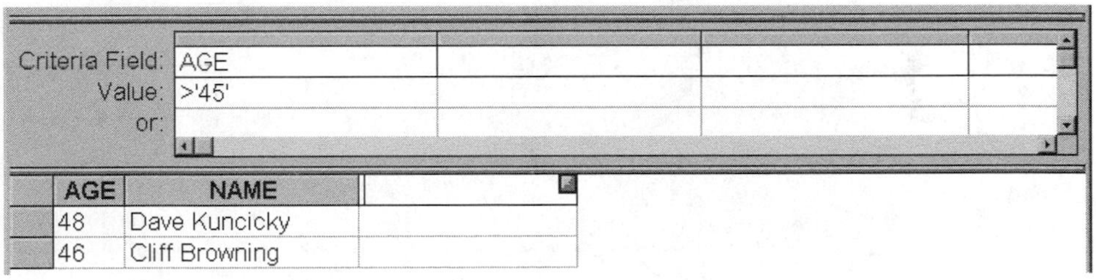

Figure 7.11.   Filtering a query

The data view can be manipulated within MS Query or the data can be copied to an Excel worksheet. Once the data are part of an Excel worksheet, the data can be modified and the database functions described in this chapter can be used. To copy the data to an Excel worksheet, choose **File, Return Data to Microsoft Excel** from the MS Query Menu bar.

Microsoft Query is a full-featured stand-alone program and contains many features that are not explained here. For example, a *Structured Query Language (SQL)* statement may be created and used to query the remote data. The criteria used in Figure 7.11 are equivalent to the following SQL statement:

```
SELECT staff.AGE, staff.NAME
FROM 'C:Dave'staff.dbf staff
WHERE (staff.AGE>'45')
```

APPLICATION - BIOPROCESSING — USING EXCEL TO ANALYZE A DATABASE.

The Human Genome Project is intended to help mankind understand how we function at the molecular level. An expected outgrowth of that understanding is the ability to design medicines that target very specific problems. They will likely be produced using bioprocessing methods. Bioprocess engineering is an emerging field that uses biological systems (typically microorganisms) to produce products. Bioprocessing is as old as the wine industry, but recent advances in our understanding of how microorganisms function has made it possible to produce a much wider array of products using this technology.

The key to manufacturing products successfully using bioprocessing techniques is very careful control of the environment in which the microorganisms are growing. The growth media is typically taken through a series of steps, or stages, as the organisms are grown, prepared to produce the desired product, allowed time to produce the product, and collected. Temperature, pH, and nutrient levels must all be carefully controlled in the various stages. This produces a lot of data, stored in a database that can be extremely valuable when an engineer is trying to understand why a bioprocess is not producing as expected.

As an example of using a database to help diagnose a problem, consider a bioprocessing plant that grows microorganisms in order to collect a valuable product. The organism produces the valuable product when it is under stress, so a pH change is used to induce the formation of the valued product. The plant follows a recipe that calls for the following processing stages:

Stage 1—Prewarming	The growth media is warmed from room temperature to 35°C.
Stage 2—Growth	The broth containing the microorganisms is added to the reactor, and allowed to acclimate and grow for six hours.
Stage 3—Ramp pH	The pH is slowly changed from 6.3 to 5.4 to induce the production of the valutable product.
Stage 4—Production	The microorganisms are kept at pH 5.4 for two hours to produce the valued product.
Stage 5—Stop Growth	The temperature is quickly raised to at least 55°C to kill the microorganisms before the broth is collected.

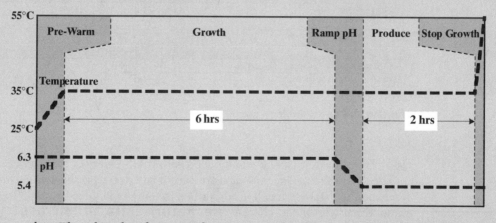

The scenario is this: The plant has been producing product for some time when Sara comes in after a long weekend to find a note from the lab technician on her desk saying,

Some of the batches failed—the bugs must have died.

Microorganisms can indeed die and not produce the product, but that explanation doesn't help much when she has to explain to the plant manager why some batches, at $20,000 per batch, failed to produce a product. Sara starts looking at the process data.

Nearly every industrial process is monitored as it is made, and in most cases the data are stored for a time in case something goes wrong. Sara goes back to the data that was collected for the past 10 batches (R1760128–R1760137). The database contains the following data:

- ID—the item number in the database
- Run Name—the unique identifier of each batch
- Time—in seconds, collected every 120 seconds
- Stage—one of the five stages mentioned above, plus "Collect" indicating the termination of the batch
- Temp—the temperature in °C
- PH—the pH value
- Nutr—the concentration of the nutrient the microorganism uses to produce the valued product (mg/L)

When Sara starts looking at the data, she quickly finds them pretty overwhelming. The data set contains over 2,300 records and over 16,000 pieces of information. Only the first few lines of the data are shown here—the first 10 minutes of 80 hours worth of data.

ID	RUNNAME	TIME	STAGE	TEMP	PH	NUTR
1	R1760128	120	PreWarm	25.70062	6.302651	19.92985
2	R1760128	240	PreWarm	26.16977	6.311809	19.76786
3	R1760128	360	PreWarm	27.0977	6.322292	19.83754
4	R1760128	480	PreWarm	27.31025	6.319426	19.95841
5	R1760128	600	PreWarm	28.26793	6.315211	20.11239

Sara realizes she'd better get some help sorting out this data, so she starts to think about writing a query.

The lab technician suspects the "bugs" have died. If that were so, the nutrient that the microorganisms use to produce the product should not have been consumed and should be close to the starting value of 20 mg/L at the end of the run. Since on a normal run the nutrient concentration falls below 10 mg/L, she begins with a query that asks for the Run Names which show a final nutrient concentration of at least 15 mg/L. Here's how she did it.

From Excel's **Data** menu, she selected **Get External Data**, then **New Database Query**.

Then she told Excel that the data were in an MS Access database, and found the database file on her company's computer network.

When Excel connected to the database, it displayed the tables that were available for use. Sara clicked on the **+** in front of the table name to see the fields available in the table.

Sara used the **>** button to move all of the fields from the left column (available fields) to the right column (fields that will be used in the query).

The next step is to design the query to select only the data you want from the available records. Sara wants to know the Run Names that ended with nutrient levels greater than 15 mg/L. Since the "Collect" stage is used in the data set to hold the values at the end of the run, Sara tells the query to use only records in which the Stage is called "Collect" ("Stage equals Collect" in the nomenclature of the query).

Note: Choosing only records in which the Stage field holds the word "Collect" reduced the number of records under consideration from 2,300 to 10 since there is one "Collect" per batch.

That's the first half of Sara's query—finding the final values. She also wants to know when the final value of nutrient concentration is greater than 15 mg/L, so she indicates there is more to the query by clicking on the **And** radio button.

and then indicates that she wants the query to consider only records that contain nutrient (Nutr) values greater than 15.

Note: The word " Stage " in the left column is in bold-face type. That is a reminder that the query also contains one or more criterion based on that field.

When Sara clicks on the **Next >** button, the Query Wizard asks how she would like the results sorted.

Since Sara doesn't need to have the results sorted, she clicks on the **Next >** button and moves on.

The Query Wizard needs to know where to put the

results, so Sara asks to have them returned to the Excel spreadsheet that was open when she began the process of getting external data from the Data menu.

When the Query Wizard sends the data to Excel, Excel needs to know where to put it. Sara asks to have the

data placed on the existing worksheet, starting with cell $A$1.

Finally, the query results are returned to the spreadsheet.

	A	B	C	D	E	F	G
1	ID	RunName	Time	Stage	Temp	pH	Nutr
2	1669	R1760134	28680	Collect	60.95771	3.722996	18.35503
3	2145	R1760136	28680	Collect	60.64491	3.76005	17.71305
4							
5							

There were two runs in which the final nutrient level was over 15 mg/L. That doesn't tell Sara what went wrong, but it tells her where to start looking for answers: runs R1760134 and R1760136.

The next step is to look at the data from the bad runs. To do this, Sara creates a query that requests time, temperature, and pH data for runs R1760134 and R176036 only. Key steps in the process are illustrated below.

Using a new sheet (Sheet 2) on the workbook, Sara begins the process of querying the database for the necessary data:

Data, Get External Data, New Database Query

Connecting to the database is the same as illustrated in the previous query. The query itself is created as follows:

1. Sara asks for only the fields that will be used in the query.

2. She requests records from only the two " bad " runs that she identified earlier.

3. Sara completes the process of creating the query and letting Excel know where the data should go. The first few lines of data are shown here.

	A	B	C	D	
1	RunName	Time	Temp	pH	
2	R1760134	120	25.48276	6.291251	
3	R1760134	240	26.453	6.296344	
4	R1760134	360	26.64769	6.286938	
5	R1760134	480	27.65522	6.271322	
6	R1760134	600	28.71442	6.271424	

Sara now has the data for the two bad runs available. To try to see what happened, she plots the time versus temperature graph and the time versus pH graph.

The temperature graph looks OK—maybe a little less control on the temperature than she would like to see, but nothing that would have killed the microorganisms. But on the pH graph she sees a problem:

There is no ramp in the pH values at 20,000 seconds—they just dropped from around 6.3 to less than 4. Somebody adjusted the pH too fast and too far—and killed the microorganisms. Sara's next step is to design a query on the personnel database to see who was responsible for adjusting the pH on runs R1760134 and R1760136.

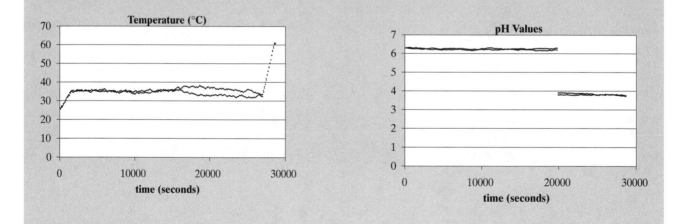

Chapter Summary

In this chapter, the Excel database features are described. These include several search and filter tools such as the AutoFilter and the Advanced Filter. Data may be retrieved from external databases by using the stand-alone program Microsoft Query.

KEY TERMS

database
database management system
DBMS
field

field name
filtering
sort key
SQL

structured query language
list
record

Problems

1. Use the AutoFilter function to list only students whose GPA is less than 3.0.
2. Use the AutoFilter function to list all *Juniors* whose last name begins with *S*.
3. Use the Advanced Filter to list all *Seniors* with a GPA less than 2.9 and all *Juniors* with a GPA greater than 3.5. Can this list be created using the AutoFilter?
4. Create a new field titled *Full Name* that contains the full name of each student. Use the CONCATENATE function to accomplish this task. Be sure to include the space between the names, for example, *Frank Washington*, not *FrankWashington*.
5. Locate or create an external database using dBase, Access, Paradox, FoxPro. Import the database into an Excel worksheet using Microsoft Query.

8

Collaborating with Other Engineers

8.1 THE COLLABORATIVE DESIGN PROCESS

Engineering design is the process of devising an effective, efficient solution to a problem. The solution may take the form of a component, a system, or a process. Engineers generally solve problems by collaborating with others as a member of a team. As a student, you will undoubtedly be asked to participate in collaborative projects with other students.

You may or may not have much experience working on a team. If a team works together effectively, more can be accomplished by the team than through any individual effort (or even the sum of individual efforts). If team members do not work together effectively, however, the group can become mired in power struggles and dissention. When this occurs, one of two things usually happens. Either the team makes little progress toward its goals, or a small subgroup of the team takes charge and does all the work.

Some guidelines for being an effective team member are presented at the end of this chapter in the Professional Success section.

8.1.1 Microsoft Excel and Collaboration

The ability to work well on a team can be learned best by participating on a successful team. Microsoft Excel includes several tools that can help to solve one of the most burdensome technical tasks of group collaboration—the preparation of the team document. In the past, collaborative document preparation has been extremely difficult. The result has been that the task is usually assigned to one or two team members. New features of Microsoft Excel make it feasible for the whole team to participate in the composition and revision of a document. Learning to use these features will require some time and practice on your team's part. The rewards will be well worth the effort.

8.2 TRACKING CHANGES

One problem that arises in document preparation by a team is keeping track of revisions. For example, one team member may be given the task of revising a portion of the team project. After the revisions are made, the team will meet and approve some or all of the revisions. Then one of the team members will incorporate the accepted changes into the document.

Excel has a feature called *Tracking Changes* that will not only mark revisions but will also keep track of whom is making each revision. The worksheet may be printed showing both the original text and the new revisions. Revisions may then be globally accepted or selectively accepted into the document.

To turn on the tracking changes feature choose **Tools**, **Track Changes**, **Highlight Changes**. The Highlight Changes dialog box should appear on the screen as depicted in Figure 8.1.

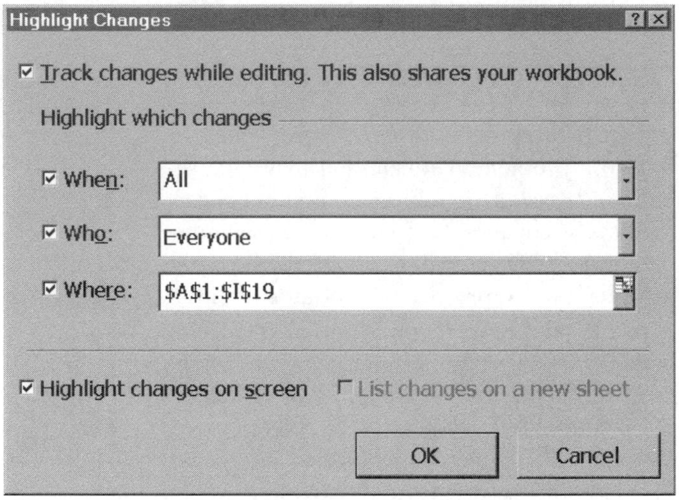

Figure 8.1. The Highlight Changes dialog box

Check the box labeled *Track changes while editing*. This will share the workbook and will turn on history tracking. The next three boxes and drop-down lists allow you to limit the changes that are highlighted by time, user, and worksheet region. The bottom two items let you decide where to display the revisions. If you select the box labeled *Highlight changes on screen*, the revisions will be highlighted in the current worksheet as depicted in Figure 8.2. The alternate selection saves the changes to a new worksheet.

Check the box labeled *Highlight changes on screen*. Now type a few words in your worksheet and notice what happens. Any modified cells are outlined in blue and a small blue tab is placed in the upper-left corner of the cell. These are called *revision marks* (see Figure 8.2).

As you review a document for which other team members have made revisions, you can see who made the revision, the date and time of the revision, and the previous contents of the cell. The identity feature works only if each reviewer has given an identity to the Excel application. To identify yourself to Excel, choose **Tools**, **Options**, and select the tab labeled **General**. Type your name in the box labeled **User Name**.

Your identity will be attached to any revisions that you make to a worksheet. You can test the feature by making a few revisions and moving the mouse cursor over a region that has revision marks. A small box should appear that displays the reviewer's name along with a date and time stamp. An example is depicted in Figure 8.3.

	A	B	C
1	32	-2.5714	6.6122
2	14	-20.5714	423.1837
3	53	18.4286	339.6122
4	26	-8.5714	73.4694
5	18	-16.5714	274.6122
6	45	10.4286	108.7551
7	54	19.4286	377.4694

Figure 8.2.   Examples of highlighted, revised cells

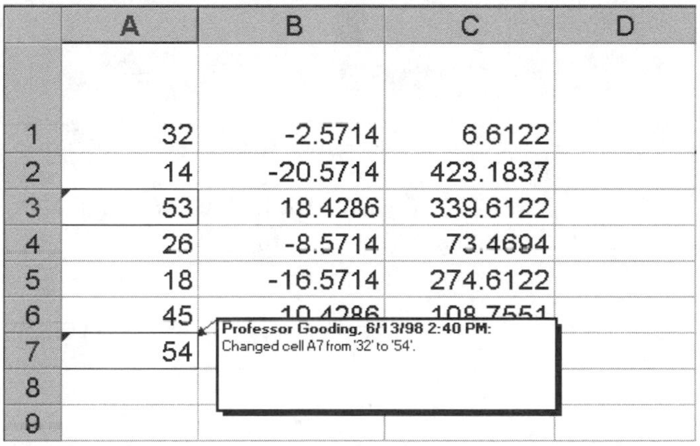

	A	B	C	D
1	32	-2.5714	6.6122	
2	14	-20.5714	423.1837	
3	53	18.4286	339.6122	
4	26	-8.5714	73.4694	
5	18	-16.5714	274.6122	
6	45	10.4286	108.7551	
7	54			
8				
9				

Professor Gooding, 6/13/98 2:40 PM:
Changed cell A7 from '32' to '54'.

Figure 8.3.   Example revision marks with reviewer's name

8.2.1   Incorporating or Rejecting Revisions

Revision marks are not wholly incorporated into the document until they are reviewed; they are then either accepted or rejected. Revision marks can be reviewed by using the Accept or Reject Changes dialog box. To accept or reject changes choose **Tools**, **Track Changes**, and **Accept or Reject Changes** from the Menu bar. The Accept or Reject Changes dialog box should appear as depicted in Figure 8.4. The three boxes and drop-down lists allow you to select which changes to review. Choose a time, reviewer, and region to review and then choose **OK**. Excel will guide you through each selected revision and give you the opportunity to accept or reject the revision.

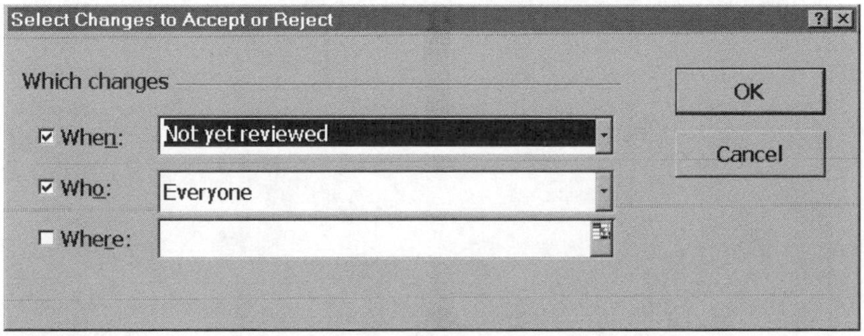

Select Changes to Accept or Reject

Which changes

☑ When: Not yet reviewed

☑ Who: Everyone

☐ Where:

OK   Cancel

Figure 8.4.   The Accept or Reject Changes dialog box

8.3   ADDING COMMENTS TO A DOCUMENT

At times, a reviewer may want to attach notes or *comments* to a cell without changing the contents of the cell. To add a comment to a cell, first select the cell, and choose **Insert**, **Comment** from the Menu bar. A Comment box will appear as depicted in Figure 8.5. Type in a comment and click outside of the Comment box to exit. A cell that is attached to a comment will be marked with a small red tab in the upper-right-hand corner of the cell.

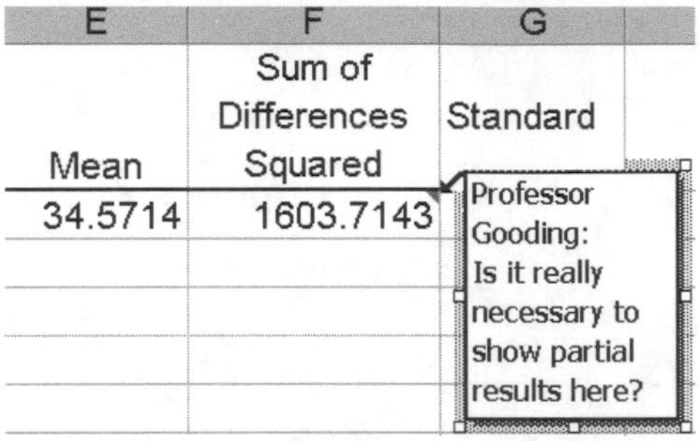

Figure 8.5.   An example of a Comment box

Comments may be reviewed, edited, or deleted by two methods. To review a single comment, first select the cell holding the comment and click the right mouse button. The drop-down Quick Edit menu will display several new items as depicted in Figure 8.6.

Figure 8.6.   Comment-related items on the Quick Edit menu

If there are a large number of comments to review, open the Reviewing toolbar by choosing **View**, **Toolbars** from the Menu bar and check the box labeled *Reviewing*. The Reviewing toolbar contains buttons for moving through the comments in a worksheet one at a time, selectively viewing, editing, or deleting each comment. The Reviewing toolbar is displayed in Figure 8.7. The buttons related to comments are described in Table 8-1.

Figure 8.7.   The Reviewing toolbar

TABLE 8-1   The Comment buttons on the Reviewing toolbar

BUTTON	ACTION
	Edit Comment
	Move to previous comment
	Move to next comment
	Show current comment
	Show all comments
	Delete current comment

8.4   MAINTAINING SHARED WORKBOOKS

Excel provides a mechanism for several users to share a workbook over a network simultaneously. A shared workbook must reside in a shared folder on the network. Other access restrictions may apply depending on your local network setup. See your network administrator for assistance in sharing folders. One other restriction to sharing workbooks is that all group members must be using Excel 97. Previous versions of Excel do not support this feature.

Once you are able to share a workbook, different users can view and modify the workbook at the same time. Sharing a document clearly requires some protocol among the group in order to keep several users from overwriting each other's work. Sharing a workbook is most effective if simultaneous users edit different parts of the workbook. Excel can be set to keep a history of changes to a shared workbook and previous versions may be recalled if necessary.

To share a workbook, choose **Tools**, **Share Workbook** from the Menu bar. The Share Workbook dialog box will appear. Select the **Editing** tab as depicted in Figure 8.8. By checking the box labeled *Allow changes...*, the workbook will be shared. Once the workbook is shared, this tab is useful to see who is currently using the workbook.

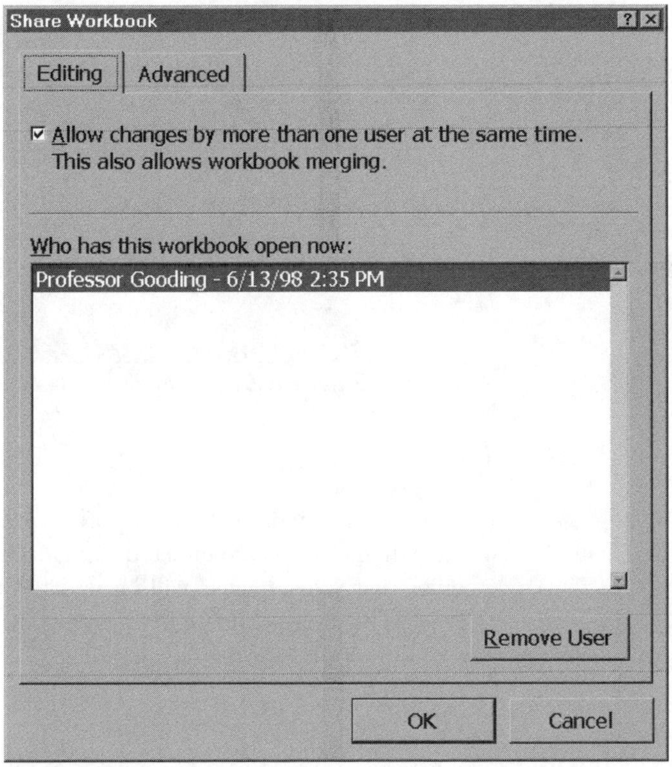

Figure 8.8.   The Editing tab on the Share Workbook dialog box

8.4.1   Keeping a Change History

Excel can keep a log of changes made by each user of a shared workgroup. The log of changes is called a *change history*. Choose the **Advanced** tab on the Shared Workbook dialog box (see Figure 8.9). The section is labeled *Track changes*. The length of time to keep a change history can be selected in this section, or the change history can be turned off. One reason to turn off the change history or to keep the time duration short is to limit the size of the workbook. A change history can significantly increase the disk space required to store a workbook. There is a trade-off between safety and storage requirements. Use of the change history feature is not a substitute for regularly backing up a workbook to some other medium such as a floppy or tape.

Note: If a shared workbook has sharing turned off, the change history is automatically deleted.

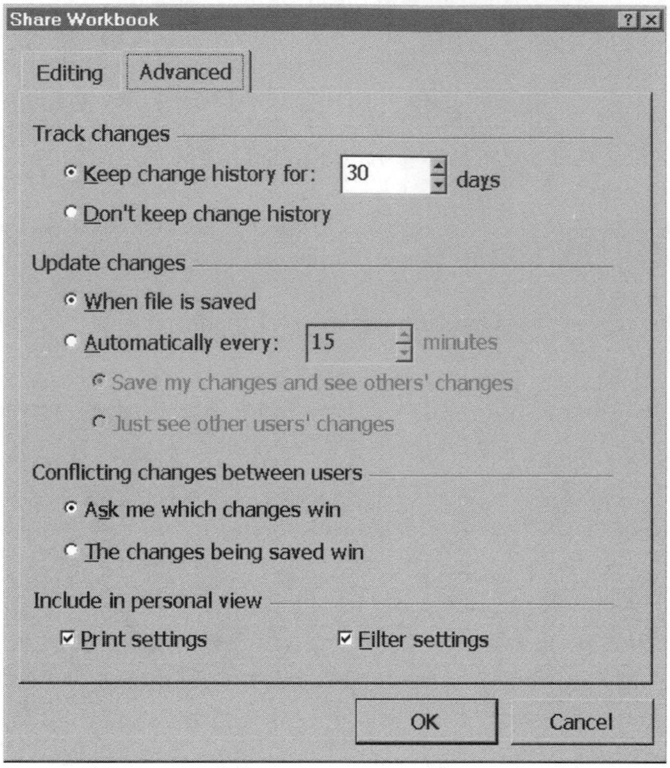

Figure 8.9. The Advanced tab on the Share Workbook dialog box

8.4.2 Timed Updates

The second section of the Shared Workbook dialog box's Advanced Setting tab is used to specify when changes are updated so that other users may see them. The first selection specifies that your changes will be updated to the group whenever you save the file. Alternatively, you can choose to have the changes automatically update the other users' view of the workbook every few minutes.

8.4.3 Managing Conflicts

If you are about to save a workbook, some of your changes may conflict with pending changes from another user. The third section of the Advanced setting tab allows you to specify how you want to resolve conflicts, if at all. If you choose the first option titled *Ask me which changes win*, the Resolve Conflicts dialog box will appear when you save the file. You will be prompted to resolve each conflict. If you don't want to resolve conflicts when you save a shared workbook, click the item titled *The changes being saved win*. The last user to save conflicting changes wins.

8.4.4   Personal Views

The last section of the Advanced setting tab allows the creation of personal printer or filter settings. When the workbook is saved, a separate personal view is saved for each user.

8.4.5   Merging Workbooks

Group members do not always have access to the same network. One scenario that occurs when groups collaborate on a workbook is that each member takes a copy of the workbook. Each group member works separately on the workbook and later the workbooks are merged into a single document.

Copies of a workbook can be revised and merged only if a change history is being maintained. Be sure to set a sufficient length of time for the change history so that the history doesn't expire before the workbook copies are merged. The number of days is set in the Share Workbook dialog box (see Figure 8.9).

To merge several copies of a workbook, open the first copy and choose **Tools**, **Merge Workbooks** from the Menu bar. You will be prompted to choose a file to merge. Continue to merge files until all of the copies have been merged into one workbook. Follow the instructions in the next section to view the history of all changes that have been made.

8.4.6   Viewing the History of Changes

To view a change history, choose **Tools**, **Track Changes**, and **Highlight Changes** from the Menu bar. The Highlight Changes dialog box will appear as previously depicted in Figure 8.1. Use the boxes and lists titled *Who*, *When*, and *Where* to limit the history list, or leave them unchecked to view all history entries.

If the box labeled *Highlight changes on screen* is checked, changes can be viewed one at a time by holding the mouse cursor over a changed cell. A pop-up box will appear with the change listed.

If the box titled *List changes on a new sheet* is checked, the history list will be displayed on a separate worksheet as depicted in Figure 8.10. This is useful if multiple changes have been made to a cell.

Note in Figure 8.10 that cell A3 has been changed twice. Also, note that the Auto-Filter feature has been turned on. This allows you to filter changes in the history list.

	A	B	C	D	E	F	G	H	I
1	Action Number	Date	Time	Who	Change	Sheet	Range	New Value	Old Value
2	1	6/13/98	2:42 PM	Professor Gooding	Cell Change	Sheet1	A3	53	52
3	2	6/13/98	2:42 PM	Professor Gooding	Cell Change	Sheet1	A7	54	32
4	3	6/13/98	3:10 PM	Dr. Doolittle	Cell Change	Sheet1	A3	43	53

Figure 8.10.   Reviewing a change history

8.4.7   Restrictions for Shared Workbooks

Some features of Excel cannot be used while a workbook is being shared. All features can be used if the workbook has sharing turned off. The disadvantage of turning off sharing is that the change history is deleted. Some of the features of Excel that cannot be used when sharing is in effect follow.

- Creation, modification, or deletion of passwords. Passwords should be set up before the workbook is shared.
- Deletion of worksheets.
- Insertion or modification of charts, pictures, or hyperlinks.
- Insertion or deletion of regions of cells. Single rows or columns can be deleted.
- Creation of data tables or pivot tables.
- Insertion of automatic subtotals.

There are other restrictions for shared workbooks. These can be viewed by choosing **Help** and then **Contents** and **Index** from the Menu bar. Select the **Index** tab from the Help dialog box. Type the keywords *shared workbook*, select **limitations** from the resulting list of keywords, and choose **Display**. A help box will appear that describes all of the limitations during the sharing of a workbook.

8.5 PASSWORD PROTECTION

Several levels of protection exist for workbooks that reside on a network. Your personal file space may be protected by the network operating system. The folder in which the workbook resides may be protected. The methods that are discussed below apply only to a single workbook. The methods below, in and of themselves, will not prevent another user from copying your workbook. Please discuss general file protection issues with your local system or network administrator.

One way to limit access to a shared workbook is with password protection. A variety of password types will be discussed. In every case, be sure to write down your password. If you lose a password, you will not be able to retrieve your work.

8.5.1 Open Protection

A password can be set that restricts a user from opening a file. This means that an unauthorized user cannot read or print the file using Excel. This type of access is called *open access* since it protects a file from being opened. A user may still be able to copy the file and interpret it using some other program. To set a password for open access, choose **File**, **Save As**, and **Options** from the Menu bar. The Save Options dialog box will appear as depicted in Figure 8.11.

The first option titled *Always create backup* specifies that Excel should create a backup copy of your workbook every time it is saved. Unless you are extremely short of disk space, this is an excellent option.

To restrict open access, type a password in the box titled *Password to open*. You will be prompted to type the password a second time for verification. Note that Excel uses case-sensitive passwords.

Hint: One of the most common reasons that a password seems to suddenly stop working is that you have the caps lock key turned on.

Figure 8.11. The Save Options dialog box

8.5.2   Write Protection

There may be times where you want to allow read access to others, but you do not want anyone to be able to modify your original file. This type of protection is called *write access*. To set a write access password, open the Save Options dialog box as depicted in Figure 8.11. Type a password in the box titled *Password to modify*. You will be prompted to type the password a second time for verification.

The next time you attempt to open the file, the Password dialog box will appear as depicted in Figure 8.12. You will be prompted for a password if you want to open the file for write access. A password is not needed to open the file for reading only. Note that a user can open a write-protected file as a read-only file and save it under a different name. The new file can be modified by the user without a password.

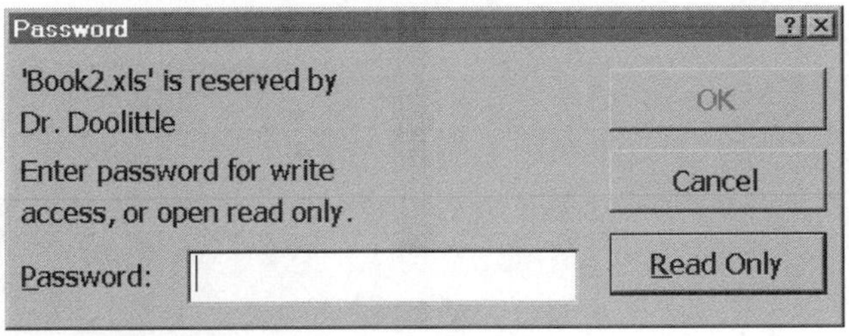

Figure 8.12.   The Password dialog box

8.5.3   Sheet Protection

Protection can be finely tuned. This is convenient when using shared documents since a user can protect part of the workbook but leave some sections available to others. Another option is to protect only the structure or window configuration of a workbook but allow others to modify the cell contents. Even if a document is not being shared, you may want to protect it. Once you have completed part of a worksheet, you may want to protect it merely to prevent yourself from inadvertently modifying that section.

To protect a single worksheet within a workbook, choose **Tools**, **Protection**, and **Protect Sheet** from the Menu bar. The Protect Sheet dialog box will appear as depicted in Figure 8.13. From the Protect Sheet dialog box, you can choose to protect the contents of cells, objects such as drawings, charts, or scenario definitions.

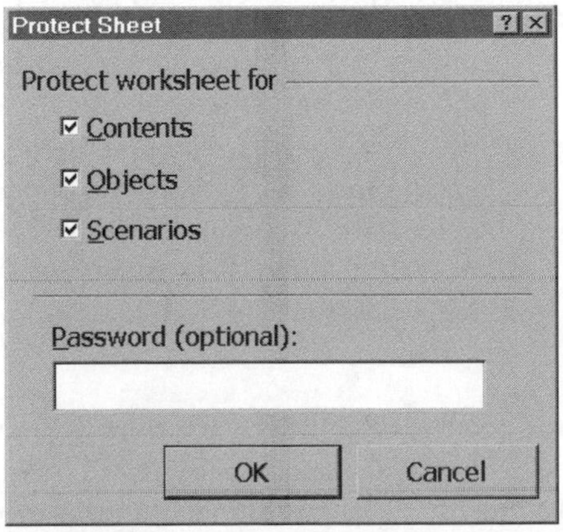

Figure 8.13.   The Protect Sheet dialog box

You may want to keep certain regions unprotected in a protected worksheet. To keep a selected region unprotected, do the following before protecting the worksheet. Select the region, choose **Format**, **Cells**, select the **Protection** tab, and remove the check from the item labeled *Locked*. Now, after the worksheet is protected, the unlocked region will be exempted but can still be modified.

8.5.4   Workbook Protection

An entire workbook can be protected in a manner similar to the protection of a worksheet. Choose **Tools**, **Protection**, and **Protect Workbook** from the Menu bar. The Protect Workbook dialog box will appear as depicted in Figure 8.14. From the Protect Workbook dialog box, you can choose to protect the workbook structure or the window setup. Protecting the workbook structure means that worksheets cannot be added, deleted, moved, or hidden. Protecting the window setup means that the workbook windows cannot be deleted, resized, or moved.

Figure 8.14.   The Protect Workbook dialog box

8.6   IMPORTING AND EXPORTING DATA FROM EXTERNAL FILE FORMATS

One side effect of working as part of a team is that each team member may not use the same application software. In addition, a large and complex project may require the use of several software packages, such as MATLAB™ , Maple, Mathcad, and so on. This implies that you may have to move data from one application to another in the process of completing a project.

Excel provides several methods for importing data. The Microsoft Query program enables the selective retrieval of data from external database files such as Oracle, dBase, or Paradox. Web queries are methods that are designed to retrieve data from sites on the World Wide Web using your default Web browser as an interface. The Microsoft query program and Web queries are discussed elsewhere in this textbook.

8.6.1   Import Using the File Open Option

In this section, we discuss the method for directly importing and exporting files to and from other file formats. A number of types of file formats may be imported directly by choosing **File** and then **Open** from the Menu bar. Click on the arrow to the right of the box labeled *Files of type*. A small drop-down menu will appear as depicted in Figure 8.15.

An external file type may be opened and viewed within Excel. If the file is modified, Excel will ask if you want to save the file in its original format or in Excel format. If the file is saved in Excel format, then the external program (e.g., dBase) will not be able to view the changes. If the file is saved in the external format (e.g., dBase), some Excel formatting may be lost. For example, formulas and macros may not be translated into the external format.

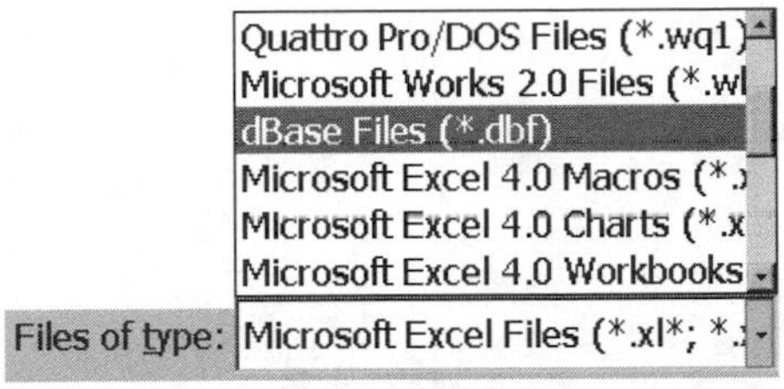

Figure 8.15.   Opening external types of files

The methods for importing from and exporting to applications not listed on the File Open menu are specific to each brand of application software. For example, Mathcad provides data input and output filters for Excel, Lotus® 1-2-3, and MATLAB. To seamlessly transfer data between Excel and MATLAB, a separate piece of software called Excel Link must be purchased. Excel Link provides a means for exchanging data between MATLAB and Excel, taking advantage of Excel's familiar spreadsheet interface and the computational and visualization capabilities of MATLAB.

8.6.2   Importing Text Data Using the Text Import Wizard

Most applications will let you export (*save as*) data as tab- or space- delimited text. In addition, you may produce data from a computer program that you have written. In either case, the Text Import Wizard helps you align and import the data. Note that formatting, macros, colors, font size, and so on cannot be imported using this method. Only data can be easily imported from text files.

To see an example of importing text, use your favorite text editor to create a tab-delimited file as displayed in Figure 8.16. If you are using a document preparation tool such as Microsoft Word, choose **Save As** from the Menu bar and save the file as type *Text Only*.

```
7.1     9.3     10.4
2.5     21.0    13.0
3.4     12.2    98.4
```

Figure 8.16.   Tab-delimited text data

Next, open the file from Excel by choosing **File** and then **Open** from the Menu bar. From the list labeled *Files of Type*; choose **All Files (*.*)** as depicted in Figure 8.17. Locate the file you created and choose **Open**.

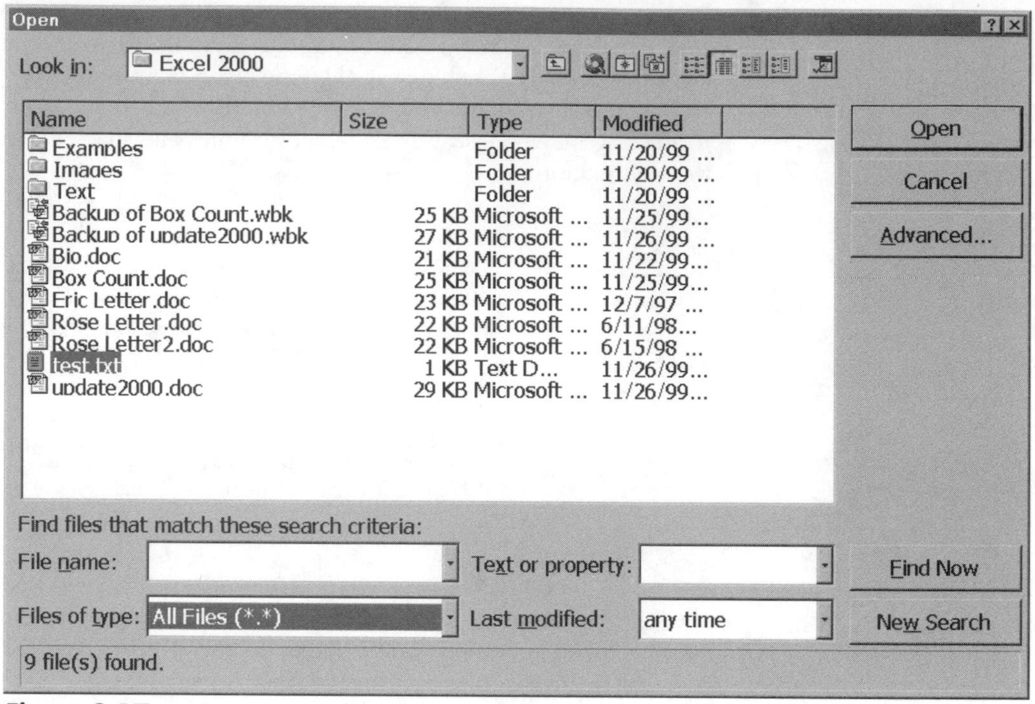

Figure 8.17. The Open dialog box

The first step of the Text Import Wizard will appear as depicted in Figure 8.18. Your data should now be visible in the Wizard dialog box. Follow the Wizard's steps to make sure that the data are aligned correctly. The result should be an Excel worksheet containing the data in Figure 8.16.

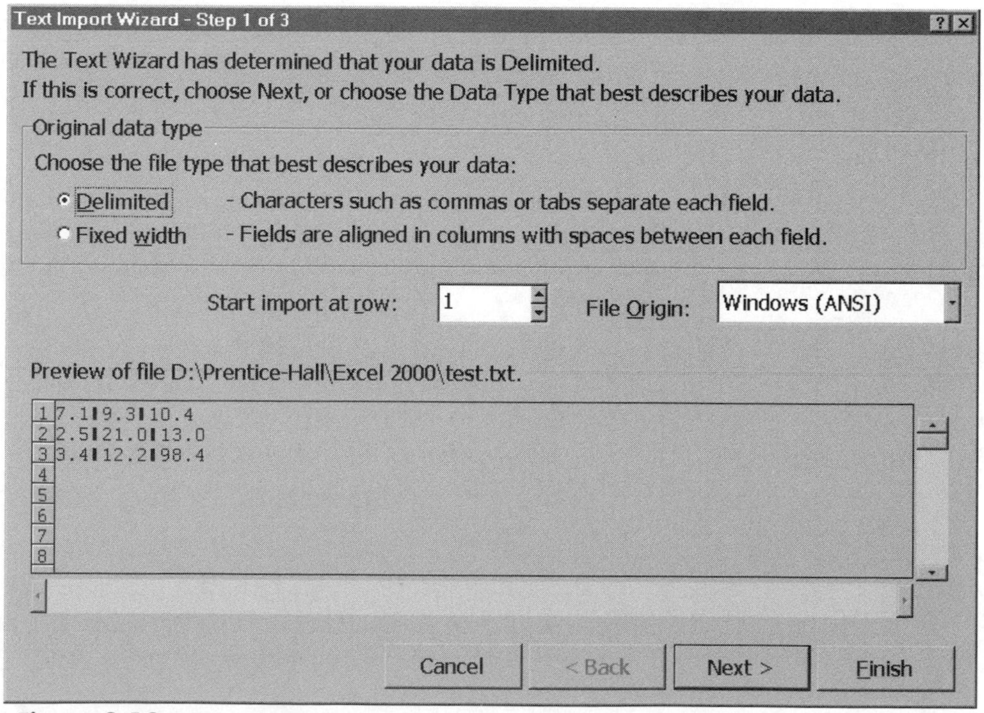

Figure 8.18. The Text Import Wizard—step 1

Mechanical Engineer: We have an immediate need for an engineer to interface an engineering automation and optimization environment with a variety of CAD and CAE systems... B.S./M.S. in mechanical engineering... Good communication skills and a strong interest to *interact with customers in problem solving situations* is a must.

Electrical Engineer: Required degree: BSEE+. Perform audio subsystem validation to verify prototypes throughout the product development program cycle. *Must work well in a team environment.*

Aerospace Engineer: Applicants selected may be subject to a government security investigation and meet eligibility requirements for access to classified information. You *must be a team player* and possess excellent written and oral communication skills.

Industrial Engineer: Investigate manufacturing processes in continuous improvement environment; recommend refinements. Design process equipment to improve processes. Must be highly skilled at planning/managing and be *able to sell ideas to team members* and company management.

Extrusion Engineer: This manufacturer of fiber optics is seeking an extrusion engineer who can handle the majority of the technical issues in production. The successful candidate must be able to *work with other disciplines in a team atmosphere* of mutual support.

Software Engineer: Looking for a well-rounded software engineer with strong experience in object-oriented design and GUI development... Must be a highly motivated self-starter who *works well in a team environment.*

8.7 CONDUCTING A TEAM MEETING

Read the Professional Success box in this chapter. All the listed positions were taken from actual job postings. What do the position announcements have in common? Teamwork! The ability of an engineer to work well in the team environment has as much to do with professional success as the engineer's scientific and technical skills. Few engineering accomplishments are produced in isolation. The following guidelines may help as you begin to conduct and participate in team meetings.

Decision Making. Attempt to make decisions by consensus. If that fails due to a single member who disagrees, move to consensus minus one.

Confidentiality. Respect confidentiality of other members. Lay ground rules about what material, if any, is to be treated confidentially. In the world of business and government contracts, you may be asked to sign a *confidentiality agreement*. These legal documents specify which of your employer's materials are protected from disclosure.

Attention. Actively listen—ask questions or request clarification of other members' comments. Reflect on the important points that other team members have made. Give acknowledgement that you have understood. Try not to mentally rehearse what you are going to say when others are speaking.

Preparation. Be adequately prepared for the meeting.

Punctuality. Be on time. If you are ten minutes late and there are six other members in the group, you are wasting one human-hour of time!

Ensure Active Contribution. If all team members are not contributing and actively participating, something is wrong with the group process. Stop the meeting and take time to get everyone involved before proceeding.

Record Keeping. Appoint someone on the team to keep records of team meetings.

Flexibility. Be prepared to think of creative solutions that every team member can accept. One of the aspects of working on a team is that you win some and you lose some. Not every one of your ideas will be accepted by the group.

Dynamics. Help improve relationships among the team members. Do not dominate the meeting or let another member dominate the meeting. If this cannot be resolved within the group, enlist the help of an outside *facilitator*. A facilitator is a nongroup member who does not take part in the content of the group issues. The facilitator exists to help smooth the group process. One of the roles of a facilitator is to prevent any single team member from dominating the others.

Quorum. Establish at the onset what a team quorum will be. Do not hold team meetings unless a quorum is present.

APPLICATION - USING TEAMWORK TO DETERMINE THE AMOUNT OF ENERGY NEEDED

Three students, Sara, Justin, and Allison, have been assigned a group project. Their assignment is to determine the energy required to pump water through a packed bed filter for a local industrial facility. Here's what they know.

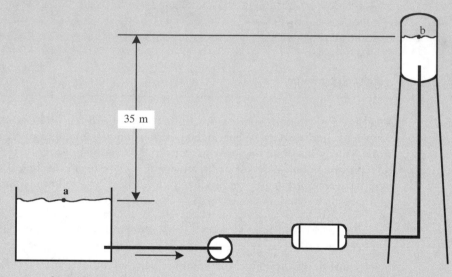

Water flows at a rate of 400 liters per minute from a holding tank that is open to the atmosphere (pressure = 1 atm = 1.01×10^5 Pa) and into a centrifugal pump (25 HP, 60% efficiency). The water then flows through the packed bed filter, and into an elevated, pressurized storage tank (pressure = 3×10^5 Pa). The elevation change between the water level in the open tank (marked 'a') and the water level in the pressurized tank (marked 'b') is 35 m.

The equation used to solve problems of this type is called the mechanical energy balance:

$$\frac{\eta\, W_p}{g} = \frac{(P_b - P_a)}{\rho\, g} + (H_b - H_a) + \frac{1}{2\, g}\left(\alpha_b V_b^2 - \alpha_a V_a^2\right) + F$$

The term on the left side of the equation represents the energy added to the system by the pump [expressed in *head* (height) of fluid—civil engineering style]. The terms on the right side represent the energy required to change the pressure of the fluid, lift the fluid from H_a to H_b, accelerate the fluid from V_a to V_b, and to overcome friction (F). The group's task is to find F.

The first thing they do is to throw out the acceleration term, since the fluid velocity at the surface of each tank (at points 'a' and 'b') will be very small. When those small velocities are squared, the acceleration term will be insignificant.

That leaves the pump energy term, the pressure energy term, and the change in height term. The students decide to each take one piece of the equation. Then they will combine their results to find F. Sara takes the pump term, Justin takes the pressure term, and Allison takes the elevation term.

SARA'S PART

W_p is the energy per unit mass to the pump (usually from a motor). ηW_p is the energy per unit mass from the pump to the fluid. Sara knows the efficiency, h, is 60% or 0.60, but she doesn't know the energy per unit mass, W_p—she knows the power rating of the pump. Power is related to W_p through the mass flow rate through the pump:

$$Power = m_{flow}\, W_p$$

Mass flow rate is related to the stated volumetric flow-rate through the fluid density, ρ.

$$m_{flow} = V_{flow}\, \rho$$

So Sara develops her spreadsheet, which looks like this:

The equations in Sara's spreadsheet are

Cell B10:	=B3/0.001341	(the 0.001341 converts HP to Watts)
Cell B12:	=B5/1000/60	(to 1000 converts liters to M³, the 60 converts minutes to seconds)
Cell B15:	=B13°B12	(density times volumetric flow rate)
Cell B16:	=B10/B15	(pump power rating divided by mass flow rate)
Cell B18:	=B11°B16/B14	($\eta W_p/g$)

JUSTIN'S PART

Justin's spreadsheet is a bit simpler, since there are fewer conversions and calculations required:

Cell B8:	=(B4-B3)/(B6°B5)

ALLISON'S PART

Allison's spreadsheet is the easiest of all:

Cell B6:   =B4-B3

COMBINING THE RESULTS

Once each of the members had their portion done, they got together and quickly finished their project:

Cell B3:   =Sara!B18   (refers to cell B 18 on the worksheet page named "Sara")
Cell B4:   =Justin!B8
Cell B5:   =Allison!B6
Cell B7:   =B3-B4-B5

While this is a very simple example of using a spreadsheet for collaborating on group assignments, it does illustrate how easily the results from different members can be combined to complete a group assignment.

Chapter Summary

In this chapter, the tools that Excel provides for collaboration are discussed. These include methods for tracking revisions, sharing workbooks, inserting comments, and importing data from other applications. This chapter also explains the various methods of data protection that Excel provides.

KEY TERMS

change history
comments
confidentiality agreement

facilitator
open access
revision marks

tracking changes
write access

Problems

1. Create a workbook and make several copies of the workbook. Make revisions to each of the separate documents using the methods described in Section 8.2. Merge the revised documents into a single document by opening the copy of the shared workbook into which you want to merge changes from another workbook file on disk and then choose **Tools**, **Merge Workbooks**. Select the shared workbook to be merged and click OK. Repeat these steps for each copy that is to be merged. You will be guided through the process of accepting and rejecting revisions.

2. Turn on the AutoSave feature to automatically save your document every two minutes. Is a new version created every two minutes? You can check this by closing Excel without manually saving your changes and testing to see if the changes have been saved.

3. Do the password protection mechanisms discussed in this chapter prevent another student from making a copy of your paper? Do any of the protection methods presented in this chapter prevent someone from printing your document without knowing the password? If so, which ones?

4. Turn sharing on and create a change history for a workbook. Then turn sharing off and see if the change history is actually deleted.

5. Set the change history timer in the Share Workbook dialog box (see Figure 8.9) for one day. Wait more than 24 hours and see if the history really expires.

9

Excel and the World Wide Web

9.1 ENGINEERING AND THE INTERNET

The Internet is one of the primary means of communication for scientists and engineers. Correspondence through electronic mail, the transfer of data and software via electronic file transfer, and research using on-line search engines and databases are everyday occurrences for engineers. The World Wide Web (WWW or simply Web) is a collection of technologies for publishing, sending, and obtaining information over the Internet. There are two new essential skills to be learned by every engineering student. First, every student must gain fluency in searching, locating, and retrieving relevant technical information from the WWW. Second, every engineering student must learn how to post written documents to the WWW. The ability to present technical results via the WWW is an essential communication skill for today's engineer.

OBJECTIVES

After reading this chapter, you should be able to

- Access the World Wide Web from within an Excel worksheet
- Obtain extra templates and other add-ins from the World Wide Web
- Retrieve files from FTP and HTTP servers into a local worksheet
- Use the Web Query feature for importing Excel data from the World Wide Web
- Create hyperlinks in a worksheet
- Convert Excel documents to HTML

The World Wide Web holds a wealth of information about your new profession. Take some time to visit the professional societies that represent your discipline.

The following LTRL's represent a few of the national and international organizations that are on-line.

Accreditation Board for Engineering and Technology (ABET)	http://www.abet.org/ABET.html
American Institute for Aeronautics and Astronautics (AIAA)	http://www.aiaa.org
American Institute of Chemical Engineers (AICHE)	http://www.aiche.org
American Society of Civil Engineers (ASCE)	http://www.asce.org
American Society of Engineering Education (ASEE)	http://www.asee.org/asee
American Society of Mechanical Engineers (ASME)	http://www.asme.org
American Society of Naval Engineers(ASNE)	http://www.jhuapl.edu/ASNE
Institute of Electrical and Electronic Engineering (IEEE)	http://www.ieee.org
National Society of Black Engineers (NSBE)	http://www.nsbe.org
National Society of Professional Engineers (NSPE)	http://www.nspe.org
Society of Women Engineers (SWE)	http://www.swe.org

9.2   ACCESSING THE WORLD WIDE WEB FROM WITHIN EXCEL

To access the Internet from within Excel, your computer must be connected to the Internet. If you are in a computer lab at school, the computer may be connected to a Local Area Network (LAN) through a network card. The LAN may or may not be connected to the Internet. Ask your lab manager or system administrator for details. If your computer is not directly connected to a LAN, you can access the Internet using a modem. This is called *dial-up networking*. For information about dial-up networking, access the Help section on the Task bar (if you are using Microsoft Windows 95 or NT). Locate the topic titled *Dial-Up Networking*. The computer systems group at your college may be able to help you with some of the details such as the assignment of an Internet Protocol address, netmasks, and so on. During the rest of this chapter, it is assumed that your computer is connected to the Internet.

Access the Web toolbar by choosing the [icon] icon on the Standard toolbar. The Web toolbar should appear as depicted in Figure 9.1. To open a Web page or local Web document, choose [Go] from the Web toolbar and then select the open button [icon] from the drop-down menu. The Open Internet Address dialog box will appear as depicted in Figure 9.2.

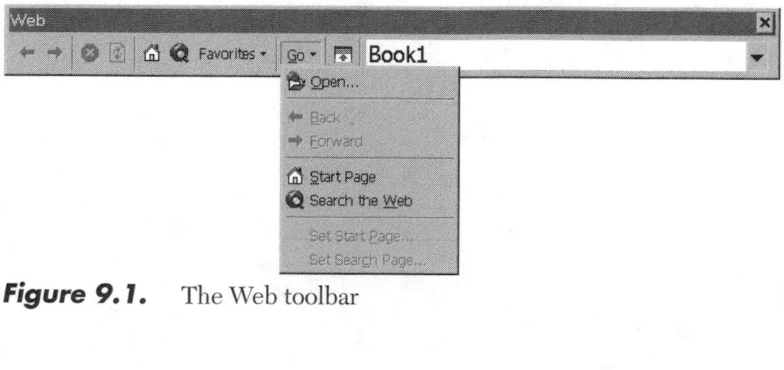

Figure 9.1.   The Web toolbar

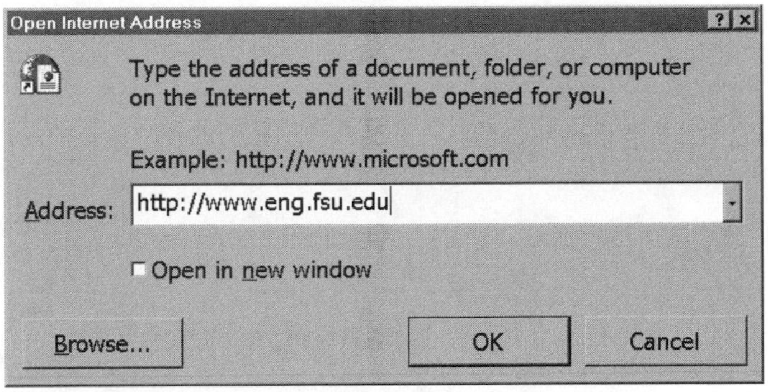

Figure 9.2. The Open Internet Address dialog box

From the Open Internet Address dialog box you can type or choose a remote or local Web page. The address of a remote Web page is called a *Uniform Resource Locator* or *URL*. A URL takes the following form:

```
http://www.eng.fsu.edu/succeed/succeed.html
```

where

`http`	stands for HyperText Transfer Protocol
`www.eng.fsu.edu`	is the name of a Web server
`succeed/succeed.html`	is the path of a Web page on that server

Figure 9.2 shows the URL for the Florida A&M University—Florida State University (FAMU-FSU) College of Engineering Web page. You can also type in the path and name of a local Web document, or select the local document by using the arrow to the right of the box labeled **Address**.

A Web document is written in a markup language called *HyperText Mark-up Language* or *HTML*. The HTML document is usually viewed using an application called a Web browser. The Web browser interprets the HTML document and displays the results as text, graphics, animations, sounds, and so on.

Excel acts as a front end to a Web browser. When you click **OK**, the selected page will be displayed through your default Web browser such as Microsoft's Internet Explorer or Netscape. Since you may already be familiar with your favorite browser, you may want to use that browser's features directly instead of the Excel front end for general Web browsing.

PRACTICE!

Practice accessing several Web sites and files from within Excel and familiarize yourself with the Web toolbar. Choose the arrow on the right-hand side of the Web toolbar and a pop-up scrollbox will appear as depicted in Figure 9.3. This box keeps a history of URLs you have previously accessed. The horizontal arrows ← → page backward and forward through sites visited in this session. The **Favorites** item is a bookmark feature. The Web Toolbar button ⬚ moves the Web toolbar from the top of the screen to a separate box (and vice versa).

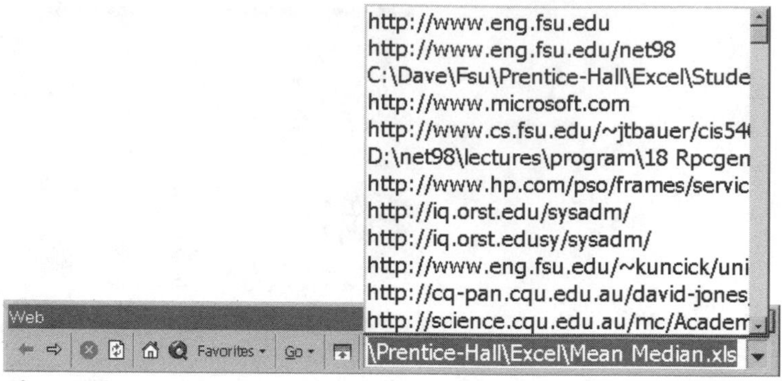

Figure 9.3. Viewing previously accessed sites

9.3   WEB SITES RELATED TO MICROSOFT EXCEL

There are sections of a Web site maintained by Microsoft specifically for Excel users. The primary page for Microsoft is located at

http://www.microsoft.com

Within the Microsoft site is an Excel tutorial, product information, and a number of free add-ins, patches, and templates.

9.4   RETRIEVING DATA FROM A WEB PAGE

The Web Query feature retrieves data from an external source over the Web and places the data in a local Excel worksheet. Before proceeding, open a new worksheet. Then **Choose Data**, **Get External Data**, **Run Web Query** from the Menu bar. The Run Query dialog box will appear as depicted in Figure 9.4. Several sample queries are provided with the standard Excel installation. If you would like to download more Web queries choose the item titled **Get More Web Queries**.

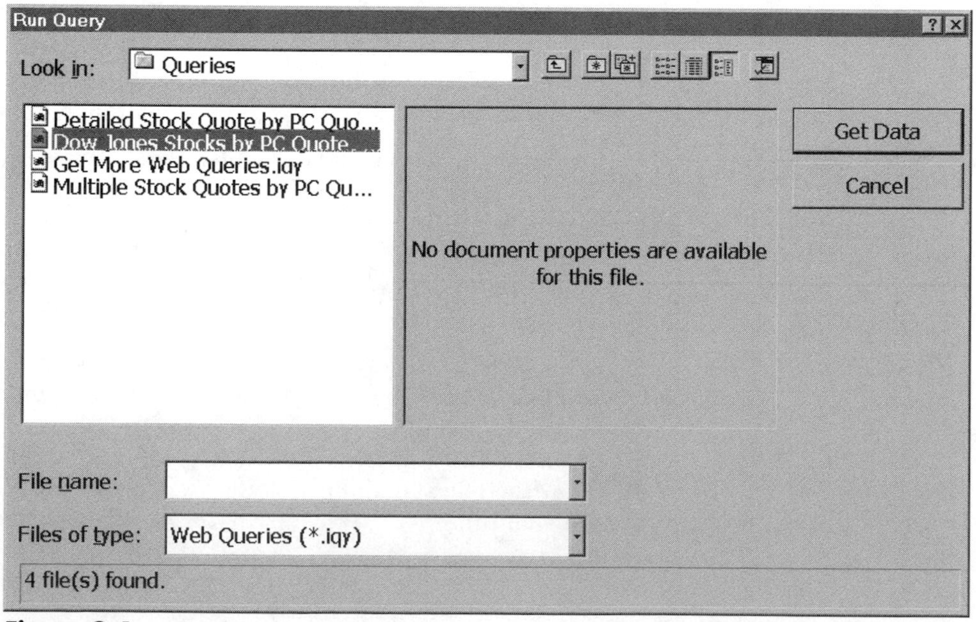

Figure 9.4. The Run Query dialog box

A *Web Query* is a formatted text file. The contents of the Dow Jones query are displayed in Figure 9.5. The effect of executing the query is to access the Web server at the URL http://webservices.pcquote.com and execute the CGI program named exceldow.exe. The results are returned and displayed in your local Excel worksheet.

```
WEB
1
http://webservices.pcquote.com/cgi-bin/exceldow.exe?
```

Figure 9.5.   Contents of Dow Jones Stock Query by PC Query, Inc

For the example, choose the item **Dow Jones Stock Quotes by PC Query, Inc**. The Returning External data dialog box will appear as depicted in Figure 9.6. From this dialog box, you can choose to place the returned data in the current worksheet, a new worksheet, or a pivot table report. Choosing the **Properties** button will allow you to modify a number of query options such as the ability to automatically refresh or update the data. If the query supports input parameters, the **Parameters** button will be active. An example of a parameter would be the addition of a particular stock symbol for a stock that you wish to download.

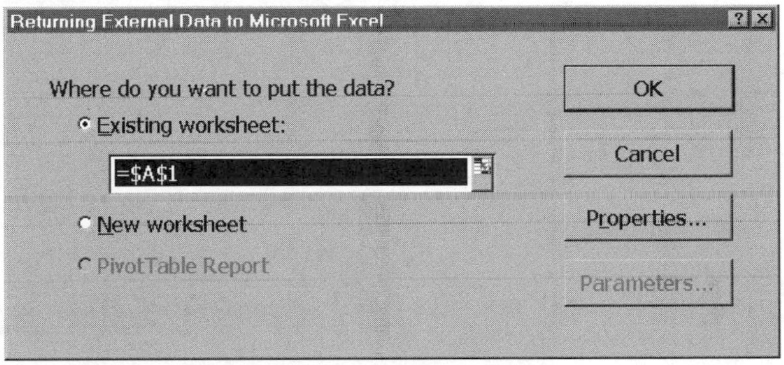

Figure 9.6.   The Returning External Data dialog box

Part of the results from the query above are displayed in Figure 9.7. Note that the AutoFilter feature has been automatically turned on. In Figure 9.7, column D has been selected to filter the top ten items for the field titled *Net Change*.

	A	B	C	D	E	F
1	Company Name & Symbol	Category	Last Price	Net Change	Open	High
7	CHEVRON CORP(CHV)	INDUSTRIALS	81 5/16	1 3/16	80 5/8	81 7/16
9	Name Not Available(DIS)	INDUSTRIALS	112 7/8	3 5/16	112 15/16	113 3/8
10	Name Not Available(EK)	INDUSTRIALS	69 5/16	5/16	69 3/8	69 3/8
15	IBM INTERNATIONAL BUSINESS MACHINES(IBM)	INDUSTRIALS	116 3/4	11/16	116 3/4	117 7/16
22	PHILIP MORRIS COMPANIES INC(MO)	INDUSTRIALS	36 5/8	3/8	36 15/16	37 1/16

Figure 9.7.   Results from PC Query, Inc. Dow quote

9.5 ACCESSING FTP SITES FROM WITHIN EXCEL

A workbook can be opened from a remote site using *FTP* or *File Transfer Protocol*. Before FTP can be used, you must be connected to the Internet using a dial-up connection (modem) or a direct network connection (network card). In addition, you must add the FTP site to a list of Internet sites.

To add an FTP site to your list, choose **File**, **Open** and then click the arrow on the right side of the box labeled **Look In**. Choose **Internet Locations (FTP)** from the drop-down list. The Add/Modify FTP Locations dialog box will appear as depicted in Figure 9.8. From the dialog box you can add, modify, and delete FTP locations.

If you have an account on the remote FTP site, check the box labeled **User** and type in your user name and password. If you do not have an account, many sites accept anonymous FTP logins. Check the box labeled **Anonymous**.

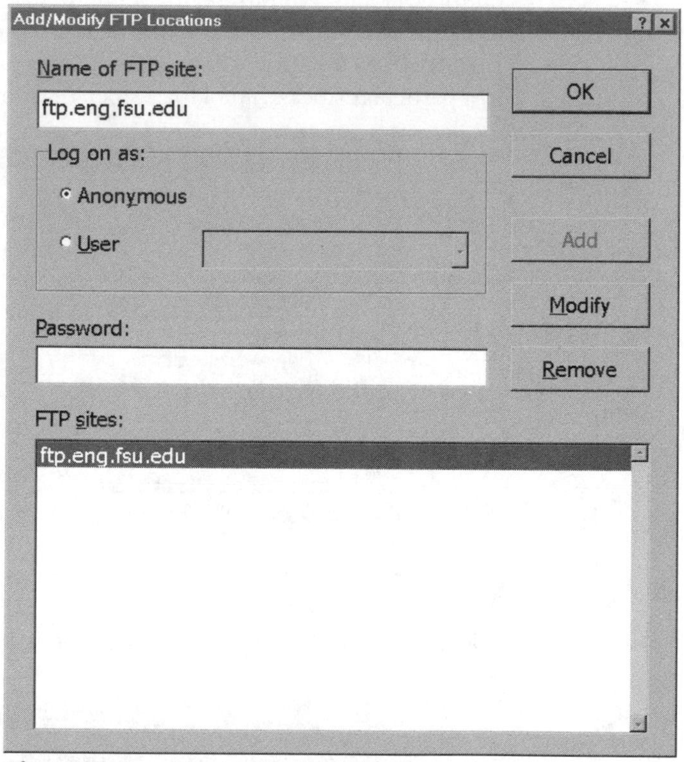

Figure 9.8. The Add/Modify FTP Locations dialog box

PRACTICE!

Practice opening a remote workbook by typing adding the site **ftp.eng.fsu.edu** to your list as shown in Figure 9.8. Check the **Anonymous** login box. Open the site and once you are anonymously logged in, select the **pub** folder, the **kuncick** folder, and then the **excel** folder. You should see a list of files similar to the list in Figure 9.9. Many of worksheets used as examples in this book are stored at this site. Download the worksheets and use them to complete the examples in this book.

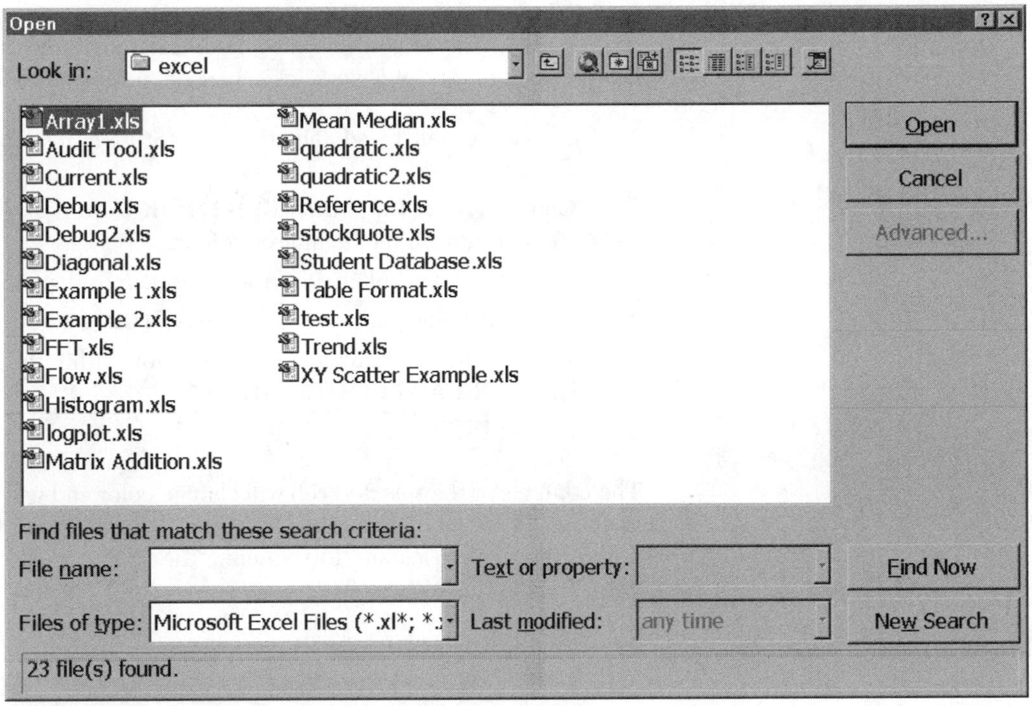

Figure 9.9.   Opening a remote workbook using FTP

9.6   CREATING HYPERLINKS WITHIN A WORKSHEET

A *hyperlink* or simply *link* can be thought of as a pointer to another document. When you click on a hyperlink, that document is displayed immediately. The linked document may be another Excel worksheet on your local computer or it may be a document from another application such as Microsoft Word. If the linked document belongs to another application, that application is automatically started for you.

A link may also point to a remote document that is retrieved from the World Wide Web using the HTTP or FTP protocols. As more computers are connected to the Internet and network speeds increase, the differences between accessing a local document and a remote document will diminish.

In this section, you will be shown how to create hyperlinks to several types of documents. The method for creating hyperlinks is the same for local or remote documents. The only difference is the address or path name of the document.

	A	B	C	D	E	F
2	Clinton	Willie	89.3		Student Database	
3	Smith	Randolph	58.2			
4	Simpson	Susie	97.0		Mean=	81.1
5	Smith	Christine	77.4		Median=	83.35
6	Washingto	Frank	65.4			
7	Granger	Linda	99.4			

Figure 9.10.   Example of a hyperlink

In the first example (see Figure 9.10), a link will be created from a grade worksheet to a student database. In this case, both documents are local Excel files. To link another worksheet or part of a worksheet to a cell, perform the following steps:

1.   Select the cell to contain the link (Student Database in the example in Figure 9.10).

2.   Choose **Insert** and then **Hyperlink** from the Menu bar, or choose the 📇 button from the Standard toolbar.

3.   The Edit Hyperlink dialog box will appear as depicted in Figure 9.11.

4.   Type a local file pathname or use the **Browse** button to select a file.

5.   You may limit the link to a name location within the file by filling in the box labeled **Name Location In File**.

6.   Choose **OK**.

The contents of the selected cell will change color and will be underlined, indicating that this cell contains a hyperlink. Click the hyperlink and the referenced file will appear. You can toggle back and forth among the source and destination files by using the ← ⇒ arrows on the Web toolbar.

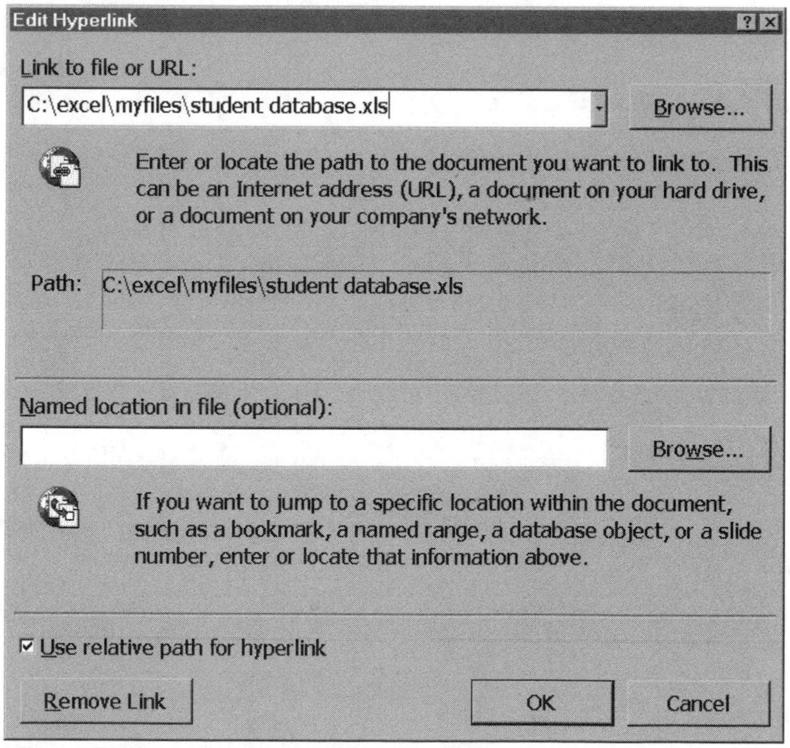

Figure 9.11.   The Edit Hyperlink dialog box

A hyperlink may contain references to an HTTP or FTP server as well as to local files. An example of an HTTP URL is

`http://www.eng.fsu.edu`

An example of an FTP URL is

`ftp://ftp.eng.fsu.edu/pub/kuncick/excel/histogram.xls`

PRACTICE!

The following ftp reference

`ftp://ftp.eng.fsu.edu/pub/kuncick/excel/mean median.xls`

will retrieve the example in Figure 9.10. The hyperlink will already be embedded in the example so you can experiment with both retrieving FTP files and following hyperlinks.

After you have retrieved and opened the file *mean median.xls*, hold the mouse over the cell with the text *Student Database* (but don't press the mouse button). Note that the URL of the hyperlink appears in a small drop-down box as depicted in Figure 9.12.

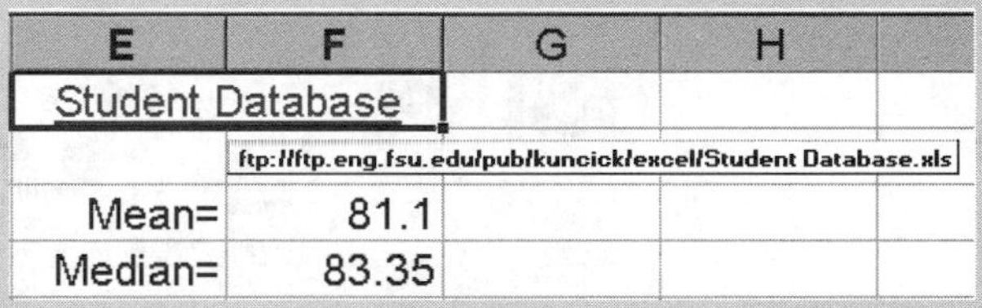

	E	F	G	H	
	Student Database				
		ftp://ftp.eng.fsu.edu/pub/kuncick/excel/Student Database.xls			
	Mean=	81.1			
	Median=	83.35			

Figure 9.12.   Viewing the URL of a hyperlink

Now click the right mouse button and choose **Hyperlink**, **Edit Hyperlink** from the drop-down menu. The Edit Hyperlink dialog box will appear and you can edit the hyperlink address. Try replacing the text *Student Database* with *Histogram*.

9.7   CONVERTING A WORKSHEET TO A WEB PAGE

Excel provides a wizard to assist with the conversion of worksheets to HTML format.

To covert a worksheet to HTML, first open the worksheet that you want to convert, then choose **File**, **Convert to HTML** from the Menu bar. The Internet Assistant Wizard (Step 1) will appear. One or more regions from the workbook will appear on the list in this dialog box. Add and remove selections until you are satisfied with the list. Then press **Next**.

Step 2 of the Internet Assistant Wizard will appear. You choices are to create a new HTML document or to insert the current selections into an existing HTML document. Choose **Create a New Document** and select the **Next** button.

Step 3 of the Internet Assistant Wizard will appear as depicted in Figure 9.13. Type in a title, heading, and text for the Web page. You may also insert horizontal lines and add author information to the Web page in this dialog box. The example in Figure 9.13 is taken from the river flow data used in Chapter 5.

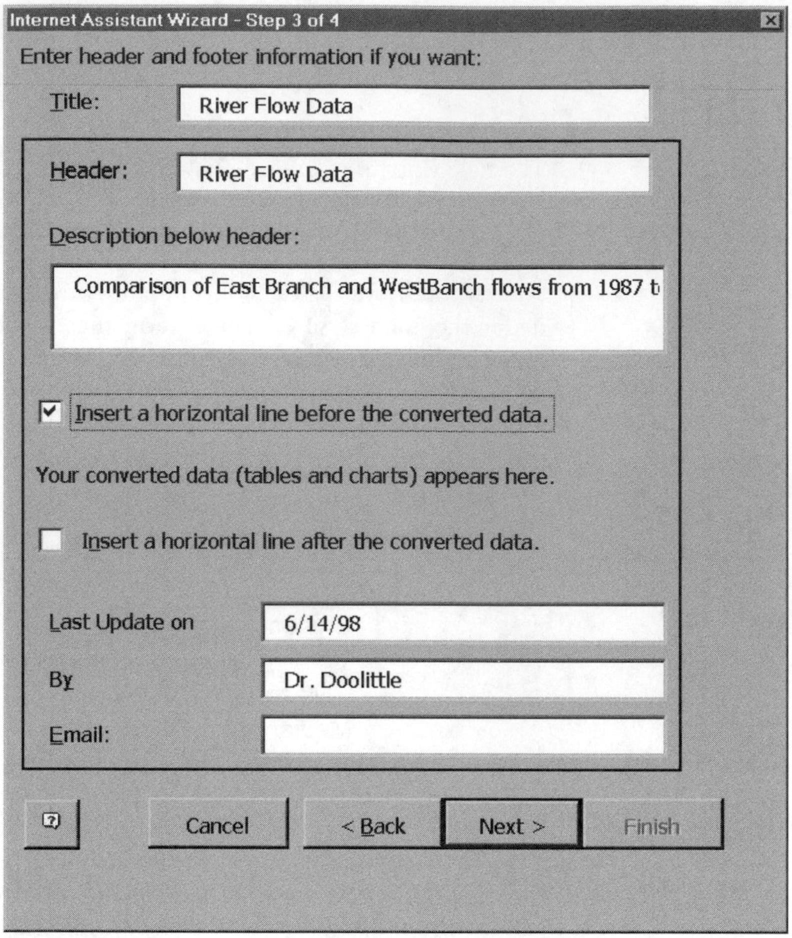

Figure 9.13. Step 3 of the Internet Assistant Wizard

After you are finished with Step 3, select the **Next** button and Step 4 of the Internet Assistant Wizard will appear. Type the pathname of where to save the HTML file and choose **Finish**. Try viewing the finished page with your favorite Web browser.

Figure 9.14 shows the River Flow Data using the Netscape browser. You can edit the HTML page with Microsoft Word or many other text editors.

Chapter Summary

This chapter introduces you to the ways that the World Wide Web and Excel can interface. The Web can be accessed from within an Excel worksheet. Excel files from remote HTTP and FTP files can be directly imported into a local worksheet. The Web Query feature automates the retrieval of remote data. Hyperlinks can be added to a worksheet and Excel will convert worksheets to HTML using the Internet Assistant Wizard.

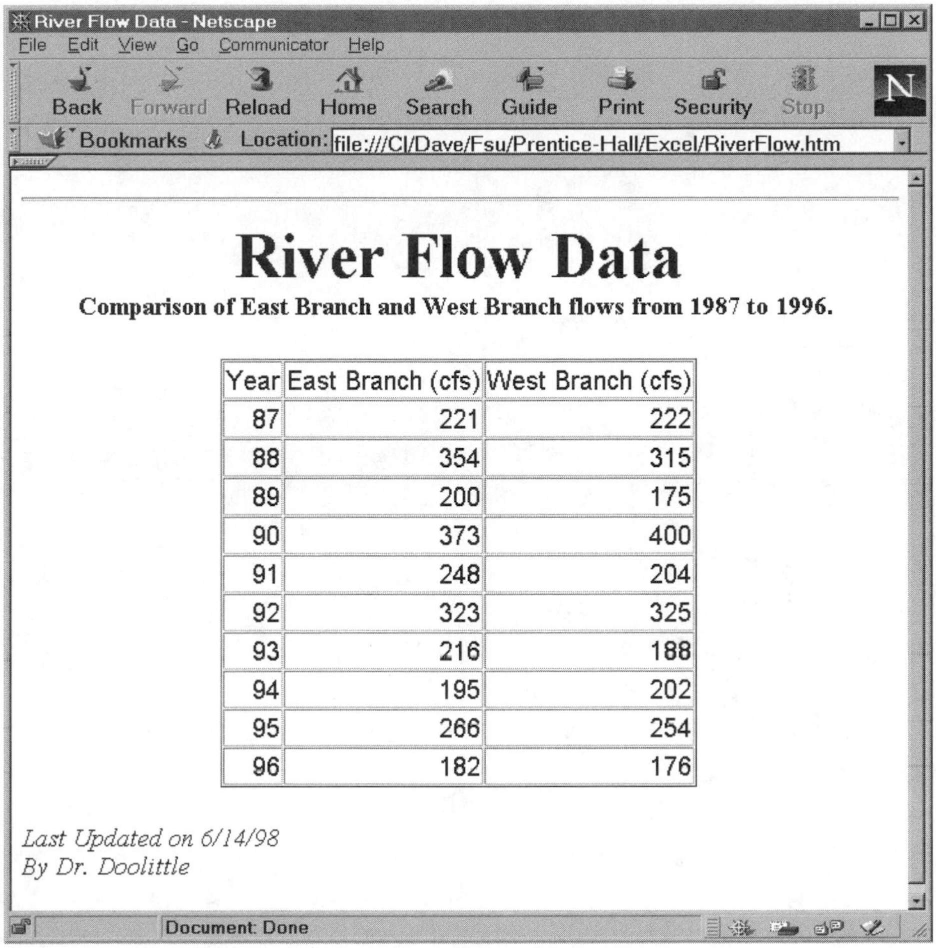

Figure 9.14. Viewing the converted worksheet with Netscape

KEY TERMS

dial-up networking	hyperlink	URL
File Transfer Protocol	HyperText Mark-up Language	Web Query
FTP	link	
HTML	Uniform Resource Locator	

Problems

1. Use the help feature to read about the HYPERLINK function. Create a valid hyperlink in a worksheet using the HYPERLINK function.

2. One advantage of using the HYPERLINK function is that the link can depend on a conditional expression. Create an IF expression that links to www.netscape.com if cell A1 = *Netscape* and links to www.microsoft.com if cell A1 = *Explorer*.

A

Commonly Used Functions

ABS(*n*)	Returns the absolute value of a number
AND(*a, b, ...*)	Returns the logical AND of the arguments (TRUE if all arguments are TRUE; otherwise FALSE)
ASIN(*n*)	Returns the arcsine of *n* in radians
AVEDEV(*n1, n2, ...*)	Returns the average of the absolute deviations of the arguments from their mean
AVERAGE(*n1, n2, ...*)	Returns the arithmetic mean of its arguments
BIN2DEC(*n*)	Converts a binary number to decimal
BIN2HEX(*n*)	Converts a binary number to hexadecimal
BIN2OCT(*n*)	Converts a binary number to octal
CALL(...)	Calls a procedure in a DLL or code resource
CEILING(*n, sig*)	Rounds a number *n* up to the nearest integer (or nearest multiple of significance *sig*)
CHAR(*n*)	Returns the character represented by the number *n* in the computer's character set
CHIDIST(*x, df*)	Returns the one-tailed probability of the chi-squared distribution using *df* degrees of freedom
CLEAN(*text*)	Removes all nonprintable characters from *text*
COLUMN(*ref*)	Returns the column number of a reference
COLUMNS(*ref*)	Returns the number of columns in a reference
COMBIN(*n, r*)	Returns the number of combinations of *n* items choosing *r* items
COMPLEX(*real, imag, suffix*)	Converts real and imaginary coefficients into a complex number
CONCATENATE(*str1, str2, ...*)	Concatenates the string arguments

CORREL(**A1**, **A2**)	Returns the correlation coefficients between two data sets
COS(n)	Returns the cosine of an angle
COUNTBLANK(*range*)	Counts the number of empty cells in a specified range
DEC2BIN(n, p)	Converts the decimal number n to binary using p places (or characters)
DELTA($n1, n2$)	Tests whether two number are equal
ISERROR(v)	Returns TRUE if value v is an error
ISNUMBER(v)	Returns TRUE if value v is a number
FACT(n)	Returns the factorial of n
FORECAST(x, *known x's*, *known y's*)	Predicts a future value along a linear trend
LN(n)	Returns the natural logarithm of n
MDETERM(**A**)	Returns the matrix determinant of array **A**
MEDIAN($n1, n2, ...$)	Returns the median of it arguments
MOD(n, d)	Returns the remainder after n is divided by d
OR($a, b, ...$)	Returns the logical OR of its arguments (TRUE if any argument is TRUE; FALSE if all arguments are FALSE)
PI()	Returns the value of pi to 15 digits of accuracy
POWER(n, p)	Returns the value of n raised to the power of p
PRODUCT($n1, n2, ...$)	Returns the product of its arguments
QUOTIENT(n,d)	Returns the integer portion of n divided by d
RADIANS(d)	Converts degrees to radians
RAND()	Returns an evenly distributed pseudorandom number $>= 0$ and < 1
ROUND(n, d)	Rounds n to d digits
ROW(*ref*)	Returns the row number of a reference
SIGN(n)	Returns the sign of a number n
SQRT(n)	Returns the square root of a number n
STDEVP($n1, n2, ...$)	Calculates the standard deviation of its arguments
SUM($n1, n2, ...$)	Returns the sum of its arguments
SUMSQ($n1, n2, ...$)	Returns the sum of the squares of its arguments
TAN(n)	Returns the tangent of an angle
TRANSPOSE(A)	Returns the transpose of an array
TREND(*known y's*, *known x's*, *new x's*, *constant*)	Returns values along a linear trend by fitting a straight line using least squares
VARP($n1, n2, ...$)	Calculates the variance of its arguments

Index